DIABETIC
COOKBOOK
FOR BEGINNERS

1200 Days Of Easy And Delicious Balanced Meals
To Manage Type 2 Diabetes Without Stress
And Improve Your Health. The Diabetic Diet Recipes
For The Newly Diagnosed

Robert Charlis

TABLE OF CONTENTS

Introduction

Diabetes is a disease in which the body releases too much glucose, a simple sugar, into the circulation; this happens when the body doesn't generate enough insulin to regulate the amount of glucose released from eating appropriately.

When a person lacks insulin, the kidneys are unable to eliminate glucose from the bloodstream quickly enough. As a result, glucose levels in the blood rise, leading to diabetes. The 2 main types of diabetes are types 1 and 2. If type 2 was not clear already, it does not mean that people who have type 2 can't or shouldn't eat junk food all day long. Type 2 happens mainly due to lifestyle choices. It is not necessarily something that people are born with or cursed with. Many people can reduce their risk for type 2 diabetes by changing their diet and doing things to manage their weight and blood sugar levels, such as exercising and managing stress.

Type 1 diabetes is an autoimmune disease marked by a fast reduction in insulin production. It is caused by a compromised immune system, which causes the pancreas to generate insufficient insulin. This means that your cells can't access nutrients properly unless accompanied by insulin when you eat food. The body makes glucose because it cannot sense that insulin is available to allow the cells to access the nutrients attached to the glucose. Symptoms of type 1 diabetes include frequent urination, high blood sugar levels, fatigue, hunger, frequent infections and extreme thirst. Unfortunately, what appears as diabetes to many people is type 1. It is critical that if you suspect that you have this type of diabetes, it must be confirmed through a blood test so people can be sure of what they are dealing with. Some doctors will prescribe medications so that patients have better control over their diabetes.

Obesity and lifestyle factors are the leading causes of type 2 diabetes. However, some people have type 2 diabetes even though they are not obese. A new study shows that even being slightly overweight can increase the risk of type 2 diabetes.

When someone has insulin resistance or "insulin sensitivity," their body does not properly respond to the hormone. As a result, instead of being absorbed by cells, glucose builds up in circulation. This is called insulin resistance because the body does not respond well to the hormone insulin, so its production gets out of control. Therefore, too much is produced, which makes an even more severe problem that needs to be taken care of.

Increased thirst, unexplained weight loss or gain, hazy vision, tiredness, and irritability are symptoms of type 2 diabetes. It is very important for people always to make sure that they see a doctor immediately if they have any of these symptoms. A blood test can confirm whether or not someone has this disease and what needs to be done to manage it appropriately.

It is always best to take preventative measures to avoid further complications from either type 1 or type 2 diabetes. Many people can prevent getting more problems from diabetes by seeing a doctor regularly and keeping track of how they manage their bodies and blood sugar levels.

When there is no insulin in the body, glucose cannot enter the cells that require it, even if it is present in the blood. As people's cells run out of energy, they become tired and frail. The difficulty to concentrate is one of the most common symptoms of diabetes. When your body doesn't get enough nutrients from food due to a shortage of insulin, it will draw from your fat reserves to get what it needs. This can cause severe weight loss or gain, depending on how low or high your blood sugar levels are at the time. If you do not have managed diabetes, this is a serious sign that you must see a doctor immediately.

In the United States, diabetes is the primary cause of blindness in individuals over 40. According to the National Diabetes Information Association (NDIA) in the United States in 2010, 10.9% of all people in this age group were diagnosed with diabetes, and 2.9% had diabetes end-stage. By 2050, if current trends continue, 30–40% of people in this age group will be diagnosed with diabetes, and 12% will have end-stage diabetes.

Recent statistics also show that people with type 2 diabetes or pre-diabetes are more likely to develop heart disease and strokes than those without it because their cholesterol levels increase significantly when they cannot produce enough insulin.

Many people with diabetes also suffer from cardiovascular diseases. While it is true that persons with high blood pressure or cholesterol are more likely to develop heart disease, having diabetes significantly enhances their risk. The amount of damage done to the body due to diabetes causes increased stiffness in the arteries, making blood circulation more difficult. The ischemic injury occurs, as a result, contributing to heart disease.

Studies show that older people but still past child-bearing age are more likely to develop type 2 diabetes. Losing weight and exercising frequently be beneficial in preventing the onset of type 2 diabetes. To avoid inflammation and oxidative damage in the body, this is in addition to maintaining a balanced diet and controlling stress.

It is estimated that in 2010 alone, 23.6 million people were diagnosed with diabetes, and 7.9 million of them did not know they had it. Many people don't know that they have it because many times, their blood sugar levels are not high enough for a doctor to notice at the regular checkups they visit when they get regular physicals, such as when they renew their driver's license or when they would go out for regular blood tests. You need to remember that there are many things you can do to help control your diabetes, but if you can't take action immediately, you should talk to your doctor about what options are best for you. Usually, some medications work well with diet and exercise.

It is recommended that you eat a diet high in fiber and lean proteins but lower in fat. Because fiber takes longer to digest, it helps avoid blood sugar surges and fills you up, allowing you to eat smaller quantities and lose weight more easily. Protein does not break down as rapidly as carbs so that you will feel fuller for a longer time. Lean proteins, such as those found in fish, beans, and other legumes, are connected with greater satiety than fattier proteins, like red meat.

Many people prefer using medicines because they believe they will immediately fix their condition and make them feel better. Instead, you have to remember that there are things that you must do on your own to help prevent the onset of diabetes. If you don't, it will just become a vicious cycle where you will have to rely on medications, but your body will not be used to them and if you go off them, you will have a hard time getting back on them.

The most important thing is the prevention of diabetes. You need to remember that there are many ways of helping yourself prevent diabetes, including eating a healthy diet and exercising regularly so that your cells can get the nutrients they need to process blood sugar properly. According to the Centres for Disease Control (CDC), about 86% of people with type 2 diabetes are overweight or obese, according to the Centers for Disease Control (CDC).

Exercising and losing weight often do not help prevent diabetes, but they can help you feel better and increase your chances of taking care of the problem. Your doctor will prescribe medications so that you can feel better. As stated, there are many things that you can do to help control your diabetes, such as exercising and eating a healthy diet. If you lose weight, your blood sugar levels will also go down, which makes it easier for you to manage your diabetes.

For it to operate effectively in the body, you may need to take insulin or other drugs. This is a huge problem for many people because it is very unpleasant and people don't want to remember to take them every time they eat something. It also makes you feel like you are reliant on medications to feel better when in fact, you just need to exercise and stick with a healthy diet to help yourself feel better.

Five servings of fruits and vegetables and whole grains, legumes, lean meats, and low-fat dairy products should be consumed each day. It's critical, though, to avoid eating anything just before or after your workouts so that your body can burn fat rather than storing it as muscle. You don't want to take too much risk, so it is best to divide your meals into 2 or 3 high carbohydrate and low-fat meals.

To help you control your diabetes, you must check with your doctor or pharmacist about what options are best for you. It would help if you did not weigh yourself too often as this will not help, but it could cause you to feel discouraged. Remember, there are other things that you can do on your own and eat a healthy diet and exercise regularly.

You should also try taking the time each day to focus on a positive attitude, eat a healthy diet, and exercise regularly so that your body can adjust itself properly and respond better to insulin medication. If you do these things and take medications as recommended by your doctor, you should start to feel better and more confident.

CHAPTER 1:

Breakfast

1. Zucchini Noodles With Creamy Avocado Pesto

Preparation time: 10 minutes
Cooking time: 20 minutes
Servings: 4
Ingredients

- 6 cup zucchini, spiralized
- 1 tbsp. olive oil
- 6 oz. avocado
- 1 basil leaf
- 3 garlic cloves
- 1/3 oz. pine nuts
- 2 tbsp. lemon juice
- 1/2 tsp. salt
- 1/4 tsp. black pepper
- 1 tbsp. parmesan cheese

Directions

1. Spiralize the zucchini and set them aside on paper towels to absorb the surplus water.
2. Put avocados, lemon juice, basil leaves, garlic, pine nuts, sea salt, and pulse until chopped in a kitchen appliance. Then put vegetable oil in a slow stream till emulsified and creamy.
3. Drizzle vegetable oil in a skillet over medium-high heat and add zucchini noodles, cooking for about 2 minutes till tender. Put zucchini noodles into a large bowl and toss with avocado pesto. Season with cracked pepper and a little Parmesan and serve.

Nutrition Calories: 115 Protein: 30 g. Fat: 0 g.Carbs: 3 g.

2. Avocado Chicken Salad

Preparation time: 5 minutes
Cooking time: 10 minutes
Servings: 2
Ingredients

- 10 oz. cooked chicken, diced

- 1/2 cup Plain Greek yogurt 2%
- 3 oz. avocado, chopped
- 12 tsp. garlic powder
- 1/4 tsp. salt
- 1/8 tsp. pepper
- 1 tbsp. + 1 tsp. lime juice
- 1/4 cup fresh cilantro, chopped

Directions

1. Combine all ingredients in a medium-sized bowl. Refrigerate until able to serve.
2. Divide the salad in half and serve with your favorite greens.

Nutrition Calories: 265 Protein: 35 g. Fat: 13 g. Carbs: 5 g.

3. Pancakes With Berries

Preparation time: 5 minutes
Cooking time: 20 minutes
Servings: 2
Ingredients
For the pancake:

- 1 egg
- 50 g. spelled flour
- 50 g. almond flour
- 15 g. coconut flour
- 150 ml. water

Direction

1. Put the flour, egg, and a few salt in a blender jar.
2. Add 150 ml. of water.
3. Mix everything into a batter.
4. Heat a coated pan.
5. Pour half the batter.
6. Once the pancake is firm, turn it over.
7. Remove the pancake, add the last half of the batter to the pan, and repeat.
8. Melt chocolate over a water bath.
9. Let the pancakes cool.
10. Brush the pancakes with the yogurt.
11. Wash the berry and let it drain.
12. Put berries on the yogurt.

13. Roll up the pancakes.
14. Sprinkle them with granulated sugar.
15. Decorate the entire thing with the melted chocolate.

Nutrition Calories: 298 Carbohydrates: 26 g. Protein: 21 g. Fat: 9 g.

4.   Omelette à la Margherita

Preparation time: 10 minutes
Cooking time: 20 minutes
Servings: 2
Ingredients:

- 3 eggs
- 50 g. Parmesan cheese
- 2 tbsp. heavy cream
- 1 tbsp. olive oil
- 1 tsp. oregano
- 1 tsp. nutmeg
- Salt and pepper to taste

For the covering:

- 3–4 stalks basil
- 1 tomato
- 100 g. Mozzarella cheese, grated

Directions:

1. Mix the cream and eggs in a medium bowl. Add the grated parmesan, nutmeg, oregano, pepper, and salt and stir everything.
2. Heat the oil in a pan.
3. Add half of the egg and cream mixture to the pan.
4. Let the omelet set over medium heat, turn it, then remove it.
5. Repeat with the last half of the egg mixture. Cut the tomato into slices and place it on top of the omelets.
6. Spread the mozzarella over the tomato.
7. Place the omelets on a baking sheet.
8. Cook at 180°F for 5–10 minutes.
9. Then, take the omelets out and decorate them with the basil leaves.

Nutrition Calories: 402 Carbohydrates: 7 g. Protein: 21 g. Fat: 34 g.

5.   Omelet With Tomatoes and Spring Onions

Preparation time: 5 minutes
Cooking time: 20 minutes
Servings: 2
Ingredients

- 6 eggs
- 2 tomatoes
- 2 spring onions
- 1 shallot
- 2 tbsp. butter
- 1 tbsp. olive oil
- 1 pinch nutmeg
- Salt to taste
- Pepper to taste

Directions

1. Whisk the eggs in a bowl.
2. Mix and season them with salt and pepper.
3. Peel the shallot and chop it up.
4. Clean the onions and cut them into rings.
5. Wash the tomatoes and cut them into pieces.
6. Heat butter and oil in a pan.
7. Braise half the shallots in it.
8. Add half the egg mixture.
9. Let everything set over medium heat.
10. Scatter a couple of tomatoes and onion rings on top.
11. Repeat with the last half of the egg mixture.
12. At the top, spread the grated nutmeg over the entire thing.

Nutrition Calories: 263 Carbohydrates: 8 g. Protein: 20.3 g. Fat: 24 g.

6.   Coconut Chia Pudding With Berries

Preparation time: 20 minutes
Cooking time: 45 minutes
Servings: 2
Ingredients

- 150 g. raspberries and blueberries
- 60 g. chia seeds
- 500 ml. coconut milk
- 1 tsp. agave syrup
- 1/2 tsp. ground bourbon vanilla

Directions

1. Put the chia seeds, agave syrup, and vanilla in a bowl.
2. Pour in the coconut milk.
3. Mix thoroughly and let it soak for 45 minutes.
4. Meanwhile, wash the berries and allow them to drain well.
5. Divide the coconut chia pudding between 2 glasses.

6. Put the berries on top.

Nutrition Calories: 662 Carbohydrates: 18 g. Protein: 8 g.Fat: 55 g.

7. Eel on Scrambled Eggs and Bread

Preparation time: 5 minutes
Cooking time: 10 minutes
Servings: 2
Ingredients

- 4 eggs
- 1 shallot
- 4 slices bread, low carb
- 2 sticks dill
- 200 g. smoked eel
- 1 tbsp. oil
- White pepper and salt to taste

Directions

1. Mix the eggs in a bowl and season with salt and pepper.
2. Peel the shallot and cut it into fine cubes.
3. Chop the dill.
4. Remove the skin from the eel and cut it into pieces.
5. Heat the oil in a pan and steam the shallot in it.
6. Add the eggs in and let them to set.
7. Use the spatula to remove the eggs several times.
8. Reduce the warmth and add the dill.
9. Stir everything.
10. Spread the scrambled eggs over 4 slices of bread.
11. Put the eel pieces on top.
12. Add some fresh dill and serve everything.

Nutrition Calories: 830 Carbohydrates: 8 g.Protein: 45 g.Fat: 64 g.

8. Chia Seed Gel With Pomegranate and Nuts

Preparation time: 5 minutes
Cooking time: 10 minutes
Servings: 3
Ingredients

- 20 g. hazelnuts
- 20 g. walnuts
- 120 ml. almond milk
- 4 tbsp. chia seeds
- 4 tbsp. pomegranate seeds
- 1 tsp. agave syrup

Directions

1. Finely chop the nuts.
2. Mix the almond milk with the chia seeds.
3. Let everything soak for 10–20 minutes.
4. Occasionally stir the mixture with the chia seeds.
5. Stir in the agave syrup.
6. Pour 2 tbsp. of every mixture into a dessert glass.
7. Layer the chopped nuts on top.
8. Cover the nuts with 1 tbsp. each of the chia mass.
9. Sprinkle the pomegranate seeds on top and serve everything.

Nutrition Calories: 248 Carbohydrates: 7 g.Protein: 1 g.Fat: 19 g.

9. Lavender Blueberry Chia Seed Pudding

Preparation time: 1 hour 10 minutes
Cooking time: 0 minutes
Servings: 4
Ingredients

- 100 g. blueberries
- 70 g. organic quark
- 50 g. soy yogurt
- 30 g. hazelnuts
- 200 ml. almond milk
- 2 tbsp. chia seeds
- 2 tsp. agave syrup
- 2 tsp. lavender

Directions

1. Bring the almond milk and lavender to a boil.
2. Let the mixture simmer for 10 minutes at a reduced temperature.
3. Allow them to calm down afterward.
4. If the milk is cold, add the blueberries and puree everything.
5. Mix the entire mixture with the chia seeds and agave syrup.
6. Let everything soak in the refrigerator for 1 hour.
7. Mix the yogurt and curd cheese.
8. Add both to the batter.
9. Divide the pudding into glasses.
10. Finely chop the hazelnuts and sprinkle them on top.

Nutrition Calories: 252 Carbohydrates: 12 g. Protein: 1 g.Fat: 11 g.

10.   Yogurt With Granola and Persimmon

Preparation time: 5 minutes
Cooking time: 5 minutes
Servings: 1
Ingredients

- 150 g. Greek-style yogurt
- 20 g. oatmeal
- 60 g. fresh persimmons
- 30 ml. tap water

Directions

1. Put the nonfat oatmeal in the pan.
2. Toast them, continually stirring, until golden brown.
3. Then, put them on a plate and allow them to calm down briefly.
4. Peel the persimmons and put them in a bowl with the water. Mix the entire thing into a fine puree.
5. Put the yogurt, the toasted oatmeal, and then puree in layers in a glass and serve.

Nutrition Calories: 286 Carbohydrates: 29 g. Protein: 1 g. Fat: 11 g.

11.   Smoothie Bowl With Spinach, Mango, and Muesli

Preparation time: 10 minutes
Cooking time: 0 minutes
Servings: 1
Ingredients

- 150 g. yogurt
- 30 g. apple
- 30 g. mango
- 30 g. low carb muesli
- 10 g. spinach
- 10 g. chia seeds

Directions

1. Soak the spinach leaves and allow them to drain.
2. Peel the mango and cut it into strips.
3. Remove the apple core and cut it into pieces.
4. Put everything except the mango alongside the yogurt in a blender and make a fine puree out of it.
5. Put the spinach smoothie in a bowl.
6. Add the muesli, chia seeds, and mango.
7. Serve and enjoy.

Nutrition Calories: 362 Carbohydrates: 21 g. Protein: 12 g. Fat: 21 g.

12.   Fried Egg With Bacon

Preparation time: 5 minutes
Cooking time: 10 minutes
Servings: 1
Ingredients

- 2 eggs
- 30 g. bacon
- 2 tbsp. olive oil
- Salt to taste
- Pepper to taste

Directions

1. Heat oil in the pan and fry the bacon.
2. Reduce the heat and beat the eggs in the pan.
3. Cook the eggs and season with salt and pepper.
4. Serve the fried eggs hot with the bacon.

Nutrition Calories: 405.Carbohydrates: 1 g.Protein: 19 g.Fat: 38 g.

13.   Smoothie Bowl With Berries, Poppy Seeds, Nuts, and Seeds

Preparation time: 15 minutes
Cooking time: 0 minutes
Servings: 2
Ingredients

- 5 almonds, chopped
- 2 walnuts, chopped
- 1 apple
- 1/4 banana
- 300 g. yogurt
- 60 g. raspberries
- 20 g. blueberries
- 20 g. rolled oats, roasted in a pan
- 10 g. poppy seeds
- 1 tsp. pumpkin seeds Agave syrup

Directions

1. Clean the fruit and let it drain.
2. Take some berries and set them aside.
3. Place the remaining berries in a tall mixing vessel.
4. Cut the banana into slices. Put a couple of aside.
5. Add the remainder of the banana to the berries.
6. Remove the core of the apple and cut it into quarters.
7. Cut the quarters into thin wedges and set a couple of aside.

8. Add the remaining wedges to the berries.
9. Add the yogurt to the fruits and blend everything into a puree.
10. Sweeten the smoothie with the agave syrup.
11. Divide it into 2 bowls.
12. Serve it with the remaining fruit, poppy seeds, oatmeal, nuts, and seeds.

Nutrition Calories: 284 Carbohydrates: 21 g.Protein: 11 g.Fat: 19 g.

14. Porridge With Walnuts

Preparation time: 5 minutes
Cooking time: 10 minutes
Servings: 1
Ingredients

- 50 g. raspberries
- 50 g. blueberries
- 25 g. ground walnuts
- 20 g. flaxseed, crushed
- 10 g. oatmeal
- 200 ml. nut drink
- 1 tsp. agave syrup
- 1/2 tsp. cinnamon salt

Directions

1. Warm the nut drink in a saucepan.
2. Add the walnuts, flaxseed, and oatmeal, stirring constantly.
3. Stir in the cinnamon and salt.
4. Simmer for 8 minutes.
5. Keep stirring everything.
6. Sweeten the entire thing.
7. Put the porridge in a bowl.
8. Wash the berries and allow them to drain.
9. Add them to the porridge and serve everything.

Nutrition Calories: 378 Carbohydrates: 11 g.Protein: 18 g.Fat: 27 g.

15. Alkaline Blueberry Spelt Pancakes

Preparation time: 6 minutes
Cooking time: 20 minutes
Servings: 3
Ingredients

- 2 cups spelt flour
- 1 cup coconut milk
- 1/2 cup alkaline water
- 2 tbsp. grapeseed oil
- 1/2 cup agave

- 1/2 cup blueberries
- 1/4 tsp. sea moss
- 2 tsp. hemp seeds

Directions

1. Mix the spelt flour, agave, grapeseed oil, hemp seeds, and sea moss in a bowl.
2. Add 1 cup of coconut milk and alkaline water to the mixture until you get the consistent mix you wish.
3. Combine the blueberries with the batter.
4. Heat the skillet to moderate heat, then lightly coat it with the grapeseed oil.
5. Pour the batter into the skillet, then allow them to cook for about 5 minutes on every side.
6. Serve and enjoy.

Nutrition Calories: 203 Fat: 1.4 g.Carbs: 41.6 g. Protein: 4.8 g.

16. Alkaline Blueberry Muffins

Preparation time: 5 minutes
Cooking time: 30 minutes
Servings: 3
Ingredients

- 1 cup coconut milk
- 3/4 cup spelt flour
- 3/4 teff flour
- 1/2 cup blueberries
- 1/3 cup agave
- 1/4 cup sea moss gel
- 1/2 tsp. sea salt
- 2 tbsp. grapeseed oil

Directions

1. Adjust the temperature of the oven to 365°F.
2. Grease 6 regular-size muffin cups with muffin liners.
3. In a bowl, mix sea salt, sea moss, agave, coconut milk, and flours until they're appropriately blended.
4. Next, introduce the blueberries.
5. Coat the muffin pan lightly with the grapeseed oil.
6. Pour in the muffin batter.
7. Bake for at least 30 minutes until it turns golden brown.
8. Serve.

Nutrition Calories: 160 Fat: 5 g.Carbs: 25 g.Protein: 2 g.

17. Coconut Pancakes

Preparation time: 5 minutes
Cooking time: 5 minutes
Servings: 4
Ingredients

- 1 cup coconut flour
- 2 tbsp. arrowroot powder
- 1 tsp.. baking powder
- 1 cup coconut milk
- 3 tbsp. coconut oil

Directions

1. In a medium container, mix all the dry ingredients.
2. Add the coconut milk and 2 tbsp. of coconut oil, then mix properly.
3. In a skillet, melt 1 tsp. of coconut oil.
4. Pour a ladle of the batter into the skillet, then swirl the pan to spread the batter evenly into a smooth pancake.
5. Cook it for 3 minutes on medium heat until it becomes firm.
6. Turn the pancake to the other side, then cook it for an additional 2 minutes until it turns golden brown.
7. Cook the remaining pancakes in the same process.
8. Serve.

Nutrition Calories: 377 Fat: 14.9 g.Carbs: 60.7 g.Protein: 6.4 g.

18. Quinoa Porridge

Preparation time: 5 minutes
Cooking time: 25 minutes
Servings: 2
Ingredients

- 2 cups coconut milk
- 1 cup rinsed quinoa
- 1/8 tsp. ground cinnamon
- 1 cup fresh blueberries

Directions

1. In a saucepan, boil the coconut milk over high heat.
2. Add the quinoa to the milk, then allow the mixture to boil.
3. Then cook over medium heat for 15 minutes until the milk is reduced.
4. Add the cinnamon, then mix it properly in the saucepan.
5. Cover the saucepan and cook for at least 8 minutes until the milk is absorbed.

6. Add in the blueberries, then cook for 30 more seconds.
7. Serve.

Nutrition Calories: 271 Fat: 3.7 g.Carbs: 54 g.Protein: 6.5 g.

19. Amaranth Porridge

Preparation time: 5 minutes
Cooking time: 30 minutes
Servings: 2.
Ingredients

- 2 cups coconut milk
- 2 cups alkaline water
- 1 cup amaranth
- 2 tbsp. coconut oil
- 1 tbsp. ground cinnamon

Directions

1. In a saucepan, mix the milk with water, then boil the mixture.
2. Stir in the amaranth, then reduce the heat to medium.
3. Cook on medium heat, then simmers for at least 30 minutes while stirring occasionally.
4. Put off the fire.
5. Add in cinnamon and coconut oil, then stir.
6. Serve.

Nutrition Calories: 434 Fat: 35 g.Carbs: 27 g.Protein: 6.7 g.

20. Banana Barley Porridge

Preparation time: 15 minutes
Cooking time: 5 minutes
Servings: 2
Ingredients

- 1 cup unsweetened coconut milk, divided
- 1 small banana, peeled and sliced
- 1/2 cup barley
- 3 drops liquid Stevia®
- 1/4 cup coconuts, chopped

Directions

1. In a bowl, properly mix barley with half the coconut milk and Stevia®
2. Cover the blending bowl, then refrigerate for 6 hours.
3. In a saucepan, mix the barley mixture with coconut milk.
4. Cook for 5 minutes on moderate heat.
5. Then top it with the chopped coconuts and, therefore, the banana slices.

6. Serve.

Nutrition Calories: 159 Fat: 8.4 g.Carbs: 19.8 g.Protein: 4.6 g.

21.   Apple Cheddar Muffins

Preparation time: 10 minutes
Cooking time: 20 minutes
Servings: 12
Ingredients

- 1 egg
- 3/4 cup tart apple, peel, and chop
- 2/3 cup reduced-fat cheddar cheese, grated
- 2/3 cup skim milk
- 2 cups baking mix, low carb
- 2 tbsp. vegetable oil
- 1 tsp. cinnamon.

Directions

1. Heat the oven to 400ºF.
2. Line a 12-cup muffin pan with paper liners.
3. In a medium bowl, lightly beat the egg. Stir in the remaining ingredients just until moistened. Divide evenly between prepared muffin cups.
4. Bake for 17–20 minutes or until golden brown.
5. Serve warm.

Nutrition Calories: 162 Total carbs: 17 g.Net carbs: 13 g.Protein: 10 g.Fat: 5 g.Sugar: 8 g.Fiber: 4 g.

22.   Apple Cinnamon Muffins

Preparation time: 15 minutes
Cooking time: 25 minutes
Servings: 12
Ingredients

- 1 cup apple, diced fine
- 2/3 cup skim milk
- 1/4 cup reduced-calorie margarine, melted
- 1 egg, lightly beaten
- 1 2/3 cups flour
- 1 tbsp. Stevia®
- 2 1/2 tsp. baking powder
- 1 tsp. cinnamon
- 1/2 tsp. sea salt
- 1/4 tsp. nutmeg
- Nonstick cooking spray

Directions

1. Heat oven to 400ºF.
2. Spray a 12-cup muffin pan with cooking spray.
3. In a large bowl, combine dry ingredients and stir to mix.
4. In another bowl, beat milk, margarine, and egg to combine.
5. Pour wet ingredients into dry ingredients and stir just until moistened. Gently fold in apples.
6. Spoon into prepared muffin pan. Bake for 25 minutes, or until tops are lightly browned.

Nutrition Calories: 119 Total carbs: 17 g.Net carbs: 16 g.Protein: 3 g.Fat: 4 g.Sugar: 3 g.Fiber: 1 g.

23.   Apple Cinnamon Scones

Preparation time: 5 minutes
Cooking time: 25 minutes
Servings: 16
Ingredients

- 2 large eggs
- 1 apple, diced
- 1/4 cup + 1/2 tbsp. margarine, melted, and divided
- 1 tbsp. half-n-half
- 3 cups almond flour
- 1/3 cup + 2 tsp. Splenda®
- 2 tsp. baking powder
- 2 tsp. cinnamon
- 1 tsp. vanilla
- 1/4 tsp. salt

Directions

1. Heat oven to 325ºF. Line a large baking sheet with parchment paper.
2. In a large bowl, whisk flour, 1/3 cup Splenda®, baking powder, 1 1/2 tsp. of cinnamon, and salt. Stir in apple.
3. Add the eggs, 1/4 cup melted margarine, cream, and vanilla. Stir until the mixture forms a soft dough.
4. Divide the dough in half and pat it into 2 circles, about 1-inch thick and 7–8 inches around.
5. In a small bowl, stir together the remaining 2 tsp. Splenda® and 1/2 tsp. cinnamon.

6. Brush the 1/2 tbsp. melted margarine over the dough and sprinkle with cinnamon mixture. Cut each into 8 equal pieces and place them on a prepared baking sheet.

7. Bake for 20–25 minutes, or until golden brown and firm to the touch.

Nutrition Calories: 176 Total carbs: 12 g.Net carbs: 9 g.Protein: 5 g.Fat: 12 g. Sugar: 8 g.Fiber: 3 g.

24. Apple Filled Swedish Pancake

Preparation time: 25 minutes
Cooking time: 30 minutes
Servings: 6
Ingredients

- 2 apples, cored and sliced thin
- 3/4 cup egg substitute
- 1/2 cup fat-free milk
- 1/2 cup sugar-free caramel sauce
- 1 tbsp. reduced-calorie margarine
- 1/2 cup flour
- 1 1/2 tbsp. brown sugar substitute
- 2 tsp. water - 1/4 tsp. cinnamon
- 1/8 tsp. cloves - 1/8 tsp. salt
- Non-stick cooking spray

Direction

1. Heat oven to 400ºF. Place margarine in cast iron or ovenproof skillet and place in oven until margarine is melted.

2. In a medium bowl, whisk together flour, milk, egg substitute, cinnamon, cloves, and salt until smooth.

3. Pour batter in hot skillet and bake 20–25 minutes until puffed and golden brown.

4. Spray a medium saucepan with cooking spray. Heat over medium heat.

5. Add apples, brown sugar, and water. Cook, occasionally stirring, until apples are tender and golden brown, about 4–6 minutes.

6. Pour the caramel sauce into a microwave-proof measuring glass and heat 30–45 seconds, or until warmed through. To serve, spoon apples into pancakes and drizzle with caramel. Cut into wedges.

Nutrition Calories:193 Total carbs: 25 g.Net carbs: 23 g.Protein: 6 g.Fat: 2 g.Sugar: 12 g.Fiber: 2 g.

25. Apple Topped French Toast

Preparation time: 10 minutes
Cooking time: 10 minutes
Servings: 2
Ingredients

- 1 apple, peel and slice thin
- 1 egg
- 1/4 cup skim milk
- 2 tbsp. margarine, divided
- 4 slices Healthy Loaf Bread, (chapter 14)
- 1 tbsp. Splenda® brown sugar
- 1 tsp. vanilla
- 1/4 tsp. cinnamon

Direction

1. Melt 1 tbsp. margarine in a large skillet over med-high heat. Add the apple slices, Splenda®, and cinnamon and cook, frequently stirring, until apples are tender.

2. In a shallow dish, whisk together egg, milk, and vanilla.

3. Melt the remaining margarine in a separate skillet over med-high heat. Dip each slice of bread in the egg mixture and cook until golden brown on both sides.

4. Place 2 slices of French toast on plates, and top with apple slices. Serve immediately.

Nutrition Calories: 3 Total carbs: 27 g.Net carbs: 22 g.Protein: 10 g.Fat: 23 g.Sugar: 19 g.Fiber: 5 g.

26. Apple Walnut Pancakes

Preparation time: 15 minutes
Cooking time: 30 minutes
Servings: 18
Ingredients

- 1 apple, peeled and diced
- 2 cup skim milk
- 2 egg whites
- 1 egg, beaten
- 1 cup flour
- 1 cup whole wheat flour
- 1/2 cup walnuts, chopped
- 2 tbsp. sunflower oil
- 1 tbsp. Splenda® brown sugar
- 2 tsp. baking powder
- 1 tsp. salt
- Non-stick cooking spray

Direction

1. In a large bowl, combine dry ingredients.
2. Combine egg whites, egg, milk, and oil in a separate bowl and add to dry ingredients. Stir just until moistened. Fold in apple and walnuts.
3. Spray a large skillet with cooking spray and heat. Pour batter, 1/4 cup onto the hot skillet. Flip when bubbles form on top. Cook until the second side is golden brown. Serve with sugar-free syrup.

Nutrition Calories: 120 Total carbs: 15 g.Net carbs: 13 g.Protein: 4 g.Fat: 5 g. Sugar: 3 g.Fiber: 2 g.

27. "Bacon" and Egg Muffins

Preparation time: 10 minutes
Cooking time: 15 minutes
Servings: 6
Ingredients

- 1 1/4 cups frozen hash browns, thawed
- 1 cup egg substitute
- 2 turkey sausage patties, diced
- 2 tbsp. onion, diced fine
- 2 tbsp. turkey bacon, cooked and chopped
- 2 tbsp. Monterey Jack cheese, grated
- 1 tbsp. fat-free sour cream
- 1 garlic clove, diced fine
- 1 tsp. vegetable oil
- 1/4 tsp. salt
- 1/8 tsp. black pepper
- Non-stick cooking spray

Directions

1. Heat oven to 400°F. Spray a 6-cup muffin pan with cooking spray.
2. Divide the hash browns evenly among the muffin cups, pressing firmly on the bottoms and up the sides.
3. In a large skillet, heat the oil until hot. Add onion, and cook, stirring until tender.
4. Add garlic and sausage and cook for 1 minute.
5. Remove the skillet from heat and stir in sour cream.
6. In a medium bowl, beat egg substitute with salt and pepper. Pour the egg mixture evenly over the potatoes.
7. Top with sausage mixture, bacon, and cheese.

8. Bake for 15–18 minutes, or until eggs are firm. Serve immediately.

Nutrition Calories: 165 Total carbs: 13 g.Net carbs: 12 g.Protein: 11 g.Fat: 7 g.Sugar: 1 g.Fiber: 1 g.

28. Berry Breakfast Bark

Preparation time: 10 minutes; freeze time: 2 hours
Cooking time: 0 minutes
Servings: 6
Ingredients

- 3–4 strawberries, sliced
- 1 1/2 cup plain Greek yogurt
- 1/2 cup blueberries
- 1/2 cup low-fat granola
- 3 tbsp. sugar-free maple syrup

Directions

1. Line a baking sheet with parchment paper.
2. In a medium bowl, mix yogurt and syrup until combined. Pour into prepared pan and spread in a thin, even layer.
3. Top with remaining ingredients. Cover with foil and freeze for 2 hours or overnight.

   To serve: Slice into squares and serve immediately. If bark thaws too much, it will lose its shape. Store any remaining bark in an airtight container in the freezer.

Nutrition Calories: 69 Total carbs: 18 g. Net carbs: 16 g.Protein: 7 g.Fat: 6 g.Sugar: 7 g.Fiber: 2 g.

29. Blueberry Cinnamon Muffins

Preparation time: 10 minutes
Cooking time: 30 minutes
Servings: 10
Ingredients

- 3 eggs
- 1 cup blueberries
- 1/3 cup half-n-half
- 1/4 cup margarine, melted
- 1 1/2 cup almond flour
- 1/3 cup Splenda®
- 1 tsp. baking powder
- 1 tsp. cinnamon

Directions

1. Heat oven to 350°F.

2. Line 10 muffin cups with paper liners.
3. In a large mixing bowl, combine dry ingredients.
4. Stir in wet ingredients and mix well.
5. Fold in the blueberries and spoon evenly into a lined muffin pan.
6. Bake for 25–30 minutes, or they pass the toothpick test.

Nutrition Calories: 194 Total carbs: 12 g.Net carbs: 10 g.Protein: 5 g.Fat: 14 g.Sugar: 9 g.Fiber: 2 g.

30. Blueberry English Muffin Loaf

Preparation time: 15 minutes
Cooking time: 1 hour
Servings: 12
Ingredients

- 6 eggs beaten
- 1/2 cup almond milk, unsweetened
- 1/2 cup blueberries
- 1/2 cup cashew butter
- 1/2 cup almond flour
- 1/4 cup coconut oil
- 2 tsp. baking powder
- 1/2 tsp. salt
- Non-stick cooking spray

Directions

1. Heat oven to 350°F.
2. Line a loaf pan with parchment paper and spray lightly with cooking spray.
3. In a small glass bowl, melt cashew butter and oil together in the microwave for 30 seconds. Stir until well combined.
4. In a large bowl, stir together the dry ingredients. Add cashew butter mixture and mix well.
5. In a separate bowl, whisk the milk and eggs together. Add to the flour mixture and stir well. Fold in blueberries.
6. Pour into the prepared pan and bake for 45 minutes or until it passes the toothpick test.
7. Cook 30 minutes, remove from pan, and slice.

Nutrition Calories: 162 Total carbs: 5 g.Net carbs: 4 g.Protein: 6 g.Fat: 14 g.Sugar: 1 g.Fiber: 1 g.

31. Blueberry Stuffed French Toast

Preparation time: 15 minutes
Cooking time: 20 minutes
Servings: 8
Ingredients

- 4 eggs
- 1 1/2 cup blueberries
- 1/2 cup orange juice
- 1 tsp. orange zest
- 16 slices bread
- 3 tbsp. Splenda®, divided
- 1/8 tsp. salt
- Blueberry Orange Dessert Sauce
- Non-stick cooking spray

Directions

1. Heat oven to 400°F. Spray a large baking sheet with cooking spray.
2. In a small bowl, combine berries with 2 tbsp. of Splenda®.
3. Lay 8 slices of bread on the work surface. Top with about 3 tbsp. of berries and place the second slice of bread on top. Flatten slightly.
4. In a shallow dish, whisk all the remaining ingredients. Carefully dip both sides of bread in egg mixture and place on prepared pan.
5. Bake for 7–12 minutes per side, or until lightly browned.
6. Heat dessert sauce until warm. Plate the French toast and top with 1–2 tbsp. of the sauce. Serve.

Nutrition Calories: 208 Total carbs: 20 g.Net carbs: 18 g.Protein: 7 g.Fat: 10 g. Sugar: 14 g.Fiber: 2 g.

32. Breakfast Pizza

Preparation time: 10 minutes
Cooking time: 30 minutes
Servings: 8
Ingredients

- 12 eggs
- 1/2 lb. breakfast sausage
- 1 cup bell pepper, sliced
- 1 cup red pepper, sliced
- 1 cup cheddar cheese, grated
- 1/2 cup half-n-half
- 1/2 tsp. salt
- 1/4 tsp. pepper

Directions

1. Heat oven to 350°F.
2. In a large cast-iron skillet, brown sausage. Transfer to a bowl.
3. Add peppers and cook for 3–5 minutes or until they begin to soften. Transfer to a bowl.
4. In a small bowl, whisk together the eggs, cream, salt, and pepper. Pour into skillet. Cook 5 minutes or until the sides start to set.
5. Bake for 15 minutes.
6. Remove from oven and set it to broil. Top "crust" with sausage, peppers, and cheese. Broil for 3 minutes, or until cheese is melted and starts to brown.
7. Let rest for 5 minutes before slicing and serving.

Nutrition Calories: 230 Total carbs: 4 g.Protein: 16 g. Fat 17 g.Sugar: 2 g.Fiber: 0 g.

33. Cafe Mocha Smoothies

Preparation time: 5 minutes
Cooking time: 0 minutes
Servings: 3
Ingredients

- 1 avocado, remove pit and cut in half
- 1 1/2 cup almond milk, unsweetened
- 1/2 cup coconut milk, canned
- 3 tbsp. Splenda®
- 3 tbsp. cocoa powder, unsweetened
- 2 tsp. instant coffee
- 1 tsp. vanilla

Directions

1. Place everything but the avocado in the blender. Process until smooth.
2. Add the avocado and blend until smooth and no chunks remain.
3. Pour into glasses and serve.

Nutrition Calories: 109 Total carbs: 15 g.Protein: 6 g.Fat: 1 g.Sugar: 13 g.Fiber: 0 g.

34. Cauliflower Breakfast Hash

Preparation time: 10 minutes
Cooking time: 20 minutes
Servings: 2
Ingredients

- 4 cups cauliflower, grated
- 1 cup mushrooms, diced
- 3/4 cup onion, diced
- 3 slices bacon

- 1/4 cup sharp cheddar cheese, grated

Directions

1. In a medium skillet over medium-high heat, fry bacon and set aside.
2. Add vegetables to the skillet and cook, occasionally stirring, until golden brown.
3. Cut bacon into pieces and return to the skillet.
4. Top with cheese and allow it to melt. Serve immediately.

Nutrition Calories: 155 Total carbs: 16 g. Net carbs: 10 g. Protein: 10 g. Fat: 7 g. Sugar: 7 g.Fiber: 6 g.

35. Cheese Spinach Waffles

Preparation time: 10 minutes
Cooking time: 20 minutes
Servings: 4
Ingredients

- 2 strips bacon, cooked and crumbled
- 2 eggs, lightly beaten
- 1/2 cup cauliflower, grated
- 1/2 cup frozen spinach, chopped (squeeze water out first)
- 1/2 cup low-fat Mozzarella cheese, grated
- 1/2 cup low-fat cheddar cheese, grated
- 1 tbsp. margarine, melted
- 1/4 cup reduced-fat Parmesan cheese, grated - 1 tsp. onion powder
- 1 tsp. garlic powder
- Non-stick cooking spray

Directions

1. Thaw spinach and squeeze out as much water as possible, place it in a large bowl.
2. Heat your waffle iron and spray with cooking spray.
3. Add the remaining ingredients to the spinach and mix well.
4. Pour small amounts on the waffle iron and cook like you would for regular waffles. Serve warm.

Nutrition Calories: 186 Total carbs: 2 g.Protein: 14 g.Fat: 14 g.Sugar: 1 g. Fiber: 0 g.

36. Cinnamon Apple Granola

Preparation time: 5 minutes
Cooking time: 35 minutes
Servings: 4
Ingredients

- 1 apple, peel, and diced fine

- 1/4 cup margarine, melted
- 1 cup walnuts or pecans
- 1 cup almond flour
- 3/4 cup flaked coconut
- 1/2 cup sunflower seeds
- 1/2 cup hemp seeds
- 1/3 cup Splenda®
- 2 tsp. cinnamon
- 2 tsp. vanilla
- 1/2 tsp. salt

Directions

1. Heat oven to 300°F. Line a large baking sheet with parchment paper.
2. Place the nuts, flour, coconut, seeds, Splenda®, and salt in a food processor. Pulse until mixture resembles coarse crumbs but leave some chunks.
3. Transfer to a bowl and add apple and cinnamon. Stir in margarine and vanilla until well coated, and the mixture starts to clump together.
4. Pour onto prepared pan and spread out evenly. Bake for 25 minutes, stirring a couple of times until it starts to brown.
5. Turn the oven off and let the granola sit inside 5–10 minutes. Remove from oven and cool completely; it will crisp up more as it cools. Store in an airtight container.

Nutrition Calories: 360 Total carbs: 19 g.Net carbs: 14 g.Protein: 10 g.Fat: 28 g.Sugar: 12 g.Fiber: 5 g.

37. Coconut Breakfast Porridge

Preparation time: 2 minutes
Cooking time: 10 minutes
Servings: 4
Ingredients

- 4 cup vanilla almond milk, unsweetened
- 1 cup unsweetened coconut, grated
- 8 tsp. coconut flour

Directions

1. Add coconut to a saucepan and cook over medium-high heat until it is lightly toasted; be careful not to let it burn.
2. Add milk and bring to a boil. While stirring, slowly add flour, cook, and stir until the mixture thickens about 5 minutes.
3. Remove from heat; the mixture will thicken more as it cools. Ladle into

bowls, add blueberries, or drizzle with a bit of honey if desired.

Nutrition Calories: 231 Total carbs: 21 g.Net carbs: 8 g.Protein: 6 g.Fat: 14 g.Sugar: 4 g.Fiber: 13 g.

38. Cottage Cheese Pancakes

Preparation time: 5 minutes
Cooking time: 5 minutes
Servings: 2
Ingredients

- 1 cup low-fat cottage cheese
- 4 egg whites
- 1/2 cup oats
- 1 tbsp. Stevia, raw, optional
- 1 tsp. vanilla
- Non-stick cooking spray

Directions

1. Place all the ingredients into a blender and process until smooth.
2. Spray a medium skillet with cooking spray and heat over medium heat.
3. Pour about 1/4cup batter into the hot pan and cook until golden brown on both sides.
4. Serve with sugar-free syrup, fresh berries, or topping of your choice.

Nutrition Calories: 250 Total carbs: 25 g. Net carbs: 23 g.Protein: 25 g.Fat: 4 g. Sugar: 7 g. Fiber: 2 g.

39. Crab and Spinach Frittata

Preparation time: 10 minutes
Cooking time: 30 minutes
Servings: 10
Ingredients

- 3/4 lb. crabmeat
- 8 eggs
- 10 oz. spinach, frozen and thawed, squeeze dry
- 2 stalks celery, diced
- 2 cup half-n-half
- 1 cup Swiss cheese
- 1/2 cup onion, diced
- 1/2 cup red pepper, diced
- 1/4 cup mushrooms, diced
- 2 tbsp. margarine
- 1 cup bread crumbs
- 1/2 tsp. salt
- 1/4 tsp. pepper

- 1/4 tsp. nutmeg
- Non-stick cooking spray

Directions

1. Heat oven to 375°F. Spray a large casserole or baking dish with cooking spray.
2. In a large bowl, beat eggs and half-n-half. Stir in crab, spinach, bread crumbs, cheese, and seasonings.
3. Melt butter in a large skillet over medium heat. Add celery, onion, rep pepper, and mushrooms. Cook, occasionally stirring, until vegetables are tender, about 5 minutes. Add to egg mixture.
4. Pour mixture into prepared baking dish and bake for 30–35 minutes, or until eggs are firm and top is light brown.
5. Cool for 10 minutes before serving.

Nutrition Calories: 261 Total carbs: 18 g.Net carbs: 16 g.Protein: 14 g.Fat: 15 g.Sugar: 4 g.Fiber: 2 g.

40. Cranberry Coffeecake

Preparation time: 10 minutes
Cooking time: 20–25 minutes
Servings: 12
Ingredients

- 1 cup whole fresh cranberries
- 4 large eggs
- 1 1/4 cup flaxseed meal
- 1/2 cup Splenda®
- 1/2 cup sugar-free vanilla syrup
- 1/4 cup olive oil
- 3 tbsp. cinnamon
- 1 tbsp. vanilla
- 1 tsp. baking powder
- 1 tsp. nutmeg
- 1/2 tsp. salt
- Non-stick cooking spray

Directions

1. Heat oven to 350°F. Coat a Bundt cake pan with cooking spray.
2. Put cranberries in a microwave-safe bowl and cover them with plastic wrap. Cook on high for 1–2 minutes, or until the berries are tender.
3. In a medium mixing bowl, combine all the wet ingredients. Mix until thoroughly combined.
4. Add the dry ingredients and mix well. Let sit for 10 minutes, so the mixture thickens.
5. Fold in the cranberries and pour into the prepared pan.
6. Bake for 20–25 minutes or until the coffee cake passes the toothpick test. Let cook 5 minutes in the pan, then invert onto a serving plate.

Nutrition Calories: 122 Total carbs: 11 g.Net carbs: 9 g.Protein: 2 g.Fat: 6 g.Sugar: 9 g.Fiber: 2 g.

CHAPTER 2:

Lunch And Dinner

41. Asparagus Frittata

Preparation time: 20 minutes
Cooking time: 20 minutes
Servings: 4
Ingredients

- 4 slices bacon, chopped
- Salt and black pepper
- 8 eggs, whisked
- 1 bunch asparagus, trimmed and chopped

Directions

1. Heat a pan, add bacon, stir and cook for 5 minutes.
2. Add asparagus, salt, and pepper; stir, and cook for an additional 5 minutes.
3. Add the chilled eggs, spread them in the pan, allow them to substitute the oven, and bake for 20 minutes at 350°F.
4. Share and divide between plates and serve for breakfast.

Nutrition Calories: 251 Carbs: 16 g.Fat: 6 g.Fiber: 8 g.Protein: 7.76 g.

42. Avocados Stuffed With Salmon

Preparation time: 5 minutes
Cooking time: 5 minutes
Servings: 2
Ingredients:

- 1 avocado, pitted and halved
- 2 tbsp. olive oil
- 1 lemon juice
- 2 oz. smoked salmon, flaked
- 1 oz. goat cheese, crumbled
- Salt and black pepper to taste

Directions

1. In your kitchen appliance, combine the salmon with juice, oil, cheese, salt, and pepper and pulsate well.
2. Divide this mixture into the avocado halves and serve.

3. Serve and enjoy!

Nutrition Calories: 300 Fat: 15 g.Fiber: 5 g.Carbs: 8 g.Protein: 16 g.

43. Bacon and Brussels Sprout Breakfast

Preparation time: 15 minutes
Cooking time: 10 minutes
Servings: 3
Ingredients

- 1 1/2 tbsp. apple cider vinegar
- Salt to taste
- 2 shallots, minced
- 2 garlic cloves, minced
- 3 medium eggs
- 12 oz. Brussels sprouts, sliced
- Black pepper to taste
- 2 oz. bacon, chopped
- 1 tbsp. butter, melted

Directions

1. Over medium heat, fry the bacon quickly until crispy, then reserve on a plate.
2. Set the pan ablaze again to fry garlic and shallots for 30 seconds.
3. Stir in apple vinegar, Brussels sprouts, and seasoning to cook for 5 minutes.
4. Add the bacon to cook for 5 minutes, then stir in the butter and set a hole in the middle.
5. Crash the eggs to the pan and let cook fully.
6. Enjoy.

Nutrition Calories: 275 Fat: 16.5 g.Fiber: 4.3 g.Carbs: 17.2 g Protein: 17.4 g.

44. Onion and Zucchini Platter

Preparation time: 15 minutes
Cooking time: 45 minutes
Servings: 4
Ingredients

- 3 large zucchinis, julienned
- 1 cup cherry tomatoes, halved

- 1/2 cup basil
- 2 red onions, thinly sliced
- 1/4 tsp. salt
- 1 tsp. cayenne pepper
- 2 tbsp. lemon juice

Directions
1. Make zucchini noodles using a vegetable peeler and shave the zucchini with a peeler lengthwise until you get to the core and seeds.
2. Turn zucchini and repeat until you have long strips.
3. Discard seeds.
4. Lay strips on a chopping board and slice lengthwise to your required thickness.
5. Mix noodles in a bowl alongside onion, basil, tomatoes, and toss.
6. Sprinkle salt and cayenne pepper on top and drizzle the juice.
7. Serve and enjoy!

Nutrition Calories: 156 Fat: 8 g.Carbohydrates: 6 g.Protein: 7 g.

45. Lemon Flavored Sprouts
Preparation time: 10 minutes
Cooking time: 0 minutes
Servings: 4
Ingredients

- 1 lb. Brussels sprouts, trimmed and shredded
- 8 tbsp. olive oil
- 1 lemon, juiced, and zested
- Salt and pepper to taste
- 3/4 cup spicy almond and seed mix

Directions
1. Take a bowl and blend in juice, salt, pepper, and vegetable oil; mix well.
2. Stir in shredded Brussels sprouts and toss. Let it sit for 10 minutes.
3. Add nuts and toss.

Nutrition Calories: 382 Fat: 36 g.Carbohydrates: 9 g.Protein: 7 g.

46. Avocado and Caprese Salad
Preparation time: 15 minutes
Cooking time: 0 minutes
Servings: 6
Ingredients:

- 2 avocados, cubed
- 1 cup cherry tomatoes, halved
- 8 ounces cashew cheese

- 2 tbsp. finely chopped fresh basil
- 2 tbsp. olive oil
- 2 tbsp. balsamic vinegar
- 1 tbsp. salt
- Fresh ground black pepper

Directions:
1. Take a bowl and add the listed ingredients; toss them well until thoroughly mixed
2. Season with salt pepper at your taste.
3. Serve and enjoy!

Nutrition Calories: 358 Fat: 30 g. Carbohydrates: 9 g. Protein: 14 g.

47. Cilantro and Kidney Beans
Preparation time: 6 minutes
Cooking time: 0 minutes
Servings: 4
Ingredients

- 1 can (15 oz.) kidney beans, drained and rinsed
- 1/2 English cucumber, chopped
- 1 medium heirloom tomato, chopped
- 1 bunch fresh cilantro, stems removed and chopped
- 1 red onion, chopped
- 1 lime juice - 3 tbsp. Dijon mustard
- 1/2 tsp. fresh garlic paste
- 1 tsp. Sumac
- Salt and pepper as needed

Directions
1. Take a medium-sized bowl and add kidney beans, chopped-up veggies, and cilantro.
2. Take a small bowl and make the vinaigrette by adding juice, oil, fresh garlic, pepper, mustard, and sumac.
3. Pour the vinaigrette over the salad and provide it with a mild stir.
4. Add some salt and pepper.
5. Cover and permit it to relax for 30 minutes.

Nutrition Calories: 74 Fat: 0.7 g.Carbohydrates: 16 g.Protein: 21 g.

48. Ginger Soup
Preparation time: 10 minutes
Cooking time: 10 minutes
Servings: 4
Ingredients

- 1 can tomatoes, diced

- 1 can peppers
- 6 cups vegetable broth
- 3 cups green onions, diced
- 2 cups mushrooms, sliced
- 3 tsp. garlic, minced
- 3 tsp. ginger, fresh and grated
- 4 tbsp. tamari
- 2 cups bok choy, chopped
- 1 tbsp. cilantro, chopped
- 3 tbsp. carrot, grated

Directions
1. Add all the ingredients apart from carrots and scallions into a saucepan, then bring it to a boil using medium-high heat.
2. Lower to medium-low, cooking for 6 minutes.
3. Stir in your carrots and green onions, cooking for an additional 2 minutes.
4. Serve with cilantro.

Nutrition Calories: 382 Fat: 36 g.Carbohydrates: 9 g.Protein: 7 g.

49. Buttery Garlic Shrimp

Preparation time: 10 minutes
Cooking time: 15 minutes
Servings: 4
Ingredients

- 6 tbsp. butter
- 1 lb. shrimp, cooked
- 2 lemons, halved
- 1/2 tsp. red pepper flakes
- 4 garlic cloves, crushed
- Sea salt and black pepper to taste

Directions
1. Start by heating your oven to 425°F, then place the butter in an 8-inch baking dish; the butter should melt.
2. Sprinkle your shrimp with salt and pepper, then slice your lemon halves into thin slices.
3. Add your shrimp, garlic, and butter to the baking dish. Sprinkle with red pepper flakes and cook for 15 minutes. Stir halfway through, then squeeze the lemon wedges across the dish before serving.

Nutrition Calories: 329Protein: 32 g.Fat: 20 g.Net carbs: 4 g.

50. Bacon and Lemon Spiced Muffins

Preparation time: 10 minutes
Cooking time: 20 minutes
Servings: 12
Ingredients

- 2 tsp. lemon thyme
- Salt to taste
- 3 cups almond flour
- 1/2 cup butter, melted
- 1 tsp. baking soda
- Black pepper to taste
- 4 medium eggs
- 1 cup bacon, diced

Directions
1. In a bowl, stir together the eggs and baking soda until well integrated.
2. Whisk in the seasonings, butter, bacon, and lemon thyme.
3. Set the mixture in a well-lined muffin pan.
4. Set the oven for 20 minutes at 350°F; allow to bake.
5. Allow the muffins to chill before serving.

Nutrition Calories: 186 Fat: 17.1 g.Fiber: 0.8 g.Carbs: 1.8 g.

51. Salmon Stew

Preparation time: 8 minutes
Cooking time: 12 minutes
Servings: 2
Ingredients

- 1 lb. salmon fillet, sliced
- 1 onion, chopped
- Salt to taste
- 1 tbsp. butter, melted
- 1 cup fish broth
- 1/2 tsp. red chili powder

Directions
1. Season the salmon fillets with salt and red chili.
2. Put butter and onions in a skillet and sauté for 3 minutes.
3. Add seasoned salmon and cook for 2 minutes on all sides.
4. Add fish broth and close the lid.
5. Cook for 7 minutes on medium heat and open the lid.
6. Dish out and serve immediately.

7. Transfer the stew to a bowl and put it aside to cool for meal prepping.
8. Divide the mixture into 2 containers. Cover the containers and refrigerate for about 2 days. Reheat in the microwave before serving.

Nutrition Calories: 272 Carbs: 4.4 g.Protein: 32.1 g.Fat: 14.2 g.Sugar: 1.9 g.

52.   Asparagus Salmon Fillets
Preparation time: 10 minutes
Cooking time: 20 minutes
Servings: 2
Ingredients

- 1 tsp. olive oil
- 4 asparagus stalks
- 2 salmon fillets
- 1/4 cup butter
- 1/4 cup champagne
- Salt and freshly ground black pepper, to taste

Directions

1. Preheat the oven to 355ºF and grease a baking dish.
2. Put all the ingredients in a bowl and blend well.
3. Put this mixture in the baking dish and transfer it to the oven.
4. Bake for 20 minutes and dish out.
5. Place the salmon fillets in a dish and put them aside to cool for meal prepping. Divide it into 2 containers and close the lid. Refrigerate for 1 day and reheat in microwave before serving.

Nutrition Calories: 475 Carbs: 1.1 g.Protein: 35.2 g.Fat: 36.8 g.Sugar: 0.5 g.Sodium: 242 mg.

53.   Crispy Baked Chicken
Preparation time: 30 minutes
Cooking time: 10 minutes
Servings: 2
Ingredients

- 2 chicken breasts, skinless and boneless
- 2 tbsp. butter
- 1/4 tsp. turmeric powder
- Salt and black pepper, to taste
- 1/4 cup sour cream

Directions

1. Preheat the oven to 360ºF and grease a baking dish with butter.
2. Season the chicken with turmeric powder, salt, and black pepper in a bowl.

3. Put the chicken on the baking dish and transfer it to the oven.
4. Bake for 10 minutes and serve topped with soured cream.
5. Transfer the chicken to a bowl and put it aside to cool for meal prepping. Divide it into 2 containers and cover them.
6. Refrigerate for up to 2 days and reheat in microwave before serving.

Nutrition Calories: 304 Carbs: 1.4 g.Protein: 26.1 g.Fat: 21.6 g.Sugar: 0.1 g.Sodium: 137 mg.

54.   Creamy Chicken
Preparation time: 12 minutes
Cooking time: 13 minutes
Servings: 2
Ingredients

- 1/2 small onion, chopped
- 1/4 cup sour cream
- 1 tbsp. butter
- 1/4 cup mushrooms
- 1/2 lb. chicken breasts

Directions

1. Heat butter in a skillet and add onions and mushrooms.
2. Sauté for 5 minutes and add chicken breasts and salt.
3. Close the lid and cook for 5 more minutes.
4. Add the soured cream and cook for 3 minutes.
5. Open the lid and serve in a dish to eat immediately.
6. Transfer the creamy chicken breasts into a dish and put them aside to chill for meal prepping.
7. Divide it into 2 containers and cover them. Refrigerate for 2–3 days and reheat in microwave before serving.

Nutrition Calories: 335 Carbs: 2.9 g.Protein: 34 g.Fat: 20.2 g.Sugar: 0.8 g.Sodium: 154 mg.

55.   Paprika Butter Shrimp
Preparation time: 15 minutes
Cooking time: 15 minutes
Servings: 2
Ingredients

- 1/4 tbsp. smoked paprika
- 1/8 cup sour cream
- 1/2 lb. shrimp
- 1/8 cup butter
- Salt and black pepper, to taste

Directions

1. Preheat the oven to 390°F and grease a baking dish.
2. Mix all the ingredients in a large bowl and transfer them into the baking dish.
3. Place in the oven and bake for 15 minutes.
4. Place paprika shrimp in a dish and put it aside to chill for meal prepping. Divide it into 2 containers and cover them. Refrigerate for 1–2 days and reheat in microwave before serving.

Nutrition Calories: 330 Carbs: 1.5 g.Protein: 32.6 g.Fat: 21.5 g.Sugar: 0.2 g.Sodium: 458 mg.

56. Almond Flour Burger With Goat Cheese

Preparation time: 10 minutes
Cooking time: 20 minutes
Servings: 2
Ingredients

- 2 almond flour bagels
- 2 tbsp. fresh goat cheese
- 4 slices smoked salmon
- 2 pinch salt and pepper
- 4 radishes
- 3 dill

Directions

1. Cut the gluten-free bagel in half. Put the 2 halves in the toaster to make them crisp.
2. Spread both slices with the fresh goat cheese and add salmon.
3. Garnish the bagel with radish and dill.
4. A pinch of salt and pepper, and it's ready.
5. Put each burger in a container and store it in the refrigerator.

Nutrition Calories: 325 Fat: 29 g.Carbs: 4 g Protein: 12 g.Sugar: 0.9 g.

57. Stuffed Bell Peppers With Quinoa

Preparation time: 10 minutes
Cooking time: 35 minutes
Servings: 2
Ingredients

- 2 bell peppers
- 1/3 cup quinoa
- 3 oz. chicken stock
- 1/4 cup onion, diced

- 1/2 tsp. salt
- 1/4 tsp. tomato paste
- 1/2 tsp. oregano, dried
- 1/3 cup sour cream
- 1 tsp. paprika

Directions

1. Trim the bell peppers and take away the seeds.
2. Then combine chicken broth and quinoa in the pan.
3. Add salt and boil the ingredients for 10 minutes or until quinoa will soak all liquid.
4. Then combine cooked quinoa with dried oregano, tomato paste, and onion.
5. Fill the bell peppers with the quinoa mixture and arrange them in the casserole mold.
6. Add the sour cream and bake the peppers for 25 minutes at 365°F.
7. Serve the cooked peppers with sour cream sauce from the casserole mold.

Nutrition Calories: 237 Fat: 10.3 g.Fiber: 4.5 g.Carbs: 31.3 g.Protein: 6.9 g.

58. Mediterranean Burrito

Preparation time: 10 minutes
Cooking time: 0 minutes
Servings: 2
Ingredients

- 2 wheat tortillas
- 2 oz. red kidney beans, canned, drained
- 2 tbsp. hummus
- 2 tsp. tahini sauce
- 1 cucumber
- 2 lettuce leaves
- 1 tbsp. lime juice
- 1 tsp. olive oil
- 1/2 tsp. oregano, dried

Directions

1. Mash the red kidney beans until you get a puree.
2. Then spread the wheat tortillas with beans mash from one side.
3. Add hummus and tahini sauce.
4. Cut the cucumber into the wedges and place them over tahini sauce.
5. Then add lettuce leaves.

To make the dressing: Mix a little vegetable oil, dried oregano, and lime juice.

6. Drizzle the lettuce leaves with the dressing and wrap the wheat tortillas in a burrito shape.

Nutrition Calories: 288 Fat: 10.2 g.Fiber: 14.6 g.Carbs: 38.2 g.Protein: 12.5 g.

59. Prosciutto Wrapped Mozzarella Balls

Preparation time: 10 minutes
Cooking time: 10 minutes
Servings: 4
Ingredients

- 8 Mozzarella balls, cherry size
- 4 oz. bacon, sliced
- 1/4 tsp. ground black pepper
- 3/4 tsp. rosemary, dried
- 1 tsp. butter

Directions

1. Sprinkle the sliced bacon with ground black pepper and dried rosemary.
2. Wrap every Mozzarella ball in the sliced bacon and secure them with toothpicks.
3. Melt butter.
4. Brush wrapped mozzarella balls with butter.
5. Line the tray with the baking paper and arrange Mozzarella balls in it.
6. Bake the balls for 10 minutes at 365°F.

Nutrition Calories: 323 Fat: 26.8 g.Fiber: 0.1 g.Carbs: 0.6 g.Protein: 20.6 g.

60. Garlic Chicken Balls

Preparation time: 15 minutes
Cooking time: 10 minutes
Servings: 4
Ingredients

- 2 cups ground chicken
- 1 tsp. garlic, minced
- 1 tsp. dill, dried
- 1/3 carrot, grated
- 1 egg, beaten
- 1 tbsp. olive oil
- 1/4 cup coconut flakes
- 1/2 tsp. salt

Directions

1. Mix the ground chicken, minced garlic, dried dill, carrot, egg, and salt in a bowl.
2. Stir the chicken mixture with the fingertips until homogeneous.
3. Then, make medium balls from the mixture.

4. Coat every chicken ball in coconut flakes.
5. Heat vegetable oil in the skillet.
6. Add chicken balls and cook them for 3 minutes from all sides. The cooked chicken balls will have a golden brown color.

Nutrition Calories: 200 Fat: 11.5 g.Fiber: 0.6 g.Carbs: 1.7 g.Protein: 21.9 g.

61. One-Pot Roast Chicken Dinner

Preparation time: 10 minutes
Cooking time: 40 minutes
Servings: 6
Ingredients

- 1/2 head cabbage
- 1 sweet onion
- 1 sweet potato
- 4 garlic cloves
- 2 tbsp. extra-virgin olive oil
- 2 tsp. fresh thyme, minced
- 2 1/2 lbs. bone-in chicken thighs and drumsticks

Directions

1. Preheat the oven to 450°F.
2. Lightly grease a large roasting pan and arrange the cabbage, onion, sweet potato, and garlic in the bottom. Drizzle with 1 tbsp. of oil, sprinkle with the thyme, and season the vegetables lightly with salt and pepper.
3. Season the chicken with salt and pepper.
4. Place a large skillet over medium-high heat and brown the chicken on both sides in the remaining 1 tbsp. of oil, for 10 minutes.
5. Put the browned chicken on top of the vegetables in the roasting pan. Roast for 30 minutes.

Nutrition Calories: 540 Carbohydrates: 14 g.Fiber: 4 g.Fat: 85.73 g.

62. Almond-Crusted Salmon

Preparation time: 10 minutes
Cooking time: 15 minutes
Servings: 4
Ingredients

- 1/4 cup almond meal
- 1/4 cup whole-wheat breadcrumbs
- 1/4 tsp. ground coriander

- 1/8 tsp. ground cumin
- 4 (6 oz.) boneless salmon fillets
- 1 tbsp. fresh lemon juice
- Salt and pepper to taste

Directions

1. Ready the oven at 500°F and line a small baking dish with foil.
2. Combine the almond meal, breadcrumbs, coriander, and cumin in a small bowl.
3. Rinse the fish in cool water, then pat dry and brush with lemon juice.
4. Season the fish with salt and pepper, then dredge in the almond mixture on both sides.
5. Put the fish in the baking dish and bake for 15 minutes.

Nutrition Calories: 232 Carbohydrates: 5.8 g. Sugar: 1.7 g. Protein: 0.73 g. Fat: 0.13 g.

63.   Chicken and Veggie Bowl With Brown Rice

Preparation time: 10 minutes
Cooking time: 20 minutes
Servings: 4
Ingredients

- 1 cup instant brown rice
- 1/4 cup tahini
- 1/4 cup fresh lemon juice
- 2 garlic cloves, minced
- 1/4 tsp. ground cumin
- Pinch salt and pepper
- 1 tbsp. olive oil
- 4 (4 oz.) chicken breast halves
- 1/2 medium yellow onion, sliced
- 1 cup green beans, trimmed
- 1 cup broccoli, chopped
- 4 cups kale, chopped
- 1 1/4 cup water, divided

Directions

1. Bring 1 cup of water to boil in a small saucepan.
2. Stir in the brown rice and simmer for 5 minutes, then cover and set aside.
3. Meanwhile, whisk together the tahini with 1/4-cup water in a small bowl.
4. Stir in the lemon juice, garlic, and cumin with a pinch of salt and stir well.
5. Heat oil in a big cast-iron skillet over medium heat.

6. Season the chicken with salt and pepper, then add to the skillet.
7. Cook for 3–5 minutes on each side until cooked through, then remove to a cutting board and cover loosely with foil.
8. Reheat the skillet and cook the onion for 2 minutes, then stir in the broccoli and beans.
9. Sauté for 2 minutes, then stir in the kale and sauté 2 minutes more.
10. Add 2 tbsp. of water, then cover and steam for 2 minutes while you slice the chicken.
11. Build the bowls with brown rice, sliced chicken, and sautéed veggies.
12. Serve hot drizzled with the lemon tahini dressing.

Nutrition Calories: 435 Carbohydrates: 24 g. Fiber: 4.8 g. Fat: 11.88 g.

64.   Beef Fajitas

Preparation time: 10 minutes
Cooking time: 15 minutes
Servings: 4
Ingredients

- 1 lb. lean beef sirloin, sliced thin
- 1 tbsp. olive oil
- 1 medium red onion, sliced
- 1 red pepper, sliced thin
- 1 green pepper, sliced thin
- 1/2 tsp. ground cumin
- 1/2 tsp. chili powder
- 8 (6-inch) whole-wheat tortillas
- 1/2 cup fat-free sour cream

Directions

1. Preheat a large cast-iron skillet over medium heat, then add the oil.
2. Add the sliced beef and cook in a single layer for 1 minute on each side.
3. Remove the beef to a bowl and cover to keep warm.
4. Reheat the skillet, then add the onions and peppers; season with cumin and chili powder.
5. Stir-fry the veggies to your liking and add them to the bowl with the beef.
6. Serve hot in small whole-wheat tortillas with sliced avocado and fat-free sour cream.

Nutrition Calories: 430 Carbohydrates: 30.5 g. Fiber: 17 g. Protein: 32.04 g. Fat: 27.76 g.

65.   Italian Pork Chops

Preparation time: 5 minutes
Cooking time: 35 minutes
Servings: 4
Ingredients

- 4 pork chops, boneless
- 3 garlic cloves, minced
- 1 tsp. dried rosemary, crushed
- 1/4 tsp. pepper
- 1/4 tsp. sea salt

Directions

1. Prepare the oven to 425°F/218°C.
2. Line baking tray with cooking spray and season pork chops with pepper and salt. Combine garlic and rosemary and rub all over pork chops.
3. Place the pork chops in a prepared baking tray.
4. Roast the pork chops in the preheated oven for 10 minutes.
5. Set temperature to 180°C and roast for 25 minutes.
6. Serve and enjoy

Nutrition Calories: 261 Carbohydrates: 1 g. Protein: 18 g Fat: 17.39 g.

66.   Chicken Mushroom Stroganoff

Preparation time: 5 minutes
Cooking time: 10 minutes
Servings: 6
Ingredients

- 1 cup fat-free sour cream
- 2 tbsp. flour
- 1 tbsp. Worcestershire sauce
- 1/2 tsp. thyme, dried
- 1 chicken bouillon cube, crushed
- Salt and pepper to taste
- 1/2 cup water
- 1 medium yellow onion
- 8 oz. mushrooms, sliced
- 1 tbsp. olive oil
- 2 garlic cloves, minced
- 12 oz. chicken breast
- 6 oz. whole-wheat noodles, cooked

Directions

1. Whisk together 2/3 cup of the sour cream with the flour, Worcestershire sauce, thyme, and crushed bouillon in a medium bowl.
2. Season with salt and pepper, then slowly stir in the water until well combined.
3. Heat the oil in a large skillet over medium-high heat.
4. Sauté the onions and mushrooms for 3 minutes.
5. Cook the garlic for 2 minutes more and add the chicken.
6. Pour in the sour cream mixture; cook until thick and bubbling. Reduce heat and simmer for 2 minutes.
7. Spoon the chicken and mushroom mixture over the cooked noodles and garnish with the remaining sour cream to serve.

Nutrition Calories: 295 Carbohydrates: 29.6 g. Fiber: 2.9 g.Protein: 16.27 g.Fat: 7.91 g.Sugar: 1.9 g.

67.   Cheesy Mushroom and Pesto Flatbreads

Preparation time: 5 minutes
Cooking time: 13–17 minutes
Servings: 2
Ingredients

- 1 tsp. extra-virgin olive oil
- 1/2 red onion, sliced
- 1/2 cup mushrooms, sliced
- Salt and freshly ground black pepper, to taste
- 1/4 cup store-bought pesto sauce
- 2 whole-wheat flatbreads
- 1/4 cup shredded Mozzarella cheese

Directions

1. Preheat the oven to 350°F (180°C).
2. Heat the olive oil in a small skillet over medium heat. Add the onion slices and mushrooms to the skillet, and sauté for 3–5 minutes, stirring occasionally, or until they start to soften. Season with salt and pepper.
3. Meanwhile, spoon 2 tbsp. of pesto sauce onto each flatbread and spread it all over. Evenly divide the mushroom mixture between 2 flatbreads, then scatter each top with 2 tbsp. of shredded Mozzarella cheese. Transfer the flatbreads to a baking sheet and bake until the cheese melts and bubbles, about 10–12 minutes.
4. Let the flatbreads cool for 5 minutes and serve warm.

Tips: If the flatbread isn't available, the Ezekiel tortilla can be used as a substitute. You can serve with any of your favorite toppings for added flavor, such as tomato slices, bell peppers, or artichoke hearts.

Nutrition Calories: 346 Fat: 22.8 g.Protein: 14.2 g.Carbs: 27.6 g.Fiber: 7.3 g.Sugar: 4.0 g.Sodium: 790 mg.

68. Roasted Brussels Sprouts With Wild Rice Bowl

Preparation time: 15 minutes
Cooking time: 12 minutes
Servings: 4
Ingredients

- 2 cups Brussels sprouts, sliced
- 2 tsp. + 2 tbsp. extra-virgin olive oil
- 1 tsp. Dijon mustard
- 1 lemon juice
- 1 garlic clove, minced
- 1/2 tsp. salt
- 1/4 tsp. freshly ground black pepper
- 1 cup radishes, sliced
- 1 cup wild rice, cooked
- 1 avocado, sliced

Directions:

1. Preheat the oven to 400°F (205°C). Line a baking sheet with parchment paper and set it aside.
2. Add 2 tsp. of olive oil and Brussels sprouts to a medium bowl and toss to coat well.
3. Spread out the oiled Brussels sprouts on the prepared baking sheet. Roast in the preheated oven for 12 minutes or until the Brussels sprouts are browned and crisp.
4. Stir the Brussels sprouts once during cooking to ensure even cooking. Meanwhile, make the dressing by whisking together the remaining olive oil, mustard, lemon juice, garlic, salt, and pepper in a small bowl.
5. Remove the Brussels sprouts from the oven to a large bowl. Add the radishes and cooked wild rice to the bowl.
6. Drizzle with the prepared dressing and gently toss to coat everything evenly. Divide the mixture into 4 bowls and place avocado slices in each bowl. Serve immediately.

Tip: To add more flavors to this meal, try adding 1/2 cup shelled edamame or 4 oz. (113 g.) of grilled tofu to the Brussels sprouts.

Nutrition Calories: 177 Fat: 10.7 g.Protein: 2.3 g.Carbs: 17.6 g.Fiber: 5.1 g.Sugar: 2.0 g.Sodium: 297 mg.

69. Sautéed Zucchini and Tomatoes

Preparation time: 10 minutes
Cooking time: 10 minutes
Servings: 4
Ingredients

- 1 tbsp. vegetable oil
- 1 sliced onion
- 2 lb. (907 g.) zucchini, peeled and cut into 1-inch-thick slices
- 2 tomatoes, chopped
- 1 green bell pepper, chopped
- Salt and freshly ground black pepper, to taste

Directions

1. Heat the vegetable oil in a non-stick skillet until it shimmers.
2. Sauté the onion slices in the oil for about 3 minutes until translucent, stirring occasionally.
3. Add the zucchini, tomatoes, bell pepper, salt, and pepper to the skillet and stir to combine.
4. Reduce the heat, cover, and continue cooking for about 5 minutes, or until the veggies are tender.
5. Remove from the heat to a large plate and serve hot.

Tip: You can store the sautéed zucchini and tomatoes in the fridge for up to 4 days.

Nutrition Calories: 110 Fat: 4.4 g.Protein: 6.9 g.Carbs: 10.7 g.Fiber: 3.4 g.Sugar: 2.2 g.Sodium: 11 mg.

70. Butternut Noodles With Mushroom Sauce

Preparation time: 10 minutes
Cooking time: 15 minutes
Servings: 4
Ingredients

- 1/4 cup extra-virgin olive oil
- 1/2 red onion, finely chopped
- 1 lb. (454 g.) cremini mushrooms, sliced
- 1 tsp. thyme, dried

- 1/2 tsp. sea salt
- 3 garlic cloves, minced
- 1/2 cup dry white wine
- Pinch red pepper flakes
- 4 cups butternut noodles
- 4 oz. (113 g.) Parmesan cheese, grated (optional)

Directions

1. Heat the olive oil in a large skillet over medium-high heat until shimmering.
2. Add the onion, mushrooms, thyme, and salt to the skillet. Sauté for 6 minutes, stirring occasionally, or until the mushrooms begin to brown. Stir in the garlic and cook for 30 seconds until fragrant.
3. Fold in the wine and red pepper flakes and whisk to combine.
4. Add the butternut noodles to the skillet and continue cooking for 5 minutes, stirring occasionally, or until the noodles are softened.
5. Divide the mixture among 4 bowls. Sprinkle the grated Parmesan cheese on top, if desired.

Tips: You can make butternut noodles with a spiralizer, vegetable peeler, or knife. The zucchini noodles or shirataki noodles can be substituted for the butternut squash.

Nutrition Calories: 243 Fat: 14.2 g.Protein: 3.7 g.Carbs: 21.9 g.Fiber: 4.1 g.Sugar: 2.1 g.Sodium: 157 mg.

71. Homemade Vegetable Chili

Preparation time: 10 minutes
Cooking time: 15 minutes
Servings: 4
Ingredients

- 2 tbsp. extra-virgin olive oil
- 1 onion, finely chopped
- 1 green bell pepper, deseeded and chopped
- 1 can (14 oz./397 g.) kidney beans, drained and rinsed
- 2 cans (14 oz./397 g.) crushed tomatoes
- 2 cups veggie crumbles
- 1 tsp. garlic powder
- 1 tbsp. chili powder
- 1/2 tsp. sea salt

Directions

1. Heat the olive oil in a large skillet over medium-high heat until shimmering.
2. Add the onion and bell pepper and sauté for 5 minutes, stirring occasionally.
3. Fold in the beans, tomatoes, veggie crumbles, garlic powder, chili powder, and salt. Stir to incorporate and bring them to a simmer. Reduce the heat and cook for 5 more minutes, stirring occasionally, or until the mixture is heated through. Allow the mixture to cool for 5 minutes and serve warm.

Tips: You can make a chili soup by adding 4 cups of vegetable broth. If you want to reduce the carbs, you can use half of the kidney beans in this recipe.

Nutrition Calories: 282 Fat: 10.1 g.Protein: 16.7 g.Carbs: 38.2 g.Fiber: 12.9 g.Sugar: 7.2 g.Sodium: 1128 mg.

72. Wilted Dandelion Greens With Sweet Onion

Preparation time: 15 minutes
Cooking time: 12 minutes
Servings: 4
Ingredients

- 1 tbsp. extra-virgin olive oil
- 1 Vidalia onion, thinly sliced
- 2 garlic cloves, minced
- 2 bunches dandelion greens, roughly chopped
- 1/2 cup low-sodium vegetable broth
- Freshly ground black pepper, to taste

Directions

1. Heat the olive oil in a large skillet over low heat. Cook the onion and garlic for 2–3 minutes until tender, stirring occasionally.
2. Add the dandelion greens and broth and cook for 5–7 minutes, stirring frequently, or until the greens are wilted.
3. Transfer to a plate and season with black pepper. Serve warm.

Tips: Be sure to add more vegetable broth for preventing the onion and garlic from burning during cooking. For extra flavor and nutrition, you can add the dandelion greens to a white bean salad.

Nutrition Calories: 81 Fat: 3.8 g.Protein: 3.1 g.Carbs: 10.7 g.Fiber: 3.8 g.Sugar: 2.0 g.Sodium: 72 mg.

73. Collard Greens With Tomato

Preparation time: 10 minutes
Cooking time: 20 minutes
Servings: 4
Ingredients

- 1 cup low-sodium vegetable broth, divided
- 1/2 onion, thinly sliced
- 2 garlic cloves, thinly sliced
- 1 medium tomato, chopped
- 1 large bunch collard greens including stems, roughly chopped
- 1 tsp. ground cumin
- 1/2 tsp. freshly ground black pepper

Directions

1. Add 1/2 cup of vegetable broth to a Dutch oven over medium heat and bring to a simmer.
2. Stir in the onion and garlic and cook for 4 minutes until tender.
3. Add the remaining broth, tomato, greens, cumin, and pepper, and gently stir to combine.
4. Reduce the heat to low and simmer uncovered for 15 minutes. Serve warm.

Tip: To add more flavors to this dish, serve it with pasta or cooked black beans and rice.

Nutrition Calories: 68 Fat: 2.1 g.Protein: 4.8 g.Carbs: 13.8 g.Fiber: 7.1 g.Sugar: 2.0 g.Sodium: 67 mg.

74. Cheesy Summer Squash and Quinoa Casserole

Preparation time: 15 minutes
Cooking time: 27–30 minutes
Servings: 8
Ingredients

- 1 tbsp. extra-virgin olive oil
- 1 Vidalia onion, thinly sliced
- 1 large portobello mushroom, thinly sliced
- 6 yellow summer squash, thinly sliced
- 1 cup Parmesan cheese, shredded and divided
- 1 cup Cheddar cheese, shredded
- 1/2 cup tri-color quinoa
- 1/2 cup whole-wheat bread crumbs
- 1 tbsp. Creole seasoning

Directions

1. Preheat the oven to 350°F (180°C).
2. Heat the olive oil in a large cast-iron pan over medium heat.
3. Sauté the onion, mushroom, and squash in the oil for 7–10 minutes, stirring occasionally, or until the vegetables are softened.
4. Remove from the heat and add 1/2 cup of Parmesan cheese and the Cheddar cheese to the vegetables. Stir well.
5. Mix the quinoa, bread crumbs, the remaining Parmesan cheese, and Creole seasoning in a small bowl, then spread the mixture over the vegetables.
6. Place the cast-iron pan in the preheated oven and bake until browned and cooked, about 20 minutes. Cool for 10 minutes and serve on plates while warm.

Tips: If you prefer a gluten-free dish, you can omit the bread crumbs in this recipe. It can be served as a wonderful lunch with a green salad or a tomato salad.

Nutrition Calories: 184 Fat: 8.9 g.Protein: 11.7 g.Carbs: 17.6 g.Fiber: 3.2 g.Sugar: 3.8 g.Sodium: 140 mg.

75. Creamy Macaroni and Cheese

Preparation time: 10 minutes
Cooking time: 25 minutes
Servings: 6
Ingredients

- 1 cup fat-free evaporated milk
- 1/2 cup skim milk
- 1/2 cup low-fat Cheddar cheese
- 1/2 cup low-fat cottage cheese
- 1 tsp. nutmeg
- Pinch cayenne pepper
- Sea salt and freshly ground black pepper, to taste
- 6 cups cooked whole-wheat elbow macaroni
- 2 tbsp. Parmesan cheese, grated

Directions

1. Preheat the oven to 350°F (180°C). Heat the milk in a large saucepan over low heat until it steams.
2. Add the Cheddar cheese and cottage cheese to the milk and keep whisking until the cheese is melted.

3. Add the nutmeg and cayenne pepper and stir well. Sprinkle the salt and pepper to season.

4. Remove from the heat. Add the cooked macaroni to the cheese mixture and stir until well combined. Transfer the macaroni and cheese to a large casserole dish and top with the grated Parmesan cheese.

5. Bake in the preheated oven for 20 minutes, or until bubbly and lightly browned.

6. Divide the macaroni and cheese among 6 bowls and serve.

Tip: You can add other kinds of pasta instead of elbow macaroni to the cheese mixture.

Nutrition Calories: 245 Fat: 2.1 g.Protein: 15.7 g.Carbs: 43.8 g.Fiber: 3.8 g.Sugar: 6.8 g.Sodium: 186 mg.

76. Roasted Tomato and Bell Pepper Soup

Preparation time: 20 minutes
Cooking time: 35 minutes
Servings: 6
Ingredients

- 2 tbsp. extra-virgin olive oil, plus more for coating the baking dish
- 16 plum tomatoes, cored and halved
- 4 celery stalks, coarsely chopped
- 4 red bell peppers, seeded, halved
- 4 garlic cloves, lightly crushed
- 1 sweet onion, cut into eighths
- Sea salt and freshly ground black pepper, to taste
- 6 cups low-sodium chicken broth
- 2 tbsp. fresh basil, chopped
- 2 oz. (57 g.) goat cheese, grated

Directions

1. Preheat the oven to 400°F (205°C). Coat a large baking dish lightly with olive oil. Put the tomatoes in the oiled dish, cut-side down.

2. Scatter the celery, bell peppers, garlic, and onion on top of the tomatoes. Drizzle with 2 tbsp. of olive oil and season with salt and pepper.

3. Roast in the preheated oven for 30 minutes, or until the vegetables are fork-tender and slightly charred. Remove the

vegetables from the oven. Let them rest for a few minutes until cooled slightly.

4. Transfer to a food processor, along with the chicken broth, and purée until fully mixed and smooth. Pour the purée soup into a medium saucepan and bring it to a simmer over medium-high heat.

5. Sprinkle the basil and grated cheese on top before serving.

Tip: You can use the yellow and orange tomatoes to replace the plum tomatoes for a great source of lycopene.

Nutrition Calories: 187 Fat: 9.7 g.Protein: 7.8 g.Carbs: 21.3 g.Fiber: 6.1 g.Sugar: 14.0 g.Sodium: 825 mg.

77. Spaghetti Puttanesca

Preparation time: 20 minutes
Cooking time: 35 minutes
Servings: 6
Ingredients

- 1 tbsp. extra-virgin olive oil
- 3 tsp. garlic, minced
- 1 sweet onion, chopped
- 2 celery stalks, chopped
- 2 cans (28 oz./794 g.) sodium-free diced tomatoes
- 1 tbsp. fresh oregano, chopped
- 2 tbsp. fresh basil, chopped
- 1/2 tsp. red pepper flakes
- 1/2 cup pitted Kalamata olives, quartered
- 1/4 cup lemon juice, freshly squeezed
- 8 oz. (227 g.) whole-wheat spaghetti, cooked

Directions

1. Heat the olive oil in a large saucepan over medium-high heat. Add the garlic, onion, and celery to the saucepan and sauté for 3 minutes, stirring occasionally, or until softened.

2. Toss in the tomatoes, oregano, basil, and pepper flakes and stir to combine. Allow the sauce to boil, often stirring to prevent it from sticking to the bottom of the pan.

3. Reduce the heat to low and bring the sauce to a simmer, occasionally stirring for about 20 minutes. Add the olives and lemon juice to the sauce and mix well.

4. Remove from the heat and spoon the sauce over the spaghetti. Toss well and serve warm.

Tip: You can add 2 tbsp. of capers to the sauce and sprinkle with a small bunch of freshly chopped parsley before serving.

Nutrition Calories: 199 Fat: 4.7 g.Protein: 7.2 g.Carbs: 34.9 g.Fiber: 3.9 g.Sugar: 8.1 g.Sodium: 89 mg.

78. Black Bean and Tomato Soup With Lime Yogurt

Preparation time: 8 hours 10 minutes
Cooking time: 1 hour 33 minutes
Servings: 8
Ingredients

- 2 tbsp. avocado oil
- 1 medium onion, chopped
- 1 can (10 oz./284 g.) tomatoes and green chilies, diced
- 1 lb. (454 g.) dried black beans, soaked in water for at least 8 hours, rinsed
- 1 tsp. ground cumin
- 3 garlic cloves, minced
- 6 cups chicken bone broth, vegetable broth, or water
- Kosher salt, to taste
- 1 tbsp. lime juice, freshly squeezed
- 1/4 cup plain Greek yogurt

Directions

1. Heat the avocado oil in a nonstick skillet over medium heat until shimmering. Add the onion and sauté for 3 minutes or until translucent.
2. Transfer the onion to a pot, add the tomatoes and green chilies and their juices, black beans, cumin, garlic, broth, and salt. Stir to combine well.
3. Bring to a boil over medium-high heat, then reduce the heat to low. Simmer for 1 hour 30 minutes or until the beans are soft.
4. Meanwhile, combine the lime juice with Greek yogurt in a small bowl. Stir to mix well. Pour the soup in a large serving bowl, then drizzle with the lime yogurt mixture before serving.

Tip: If you want to make a thicker soup, remove 1 cup of beans from the pot after simmering, then pour the remaining soup into a food processor. Process to purée the soup until smooth, then move 1 cup of beans back to the soup and serve.

Nutrition Calories: 285 Fat: 6.0 g.Protein: 19.0 g.Carbs: 42.0 g.Fiber: 10.0 g.Sugar: 3.0 g.Sodium: 174 mg.

79. Grilled Tuna Kebabs

Preparation time: 5 minutes
Cooking time: 25 minutes
Servings: 4
Ingredients

- 2 1/2 tbsp. rice vinegar
- 2 tbsp. ginger, fresh grated
- 2 tbsp. sesame oil
- 2 tbsp. soy sauce
- 2 tbsp. cilantro, fresh chopped
- 1 tbsp. green chili, minced
- 1 1/2 lbs. fresh tuna, cut into 1 1/4-inch cubes
- 1 large red pepper, cut into 1-inch pieces
- 1 large red onion, cut into 1-inch pieces

Directions

1. Whisk together the rice vinegar, ginger, sesame oil, soy sauce, cilantro, and chili in a medium bowl; add a few drops of liquid stevia extract to sweeten.
2. Toss in the tuna and chill for 20 minutes, covered.
3. Meanwhile, grease a grill pan with cooking spray and soak wooden skewers in water.
4. Slide the tuna cubes onto the skewers with red pepper and onion.
5. Grill for 3–4 minutes on each side until done to your liking and serve hot.

Nutrition Calories: 240 Total fat: 8.2 g.Saturated fat: 1 g.Total carbs: 8.5 g.Net carbs: 6.8 g.Protein: 31.5 g.Sugar: 3.4 g.Fiber: 1.7 g.Sodium: 503 mg.

80. Strawberry-Arugula Salad

Preparation time: 10 minutes
Cooking time: 0
Servings: 2
Ingredients

- 1/4 cup parsley leaves, fresh chopped
- 2 cups arugula
- 1/2 cup strawberries
- 1/4 cup basil leaves, fresh
- 3 tbsps. lemon vinaigrette
- 1/4 cup red onion, thinly sliced

- Salt and pepper to taste
- Thinly sliced almonds (optional) for topping

Directions

1. Toss parsley, arugula, and basil in a salad bowl.
2. Add the dressing, quartered berries along with the red onion, and toss again.
3. Season prepared salad with salt and pepper to taste, then top with thinly sliced almonds for topping. Serve and enjoy!

Nutrition Calories: 41 Protein: 0.2 g.Fat: 0.4 g.Carbs: 20 g.

CHAPTER 3:

Snack And Appetizer

81. Garlic Kale Chips

Preparation time: 6–7 minutes
Cooking time: 10 minutes
Servings: 2
Ingredients

- 1 tbsp. yeast flakes
- Sea salt to taste
- 1 tsp. vegan seasoning
- 4 cups kale, packed
- 2 tbsp. olive oil
- 1 tsp. garlic, minced

Directions

1. In a bowl, place the oil, kale, garlic, and ranch seasoning pieces. Add the yeast and mix well. Dump the coated kale into the air fryer basket and cook at 375°F for 5 minutes.
2. Shake after 3 minutes and serve.

Nutrition Calories: 50 Total fat: 1.9 g.Carbs: 10 g. Protein: 46 g.

82. Garlic Salmon Balls

Preparation time: 6–7 minutes
Cooking time: 15 minutes
Servings: 2
Ingredients

- 6 oz. salmon, tinned
- 1 large egg
- 3 tbsp. olive oil
- 5 tbsp. wheat germ
- 1/2 tsp. garlic powder
- 1 tbsp. dill, fresh chopped
- 4 tbsp. spring onion, diced
- 4 tbsp. celery, diced

Directions

1. Preheat your air fryer to 370°F. Mix the salmon, egg, celery, onion, dill, and garlic in a large bowl.
2. Shape the mixture into golf ball-sized balls and roll them in the wheat germ.

3. In a small pan, warm olive oil over medium-low heat.
4. Add the salmon balls and slowly flatten them. Transfer them to your air fryer and cook for 10 minutes.

Nutrition Calories: 219 Total fat: 7.7 g.Carbs: 14.8 g.Protein: 23.1 g.

83. Onion Rings

Preparation time: 7 minutes
Cooking time: 10 minutes
Servings: 3
Ingredients

- 1 onion, cut into slices then separate into rings
- 1 1/2 cups almond flour
- 3/4 cup pork rinds
- 1 cup milk
- 1 egg
- 1 tbsp. baking powder
- 1/2 tsp. salt

Directions

1. Preheat your air fryer for 10 minutes. Cut the onion into slices, then separate into rings.
2. In a container, add the flour, baking powder, and salt. Whisk the eggs and the milk, then combines with flour.
3. Gently dip the floured onion rings into the batter to coat them. Spread the pork rinds on a plate and dredge the rings in the crumbs.
4. Place the onion rings in your air fryer and cook for 10 minutes at 360°F.

Nutrition Calories: 304 Total fat: 18 g. Carbs: 31 g. Protein: 38 g.

84. Crispy Eggplant Fries

Preparation time: 7 minutes
Cooking time: 12 minutes
Servings: 3
Ingredients

- 2 eggplants

- 1/4 cup olive oil
- 1/4 cup almond flour
- 1/2 cup water

Directions

1. Preheat your air fryer to 390°F.
2. Cut the eggplants into half-inch slices.
3. In a mixing bowl, mix the flour, olive oil, water, and eggplants.
4. Slowly coat the eggplants. Add eggplants to the air fryer and cook for 12 minutes.
5. Serve with yogurt or tomato sauce.

Nutrition Calories: 103 Total fat: 7.3 g.Carbs: 12.3 g.Protein: 1.9 g.

85.   Charred Bell Peppers

Preparation time: 7 minutes
Cooking time: 4 minutes
Servings: 3
Ingredients

- 20 bell peppers, sliced and seeded
- 1 tsp. olive oil
- Pinch sea salt
- 1 lemon

Directions

1. Preheat your air fryer to 390°F.
2. Sprinkle the peppers with oil and salt. Cook the peppers in the air fryer for 4 minutes.
3. Place the peppers in a large bowl, and squeeze lemon juice over the top. Season with salt and pepper.

Nutrition Calories: 30 Total fat: 0.25 g.Carbs: 6.91 g.Protein: 1.28 g.

86.   Garlic Tomatoes

Preparation time: 7 minutes
Cooking time: 15 minutes
Servings: 4
Ingredients

- 3 tbsp. vinegar
- 1/2 tsp. thyme, dried
- 4 tomatoes
- 1 tbsp. olive oil
- Salt and black pepper to taste
- 1 garlic clove, minced

Directions

1. Preheat your air fryer to 390°F.
2. Cut the tomatoes into halves and remove the seeds.
3. Place them in a large bowl and toss with oil, salt, pepper, garlic, and thyme. Put

them into the air fryer and cook for 15 minutes.
4. Drizzle with vinegar and serve.

Nutrition Calories: 28.9 Total fat: 2.4 g.Carbs: 2.0 g.Protein: 0.4 g.

87.   Mushroom Stew

Preparation time: 7 minutes
Cooking time: 1 hour 22 minutes
Servings: 6
Ingredients

- 1 lb. chicken, cubed, boneless, skinless
- 2 tbsp. canola oil
- 1 lb. fresh mushrooms, sliced
- 1 tbsp. thyme, dried
- 3/4 cup water
- 2 tbsp. tomato paste
- 3 large tomatoes, chopped
- 4 garlic cloves, minced
- 1 cup green peppers, sliced
- 3 cups zucchini, diced
- 1 large onion, diced
- 1 tbsp. basil
- 1 tbsp. marjoram
- 1 tbsp. oregano

Directions

1. Cut the chicken into cubes. Put them in the air fryer basket and pour olive oil over them. Add mushrooms, zucchini, onion, and green pepper.
2. Mix and add the garlic, cook for 2 minutes, and add tomato paste, water, and seasonings.
3. Close the air fryer and cook the stew for 50 minutes. Set the heat to 340°F and cook for 20 more minutes.
4. Remove from the air fryer and transfer into a large pan.
5. Add a little water and simmer for 10 minutes.

Nutrition Calories: 53 Total fat: 3.3 g.Carbs: 4.9 g.Protein: 2.3 g.

88.   Cheese and Onion Nuggets

Preparation time: 7 minutes
Cooking time: 12 minutes
Servings: 4
Ingredients

- 7 oz. Edam cheese, grated
- 2 spring onions, diced
- 1 egg, beaten

- 1 tbsp. coconut oil
- 1 tbsp. thyme, dried
- Salt and pepper to taste

Directions

1. Mix the onion, cheese, coconut oil, salt, pepper, and thyme in a bowl.
2. Make 8 small balls and place the cheese in the center.
3. Put them in the fridge for 1 hour. With a pastry brush, carefully brush beaten egg over the nuggets.
4. Cook for 12 minutes in the air fryer at 350°F.

Nutrition Calories: 227 Total fat: 17.3 g.Carbs: 4.5 g.Protein: 14.2 g.

89. Spiced Nuts

Preparation time: 7 minutes
Cooking time: 25 minutes
Servings: 3 cups
Ingredients

- 1 cup almonds
- 1 cup pecan halves
- 1 cup cashews
- 1 egg white, beaten
- 1/2 tsp. cinnamon, ground
- Pinch cayenne pepper
- 1/4 tsp. cloves, ground
- Dash salt to taste

Directions

1. Combine the egg white with spices.
2. Preheat your air fryer to 300°F.
3. Toss the nuts in the spiced mixture.
4. Cook for 25 minutes, stirring several times throughout cooking time.

Nutrition Calories: 88.4 Total fat: 7.6 g. Carbs: 3.9 g.Protein: 2.5 g.

90. Keto French Fries

Preparation time: 7 minutes
Cooking time: 20 minutes
Servings: 4
Ingredients

- 1 large (1/4-inch) rutabaga, peeled, cut into spears
- Salt and pepper to taste
- 1/2 tsp. paprika
- 2 tbsp. coconut oil

Directions

1. Preheat your air fryer to 450°F.
2. Mix the oil, paprika, salt, and pepper.

3. Pour the oil mixture over the fries, making sure all pieces are well coated.
4. Cook in the air fryer for 20 minutes or until crispy.

Nutrition Calories: 113 Total fat: 7.2 g.Carbs: 12.5 g.Protein: 1.9 g.

91. Fried Garlic Green Tomatoes

Preparation time: 7 minutes
Cooking time: 12 minutes
Servings: 2
Ingredients

- 3 green tomatoes, sliced
- 1/2 cup almond flour
- 2 eggs, beaten
- Salt and pepper to taste
- 1 tsp. garlic, minced

Directions

1. Preheat your air fryer to 400°F.
2. Season the tomatoes with salt, garlic, and pepper.
3. Dip the tomatoes first in flour and then in the egg mixture.
4. Drizzle the tomato rounds with olive oil and place them in the air fryer basket.
5. Cook for 8 minutes, then flip over and cook for additional 4 minutes.
6. Serve with zero-carb mayonnaise.

Nutrition Calories: 123 Total fat: 3.9 g. Carbs: 16 g. Protein: 8.4 g.

92. Garlic Cauliflower Tots

Preparation time: 7 minutes
Cooking time: 20 minutes
Servings: 6
Ingredients

- 1 crown cauliflower, chopped in a food processor
- 1/2 cup Parmesan cheese, grated
- Salt and pepper to taste
- 1/4 cup almond flour
- 2 eggs
- 1 tsp. garlic, minced

Directions

1. Preheat your air fryer to 400°F.
2. Mix all the ingredients.
3. Shape the tots and drizzle with olive oil.
4. Cook for 10 minutes on each side.

Nutrition Calories: 18 Fat: 0.6 g.Carbs: 1.3 g.Protein: 1.8 g.

93. Green Onions and Parmesan Tomatoes

Preparation time: 7 minutes
Cooking time: 15 minutes
Servings: 4
Ingredients

- 4 large tomatoes, cut into slices
- 1 tbsp. olive oil
- Salt and pepper to taste
- 1/2 tsp. thyme, dried
- 2 garlic cloves, minced
- 2 green onions, finely chopped
- 1/2 cup Parmesan cheese, freshly grated

Directions

1. Preheat your air fryer to 390°F.
2. Coat the tomato slices with olive oil and season with garlic, thyme, salt, and pepper.
3. Top with Parmesan and chopped green onions.
4. Place the tomatoes in the air fryer and cook for 15 minutes.
5. Serve on top of crostini or any meat, poultry, or fish.

Nutrition Calories: 69 Total fat: 3.9 g.Carbs: 69 g. Protein: 1.6 g.

94. Green Bell Peppers With Cauliflower Stuffing

Preparation time: 7 minutes
Cooking time: 20 minutes
Servings: 4
Ingredients

- 4 green bell peppers, top cut, deseeded
- 1 tsp. lemon juice
- 2 tbsp. coriander leaves, finely chopped
- 2 green chilies, finely chopped
- 2 cups cauliflower, cooked and mashed
- 2 onions, finely chopped
- 1 tsp. cumin seeds
- 1/4 tsp. turmeric powder
- 1/4 tsp. chili powder
- 1/4 tsp. garam masala
- Salt to taste
- Olive oil as needed

Directions

1. In a saucepan, warm the oil and sauté the chilies, onion, and cumin seeds. Swell the rest of the ingredients except the bell peppers and mix well.

2. Preheat your air fryer to 390°F for 10 minutes.
3. Brush the green bell peppers with olive oil inside and out and stuff each pepper with cauliflower mixture.
4. Place them into the air fryer and grill for 10 minutes.

Nutrition Calories: 257 Total fat: 4.0 g.Carbs: 44.8 g.Protein: 12.3 g.

95. Cheesy Chickpea and Zucchini Burgers

Preparation time: 7 minutes
Cooking time: 15 minutes
Servings: 4
Ingredients

- 1 can chickpeas, drained
- 3 tbsp. coriander
- 1 oz. cheddar cheese, shredded
- 2 eggs, beaten
- 1 tsp. garlic puree
- 1 zucchini spiralized
- 1 red onion, diced
- 1 tsp. chili powder
- 1 tsp. mixed spice
- Salt and pepper to taste
- 1 tsp. cumin

Directions

1. Mix all the ingredients in a mixing bowl.
2. Shape portions of the mixture into burgers.
3. Place in the air fryer at 300°F for 15 minutes.

Nutrition Calories: 184.8 Total fat: 10.1 g.Carbs: 18.4 g.Protein: 13.2 g.

96. Spicy Sweet Potatoes

Preparation time: 7 minutes
Cooking time: 23 minutes
Servings: 4
Ingredients

- 3 sweet potatoes, peeled and chopped into chips
- 1 tsp. chili powder
- 1 tsp. paprika
- 2 tbsp. olive oil
- 1 tbsp. red wine vinegar
- 1 tomato, thinly sliced
- 1/2 cup tomato sauce
- 1 onion, peeled and diced

- Salt and pepper to taste
- 1 tsp. rosemary
- 1 tsp. oregano
- 1 tsp. mixed spice
- 2 tsp. thyme
- 2 tsp. coriander

Directions

1. Toss the chips in a bowl with olive oil.
2. Add to the air fryer and cook for 15 minutes at 360°F.
3. Mix the remaining ingredients in a baking dish.
4. Place the sauce in the air fryer for 8 minutes.
5. Toss the potatoes in the sauce and serve warmly.

Nutrition Calories: 303 Total fat: 5 g.Carbs: 57 g.Protein: 8 g.

97.   Olive, Cheese, and Broccoli

Preparation time: 7 minutes
Cooking time: 15 minutes
Servings: 4
Ingredients

- 2 lbs. broccoli florets
- 2 tbsp. olive oil
- 1/4 cup Parmesan cheese shaved
- 2 tsp. lemon zest, grated
- 1/3 cup Kalamata olives (halved, pitted
- 1/2 tsp. ground black pepper
- 1 tsp. sea salt
- Water

Directions

1. Boil the water in a pan over medium heat and cook the broccoli for about 4 minutes. Drain. Add the broccoli with salt, pepper, and olive oil in a bowl.
2. Place in the air fryer and cook at 400°F for 15 minutes.
3. Stir twice during the cooking time.
4. Place on a plate and toss with lemon zest, cheese, and olives.

Nutrition Calories: 214 Total fat: 13.45 g.Carbs: 13.22 g.Protein: 12.56 g.

98.   Veggie Mix

Preparation time: 7 minutes
Cooking time: 35 minutes
Servings: 4
Ingredients

- 1/2 lb. carrots, peeled, cubed

- 6 tsp. olive oil
- 1/2 tsp. tarragon leaves
- 1/2 tsp. white pepper
- Salt to taste
- 1 lb. yellow squash, chopped into wedges
- 1 lb. zucchini, chopped into wedges

Directions

1. Toss the carrots with 2 tsp. of olive oil in your air fryer basket.
2. Cook at 400°F for 5 minutes.
3. Pour the squash and zucchini along with the remaining oil, salt, and pepper into the air fryer. Cook for 30 more minutes, stirring twice during the cooking time.
4. Toss with tarragon and serve.

Nutrition Calories: 162 Total fat: 1.2 g.Carbs: 30.3 g.Protein: 7.5 g.

99.   Garlic and Cheese Potatoes

Preparation time: 7 minutes
Cooking time: 40 minutes
Servings: 4
Ingredients

- 4 Idaho baking potatoes, halved
- 1 tbsp. garlic powder
- Salt to taste
- 1/2 cup cheddar cheese, shredded
- 1 tsp. parsley

Directions

1. Toss all your ingredients in a bowl except cheese.
2. Place the potatoes in a baking dish and sprinkle cheese over top of them.
3. Cook for 40 minutes at 390°F.

Nutrition Calories: 498 Total fat: 19.09 g.Carbs: 67.27 g. Protein: 16.5 g.

100. Garlic Baby Potatoes

Preparation time: 7 minutes
Cooking time: 15 minutes
Servings: 2
Ingredients

- 8 oz. boiled baby potatoes
- 1/2 tsp. sesame seeds
- Red chili powder to taste
- Salt and pepper to taste
- 1/2 tsp. garlic paste
- 1/4 tsp. coriander seeds, dry roasted
- 1/4 tsp. cumin seeds, dry roasted
- 1/2 cup fresh cream

Directions

1. Grind the coriander and cumin seeds to form a powder.
2. Toss all the ingredients in a baking dish except the cream.
3. Preheat your air fryer for 5 minutes at 360°F. Cook the potatoes for 5 minutes.
4. Mix with the cream and air fry for 5 extra minutes. Garnish with sesame seeds.

Nutrition Calories: 498 Total fat: 19.09 g.Carbs: 67.27 g.Protein: 16.5 g.

101. Sweet Potato Fries

Preparation time: 5 minutes
Cooking time: 13 minutes
Servings: 4
Ingredients

- 2 medium sweet potatoes, peeled
- 1 tbsp. arrowroot starch
- 2 tbsp. cinnamon
- 1/4 cup coconut sugar
- 2 tsp. melted butter, unsalted
- 1/2 tbsp. olive oil
- Confectioners Swerve® as needed

Directions

1. Switch on the air fryer, insert the fryer basket, grease it with olive oil, and close the lid. Set the fryer to 370°F, and preheat for 5 minutes. Meanwhile, cut peeled sweet potatoes into 1/2-inch thick slices, place them in a bowl, add oil and starch and toss until well coated. Open the fryer, add sweet potatoes, close the lid again, and cook for 8 minutes until nicely golden, shaking halfway through the frying.
2. When the air fryer beeps, open the lid, transfer sweet potato fries in a bowl, add butter, sprinkle with coconut sugar and cinnamon, and toss until well mixed.
3. Sprinkle confectioners Swerve® on the fries and serve.

Nutrition Calories: 130 Carbs: 27 g Fat: 2.3 g Protein: 1.2 g Fiber: 3 g.

102. Cheese Sticks

Preparation time: 5–7 minutes
Cooking time: 10 minutes
Servings: 2
Ingredients

- 10 pieces spring roll wrappers, separated, quartered
- 1/4 lb. sharp cheddar cheese, reduced-fat, sliced into 2-inchx1/2-inch matchsticks
- Oil for spraying

Directions

1. Preheat the air fryer to 400°F.
2. Place the cheese matchstick on the wider end of the quartered spring roll wrapper.
3. Moisten the edges and tip of the wrap with water.
4. Fold the spring roll wrapper over the cheese, and tuck in both ends. Roll the spring rolls tightly to the tip.
5. Place them into a freezer-safe container lined with saran wrap.
6. Repeat the steps for all cheese and spring roll wrappers.
7. Freeze for 1 hour before frying.
8. Drizzle a small amount of oil all over cheese matchsticks.
9. Place a generous handful inside the air fryer basket. Fry for 3–5 minutes, or only until wrappers turn golden brown. Shake contents of the basket once midway through.
10. Remove from the basket and set on plates. Repeat the steps for the remaining breaded cheese sticks.
11. Serve.

Nutrition Calories: 229 Carbohydrates: 16 g.Fat: 10 g.Protein: 15 g.Fiber: 1.8 g.

103. Zucchini Crisps

Preparation time: 30 minutes
Cooking time: 1 hour
Servings: 2
Ingredients

- 2 zucchinis, sliced into a 1/8-inch-thick disk - Pinch sea salt
- White pepper to taste
- Olive oil for drizzling

Directions

1. Preheat the air fryer to 330°F.
2. Put the zucchinis in a bowl with salt. Let it sit in a colander to drain for 30 minutes. Layer zucchinis in a baking dish. Drizzle with oil and season with pepper. Place a baking dish in the air fryer basket; cook for 30 minutes.
3. Adjust seasoning and serve.

Nutrition Calories: 15.2 Carbohydrates: 3.6 g.Fat: 0.1 g.Protein: 0.6 g.Fiber: 1.3 g.

104. Tortillas in Green Mango Salsa

Preparation time: 30 minutes
Cooking time: 10 minutes
Servings: 4
Ingredients
For the tortillas

- 4 pieces corn tortillas
- 1 tbsp. olive oil
- 1/16 tsp. sea salt

For the green mango and tomato salsa

- 1 green/unripe mango, minced
- 1 red/ripe Roma tomato, preferably minced
- 1 shallot, peeled, minced
- 1 fresh jalapeño pepper, minced
- 1/4 red bell pepper, minced
- 4 tbsp. fresh cilantro, minced
- 1/4 cup lime juice, freshly squeezed
- 1/16 tsp. salt

Directions

1. Preheat the air fryer to 400°F.
2. Mix the lime juice and salt in a bowl. Stir until the solids are dissolved. Add in the remaining salsa ingredients. Chill in the fridge for at least 30 minutes. Stir again just before using.
3. Lightly brush oil on both sides of tortillas. Cut them into large triangles.
4. Place a generous handful of sliced tortillas in the air fryer basket. Fry these for 10 minutes or until bread blisters and turns golden brown. Shake contents of the basket once midway through.
5. Place cooked pieces on a plate.
6. Repeat the steps for the remaining tortillas. Season with salt.
7. Place equal portions of crispy tortillas on plates. Serve with green mango and tomato salsa on the side.

Nutrition Calories: 128 Carbohydrates: 8.6 g.Fat: 3.6 g.Protein: 2.7 g.Fiber: 5.7 g.

105. Skinny Pumpkin Chips

Preparation time: 20 minutes
Cooking time: 13 minutes
Servings: 2
Ingredients

- 1 lb. pumpkin, cut into sticks
- 1 tbsp. coconut oil
- 1/2 tsp. rosemary
- 1/2 tsp. basil
- Salt and ground black pepper, to taste

Directions

1. Start by preheating the air fryer to 395°F.
2. Brush the pumpkin sticks with coconut oil; add the spices and toss to combine.
3. Cook for 13 minutes, shaking the basket halfway through the cooking time.
4. Serve with mayonnaise. Bon appétit!

Nutrition Calories: 118 Fat: 14.7 g.Carbs: 2.2 g.Protein: 6.2 g.Sugar: 2 g.

106. Garlic Bread With Cheese Dip

Preparation time: 10 minutes
Cooking time: 10 minutes
Servings: 8
Ingredients
For the fried garlic bread

- 1 medium baguette, halved lengthwise, cut sides toasted
- 2 garlic cloves, whole
- 4 tbsp. extra virgin olive oil
- 2 tbsp. fresh parsley, minced

For the blue cheese dip

- 1 tbsp. fresh parsley, minced
- 1/4 cup fresh chives, minced
- 1/4 tsp. Tabasco sauce
- 1 tbsp. lemon juice, freshly squeezed
- 1/2 cup Greek yogurt, low fat
- 1/4 cup blue cheese, reduced fat
- 1/16 tsp. salt
- 1/16 tsp. white pepper

Directions

1. Preheat the air fryer to 400°F.
2. Mix the oil and parsley in a small bowl.
3. Vigorously rub the garlic cloves on cut/toasted sides of the baguette. Discard the garlic nubs.
4. Using a pastry brush, spread parsley-infused oil on the cut side of the bread.
5. Place the bread cut-side down on a chopping board. Slice into inch-thick half-moons.
6. Place the bread slices in the air fryer basket. Fry for 3–5 minutes or until bread browns a little. Shake contents of the basket once midway through.

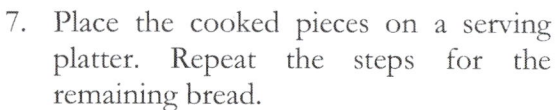

7. Place the cooked pieces on a serving platter. Repeat the steps for the remaining bread.

To prepare blue cheese dip

8. Mix all the ingredients in a bowl.
9. Place equal portions of fried bread on plates and serve with blue cheese dip on the side.

Nutrition Calories: 209 Carbohydrates: 29 g.Fat: 8 g.Protein: 2.9 g.Fiber: 3.5 g.

107. Fried Mixed Veggies With Avocado Dip

Preparation time: 10 minutes
Cooking time: 10 minutes
Servings: 4
Ingredients

- Oil for spraying

For the avocado-feta dip

- 1 avocado, pitted, peeled, flesh scooped out
- 4 oz. feta cheese, reduced fat
- 2 leeks, minced
- 1 lime, freshly squeezed
- 1/4 cup fresh parsley, chopped roughly
- 1/16 tsp. black pepper
- 1/16 tsp. salt

For the vegetables

- 1 zucchini, sliced into matchsticks
- 1 carrot, sliced into matchsticks
- 1 cup panko breadcrumbs. Add more if needed
- 1 parsnip, sliced into matchsticks
- 1 large egg, whisked, add more if needed
- 1 cup all-purpose flour, add more if needed
- 1/8 tsp. flaky sea salt

Directions

1. Preheat the air fryer to 400°F.
2. Season carrots, parsnips, and zucchini with salt.
3. Dredge the carrots with flour first, then dip them into the whisked egg, and finally in the breadcrumbs. Place breaded pieces on a baking sheet lined with parchment paper. Repeat the step for all carrots. Then do the same for parsnips and zucchini.

4. Lightly spray vegetables with oil. Place a generous handful of carrots in the air fryer basket. Fry for 10 minutes or until breading turns golden brown, shaking contents of the basket once midway. Place cooked pieces on a plate. Repeat the step for the remaining carrots.
5. Do the previous step for parsnips and then zucchini.
6. For the dip, except for salt, place the remaining ingredients in a food processor. Pulse a couple of times, and then process to desired consistency scraping the bottom of the machine often. Taste and add salt only if needed; place in an airtight container. Chill until needed.
7. Place equal portions of cooked vegetables on plates. Serve with a small amount of avocado-feta dip on the side.

Nutrition Calories: 109 Carbohydrates: 4.0 g.Fat: 2.6 g.Protein: 2.9 g. Fiber: 2.5 g.

108. Air Fried Plantains in Coconut Sauce

Preparation time: 10 minutes
Cooking time: 10 minutes
Servings: 8
Ingredients

- 6 ripe plantains, peeled, quartered lengthwise
- 1 can coconut cream
- Honey
- Coconut oil

Directions

1. Preheat the air fryer to 330°F.
2. Pour coconut cream in a thick-bottomed saucepan set over high heat; bring to boil.
3. Reduce heat to a minimum; simmer uncovered until the cream is reduced by half and darkens in color. Turn off heat.
4. Whisk in honey until smooth. Cool completely before using. Lightly grease a non-stick skillet with coconut oil.
5. Layer plantains in the air fryer basket and fry until golden on both sides; drain on paper towels. Place plantain into plates.
6. Drizzle in a small amount of coconut sauce. Serve.

Nutrition Calories: 236 Carbohydrates: 0 g.Fat: 1.5 g.Protein: 1 g.Fiber: 1.8 g.

109. Kale Chips With Lemon Yogurt Sauce

Preparation time: 10 minutes
Cooking time: 5 minutes
Servings: 4
Ingredients

- 1 cup plain Greek yogurt
- 3 tbsp. lemon juice, freshly squeezed
- 2 tbsp. honey mustard
- 1/2 tsp. oregano, dried
- 1 bunch curly kale
- 2 tbsp. olive oil
- 1/2 tsp. salt
- 1/8 tsp. pepper

Directions

1. Mix the yogurt, lemon juice, honey mustard, and oregano in a small bowl, and set aside.
2. Remove the stems and ribs from the kale with a sharp knife. Cut the leaves into 2–3-inch pieces.
3. Toss the kale with olive oil, salt, and pepper. Rub the oil into the leaves with your hands.
4. Air fry the kale in batches at 390°F (199°C) until crisp, for 5 minutes, shaking the basket once during cooking time.
5. Serve with the yogurt sauce.

Nutrition Calories: 155 Fat: 8 g.Protein: 8 g.Carbs: 13 g.Fiber: 1 g.Sugar: 3 g.Sodium: 378 mg.

110. Basil Pesto Bruschetta

Preparation time: 10 minutes
Cooking time: 4–8 minutes
Servings: 4
Ingredients

- 8 (1/2-inch) thick slices French bread
- 2 tbsp. softened butter
- 1 cup Mozzarella cheese, shredded
- 1/2 cup basil pesto
- 1 cup grape tomatoes, chopped
- 2 green onions, thinly sliced

Directions

1. Spread the bread with the butter and place butter-side up in the air fryer basket. Bake at 350°F (177°C) for 3–5 minutes or until the bread is light golden brown.
2. Remove the bread from the basket and top each piece with some of the cheese. Return to the basket in batches and bake until the cheese melts for 1–3 minutes.
3. Meanwhile, combine the pesto, tomatoes, and green onions in a small bowl.
4. When the cheese has melted, remove the bread from the air fryer and place it on a serving plate.
5. Top each slice with some of the pesto mixture and serve.

Nutrition Calories: 463 Fat: 25 g.Protein: 19 g.Carbs: 41 g.Fiber: 3 g.Sugar: 2 g.Sodium: 822 mg.

111. Cinnamon Pear Chips

Preparation time: 15 minutes
Cooking time: 9–13 minutes
Servings: 4
Ingredients

- 2 firm Bosc pears, cut crosswise into 1/8-inch-thick slices
- 1 tbsp. lemon juice, freshly squeezed
- 1/2 tsp. ground cinnamon
- 1/8 tsp. ground cardamom or ground nutmeg

Directions

1. Separate the smaller pear slices from the larger ones with seeds.
2. Remove the core and seeds from the larger slices.
3. Sprinkle all the slices with lemon juice, cinnamon, and cardamom.
4. Put the smaller chips into the air fryer basket. Air fry at 380°F (193°C) for 3–5 minutes, until light golden brown, shaking the basket once during cooking. Remove from the air fryer.
5. Repeat with the larger slices, air frying for 6–8 minutes, until light golden brown, shaking the basket once during cooking.
6. Remove the chips from the air fryer.
7. Cool and serve or store in an airtight container at room temperature for up to 2 days.

Nutrition Calories: 31 Fat: 0 g.Protein: 7 g.Carbs: 8 g.Fiber: 2 g.Sugar: 5 g.Sodium: 0 mg.

112. Phyllo Vegetable Triangles

Preparation time: 15 minutes
Cooking time: 6–11 minutes
Servings: 6
Ingredients

- 3 tbsp. onion, minced
- 2 garlic cloves, minced
- 2 tbsp. carrot, grated
- 1 tsp. olive oil
- 3 tbsp. frozen baby peas, thawed
- 2 tbsp. nonfat cream cheese, at room temperature
- 6 sheets frozen phyllo dough, thawed
- Olive oil spray, for coating the dough

Directions

1. In a baking pan, combine the onion, garlic, carrot, and olive oil. Air fry at 390°F (199°C) for 2–4 minutes, or until the vegetables are crisp-tender. Transfer them to a bowl.
2. Stir in the peas and cream cheese to the vegetable mixture. Let it cool while you prepare the dough.
3. Lay one sheet of phyllo on a work surface and spray lightly with olive oil spray. Top with another sheet of phyllo. Repeat with the remaining 4 phyllo sheets; you'll have 3 stacks with 2 layers each. Cut each stack lengthwise into 4 strips (12 strips total).
4. Place a small 2 tsp. of the filling near the bottom of each strip. Bring one corner up over the filling to make a triangle; continue folding the triangles over as you fold a flag. Seal the edge with a bit of water. Repeat with the remaining strips and filling.
5. Air fry the triangles, in 2 batches, for 4–7 minutes or until golden brown. Serve.

Nutrition Calories: 67 Fat: 2 g.Protein: 2 g.Carbs: 11 g.Fiber: 1 g.Sugar: 1 g.Sodium: 121 mg.

113. Red Cabbage and Mushroom Pot Stickers

Preparation time: 12 minutes
Cooking time: 11–18 minutes
Servings: 12 potstickers
Ingredients

- 1 cup red cabbage, shredded
- 1/4 cup button mushrooms, chopped
- 1/4 cup carrot, grated
- 2 tbsp. onion, minced
- 2 garlic cloves, minced
- 2 tsp. fresh ginger, grated
- 12 Gyoza® potsticker wrappers
- 2 1/2 tsp. olive oil, divided
- 1 tbsp. water

Directions

1. Combine the red cabbage, mushrooms, carrot, onion, garlic, and ginger in a baking pan. Add 1 tbsp. of water. Place in the air fryer and bake at 370°F (188°C) for 3–6 minutes, until the vegetables are crisp-tender. Drain and set aside.
2. Working one at a time, place the potsticker wrappers on a work surface. Top each wrapper with a scant 1 tbsp. of the filling. Fold half of the wrapper over the other half to form a half-circle. Dab one edge with water and press both edges together.
3. Spread 1 1/4 tsp. of olive oil on the baking pan. Put half of the potstickers, seam-side up, in the pan. Air fry for 5 minutes, or until the bottoms are light golden brown. Add 1 tbsp. of water and return the pan to the air fryer.
4. Air fry for 4–6 minutes more, or until hot. Repeat with the remaining potstickers, the remaining 1 1/4 tsp. of oil, and another tbsp. of water. Serve immediately.

Nutrition Calories: 88 Fat: 3 g. Protein: 2 g.Carbs: 14 g.Fiber: 1 g.Sugar: 1 g.Sodium: 58 mg.

114. Garlic Roasted Mushrooms

Preparation time: 3 minutes
Cooking time: 22–27 minutes
Servings: 4
Ingredients

- 16 garlic cloves, peeled
- 2 tsp. olive oil, divided
- 16 button mushrooms
- 1/2 tsp. marjoram, dried
- 1/8 tsp. freshly ground black pepper
- 1 tbsp. white wine or low-sodium vegetable broth

Directions

1. In a baking pan, mix the garlic with 1 tsp. of olive oil. Roast in the air fryer at 350°F (177°C) for 12 minutes.
2. Add the mushrooms, marjoram, and pepper; stir to coat.
3. Drizzle with the remaining 1 tsp. of olive oil and white wine.
4. Return to the air fryer and roast for 10–15 minutes more, or until the mushrooms and garlic cloves are tender.
5. Serve.

Nutrition Calories: 128 Fat: 4 g.Protein: 13 g.Carbs: 17 g.Fiber: 4 g.Sugar: 8 g.Sodium: 20 mg.

115. Mini Onion Bites

Preparation time: 10 minutes
Cooking time: 16–20 minutes
Servings: 20 onion bites

Ingredients

- 20 white boiler onions
- 1 cup buttermilk
- 2 eggs - 1 cup flour
- 1 cup whole-wheat bread crumbs
- 1 tbsp. smoked paprika
- 1 tsp. salt
- 1 tsp. ground black pepper
- 1 tsp. garlic, granulated
- 3/4 tsp. chili powder
- Olive oil spray

Directions

1. Place a parchment liner in the air fryer basket.
2. Slice off the root end of the onions, taking off as little as possible.
3. Peel off the papery skin and make cuts halfway through the tops of the onions. Don't cut too far down; you want the onion to hold together still.
4. In a large bowl, beat the buttermilk and eggs together.
5. Mix the flour, bread crumbs, paprika, salt, pepper, garlic, and chili powder in a medium bowl.
6. Add the prepared onions to the buttermilk mixture and allow to soak for at least 10 minutes.
7. Working in batches, remove the onions from the batter and dredge them with the bread crumb mixture.

8. Place the prepared onions in the air fryer basket in a single layer.
9. Spray lightly with olive oil and air fry at 360°F (182°C) for 8–10 minutes, until golden and crispy. Repeat with any remaining onions and serve.

Nutrition Calories: 166 Fat: 2 g.Protein: 6 g.Carbs: 31 g.Fiber: 4 g.Sugar: 7 g.Sodium: 372 mg.

116. Crispy Parmesan Cauliflower

Preparation time: 12 minutes
Cooking time: 14–17 minutes
Servings: 20 cauliflower bites

Ingredients

- 4 cups cauliflower florets
- 1 cup whole-wheat bread crumbs
- 1 tsp. coarse sea salt or kosher salt
- 1/4 cup Parmesan cheese, grated
- 1/4 cup butter
- 1/4 cup mild hot sauce
- Olive oil spray

Directions

1. Place a parchment liner in the air fryer basket.
2. Cut the cauliflower florets in half and set them aside.
3. In a small bowl, mix the bread crumbs, salt, and Parmesan; set aside.
4. In a small microwave-safe bowl, combine the butter and hot sauce. Heat in the microwave until the butter is melted, about 15 seconds. Whisk.
5. Holding the stems of the cauliflower florets, dip them in the butter mixture to coat. Shake off any excess mixture.
6. Dredge the dipped florets with the bread crumb mixture, then put them in the air fryer basket. There's no need for a single layer; just toss them all in there.
7. Spray the cauliflower lightly with olive oil and air fry at 350°F (177°C) for 14–17 minutes, shaking the basket a few times throughout the cooking process. The florets are done when they are lightly browned and crispy. Serve warm.

Nutrition Calories: 106 Fat: 6 g.Protein: 3 g.Carbs: 10 g.Fiber: 1 g.Sugar: 1 g.Sodium: 416 mg.

117. Cream Cheese Stuffed Jalapeños

Preparation time: 12 minutes
Cooking time: 6–8 minutes
Servings: 10 poppers
Ingredients

- 8 oz. (227 g.) cream cheese, at room temperature
- 1 cup whole-wheat bread crumbs, divided
- 2 tbsp. fresh parsley, minced
- 1 tsp. chili powder
- 10 jalapeño peppers, halved and seeded

Directions

1. In a small bowl, combine the cream cheese, 1/2 cup of bread crumbs, the parsley, and the chili powder. Whisk to combine.
2. Stuff the cheese mixture into the jalapeños.
3. Sprinkle the tops of the stuffed jalapeños with the remaining 1/2 cup of breadcrumbs.
4. Place in the air fryer basket and air fry at 360°F (182°C) for 6–8 minutes, until the peppers are softened and the cheese is melted.
5. Serve warm.

Nutrition Calories: 244 Fat: 16 g.Protein: 6 g.Carbs: 19 g.Fiber: 2 g.Sugar: 4 g.Sodium: 341 mg.

118. Parmesan French Fries

Preparation time: 5 minutes
Cooking time: 20–25 minutes
Servings: 16 fries
Ingredients

- 2 russet potatoes, washed
- 1 tbsp. olive oil
- 1 tbsp. garlic, granulated
- 1/4 cup Parmesan cheese, grated
- 1/4 tsp. salt
- 1/4 tsp. ground black pepper
- 1 tbsp. fresh parsley, finely chopped (optional)

Directions

1. Cut the potatoes into thin wedges and place them in a large bowl.
2. Drizzle the olive oil over the potatoes, and toss to coat.

3. Sprinkle with the garlic, Parmesan cheese, salt, and pepper, and toss again.
4. Place in the air fryer basket and air fry at 400°F (204°C) for 20–25 minutes, until golden and crispy, stirring halfway through to ensure even cooking.
5. Top with the parsley (if using), and serve warm.

Nutrition Calories: 209 Fat: 5 g.Protein: 6 g.Carbs: 35 g.Fiber: 2 g.Sugar: 1 g.Sodium: 268 mg.

119. Simple Corn Tortilla Chips

Preparation time: 5 minutes
Cooking time: 10 minutes
Servings: 4
Ingredients

- 4 (6-inch) corn tortillas
- 1 tbsp. canola oil
- 1/4 tsp. kosher salt

Directions

1. Stack the corn tortillas, cut them in half, then slice them into thirds.
2. Spray the air fryer basket with non-stick cooking spray, brush the tortillas with canola oil and place them in the basket. Air fry at 360°F (182°C) for 5 minutes.
3. Pause the fryer to shake the basket, then air fry for 3–5 more minutes or until golden brown and crispy.
4. Remove the chips from the fryer and place them on a plate lined with a paper towel. Sprinkle with the kosher salt on top before serving warm.

Nutrition Calories: 72 Fat: 4 g.Protein: 1 g.Carbs: 8 g.Fiber: 1 g.Sugar: 0 g.Sodium: 79 mg.

120. Corn on the Cob With Herb Butter

Preparation time: 15 minutes
Cooking time: 10 minutes
Servings: 2
Ingredients

- 2 ears fresh corn, shucked and cut into halves
- 2 tbsp. butter, room temperature
- 1 tsp. garlic, granulated
- 1/2 tsp. fresh ginger, grated
- Salt and black pepper to taste
- 1 tbsp. fresh rosemary, chopped
- 1 tbsp. fresh basil, chopped

- 2 tbsp. fresh chives, roughly chopped
- Non-stick cooking spray

Directions

1. Spray the corn with cooking spray. Cook at 395°F for 6 minutes, turning them over halfway through the cooking time.
2. In the meantime, mix the butter with the granulated spices: garlic, ginger, salt, black pepper, rosemary, and basil.
3. Spread the butter mixture all over the corn cob. Cook in the preheated air fryer for 2 more minutes. Bon appétit!

Nutrition Calories: 239 Fat: 13.3 g.Carbs: 30.2 g.Protein: 5.4 g.Sugar: 5.8 g.

CHAPTER 4:

Poultry And Lamb

121. Blackened Spatchcock With Lime Aioli

Preparation time: 15 minutes
Cooking time: 45 minutes
Servings: 6
Ingredients

- 4 lbs. (1.8 kg.) chicken, spatchcocked
- 3 tbsp. blackened seasoning
- 2 tbsp. olive oil

For the lime aioli

- 1/2 cup mayonnaise
- Juice and zest of 1 lime
- 1/4 tsp. kosher salt
- 1/4 tsp. ground black pepper

Directions

1. Preheat the grill to medium-high heat.
2. On a clean work surface, rub the chicken with blackened seasoning and olive oil.
3. Place the chicken on the preheated grill, skin side up, and grill for 45 minutes or until the internal temperature of the chicken reaches at least 165°F (74°C).
4. Meanwhile, combine the ingredients for the aioli in a small bowl and stir to mix well.
5. Once the chicken is fully grilled, transfer it to a large plate and baste with the lime aioli. Allow to cool and serve.

Tip: To make this a complete meal, you can serve it with roasted Brussels sprouts or radish soup.
Nutrition Calories: 436 Fats: 16.3 g.Protein: 61.8 g.Carbs: 6.8 g. Fiber: 0.7 g.Sugar: 1.5 g.Sodium: 653 mg.

122. Citrus Chicken Thighs

Preparation time: 15 minutes
Cooking time: 30 minutes
Servings: 4
Ingredients

- 1 tbsp. fresh ginger, grated

- Sea salt to taste
- 4 chicken thighs, bone-in, skinless
- 1 tbsp. extra-virgin olive oil
- 1/2 orange juice and zest
- 1/2 lemon juice and zest
- 1 tbsp. low-sodium soy sauce
- Pinch red pepper flakes
- 2 tbsp. honey
- 1 tbsp. fresh cilantro, chopped

Directions

1. In a large bowl, combine the ginger and salt. Soak the chicken thighs and toss to coat well.
2. Heat the olive oil in a non-stick skillet over medium-high heat until shimmering.
3. Add the chicken thighs and cook for 10 minutes or until well browned. Flip halfway through the cooking time.
4. Meanwhile, combine the orange juice and zest, lemon juice and zest, soy sauce, red pepper flakes, and honey. Stir to mix well.
5. Pour the mixture into the skillet. Reduce the heat to low, then cover and braise for 20 minutes. Add tbsp. of water, if too dry. Serve the chicken thighs garnished with cilantro.

Tip: To make this a complete meal, you can serve it with roasted asparagus, spinach, and tomato soup. **Nutrition** Calories: 114 Fats: 5.0 g. Protein: 9.0 g. Carbs: 9.0 g. Fiber: 0 g. Sugar: 9.0 g. Sodium: 287 mg.

123. Creamy and Aromatic Chicken

Preparation time: 15 minutes
Cooking time: 30 minutes
Servings: 4
Ingredients

- 4 (4 oz./113 g.) boneless, skinless chicken breasts

- Salt and freshly ground black pepper, to taste
- 1 tbsp. extra-virgin olive oil
- 1/2 sweet onion, chopped
- 2 tsp. fresh thyme, chopped
- 1 cup low-sodium chicken broth
- 1/4 cup heavy whipping cream
- 1 scallion, white and green parts, chopped

Directions

1. Preheat the oven to 375ºF (190ºC).
2. On a clean work surface, rub the chicken with salt and pepper.
3. Heat the olive oil in an oven-safe skillet over medium-high heat until shimmering.
4. Put the chicken in the skillet and cook for 10 minutes or until well browned. Flip halfway through. Transfer onto a platter and set it aside.
5. Add the onion to the skillet and sauté for 3 minutes or until translucent.
6. Add the thyme, the broth, and simmer for 6 minutes or until the liquid reduces in half.
7. Mix in the cream, then put the chicken back to the skillet.
8. Arrange the skillet in the oven and bake for 10 minutes.
9. Remove the skillet from the oven and serve them with scallion.

Tip: You can also garnish the chicken with black olives, sliced cherry tomatoes, or parsley for more flavor. **Nutrition** Calories: 287 Fats: 14.0 g.Protein: 34.0 g. Carbs: 4.0 g. Fiber: 1.0 g. Sugar: 1.0 g. Sodium: 184 mg.

124. Creamy and Cheesy Chicken Chile Casserole

Preparation time: 25 minutes
Cooking time: 32 minutes
Servings: 4
Ingredients

- 1 tbsp. olive oil
- 4 eggs, beaten
- 3 tbsp. cream cheese, softened
- 3/4 cup heavy whipping cream
- 1 tsp. cumin
- 1/2 garlic powder
- 1/2 tsp. salt
- 1/2 tsp. ground black pepper

- 2 (6–8 oz./170–227 g.) chicken breast, cooked and shredded
- 4 large whole green chiles, rinsed and patted dry, flattened
- 1 cup Jack cheese, shredded
- 1 cup Cheddar cheese, shredded
- 1/4 tsp. red pepper flakes, optional

Directions

1. Preheat the oven to 350ºF (180ºC).
2. Grease a casserole dish with olive oil.
3. Combine the eggs, cream cheese, cream, cumin, garlic powder, salt, and black pepper in a large bowl. Stir to mix well.
4. Soak the chicken in the mixture. Press to coat well. Set aside.
5. Lay 2 chiles on the casserole dish, then flatten to cover the bottom. Pour half of the cream chicken mixture over the chiles.
6. Spread 1/2 cup of Jack cheese and 1/2 cup of Cheddar cheese on the cream chicken, then top them with the remaining 2 flattened chiles.
7. Pour the remaining cream chicken mixture over, scatter the remaining cheeses and sprinkle them with red pepper flakes.
8. Arrange the casserole dish in the preheated oven and bake for 30 minutes, then turn the oven to broil for 2 minutes until the top of the casserole is well browned.
9. Remove the casserole from the oven. Allow to cool for 15 minutes, then serve warm.

Tip: To make this a complete meal, you can serve it with arugula salad and gazpacho.
Nutrition Calories: 412 Fats: 30.0 g. Protein: 30.0 g. Carbs: 4.0 g. Fiber: 1.0 g. Sugar: 1.0 g. Sodium: 727 mg.

125. Herbed Chicken and Artichoke Hearts

Preparation time: 10 minutes
Cooking time: 20 minutes
Servings: 4
Ingredients

- 2 tbsp. olive oil, divided
- 4 (6 oz./170 g.) chicken breast halves, boneless, skinless
- 1/2 tsp. dried thyme, divided

- 1 tsp. crushed rosemary, dried and divided
- 1/2 tsp. ground black pepper, divided
- 2 cans (14 oz./397 g.) water-packed, low-sodium artichoke hearts, drained and quartered
- 1/2 cup low-sodium chicken broth
- 2 garlic cloves, chopped
- 1 medium onion, coarsely chopped
- 1/4 cup Parmesan cheese, shredded
- 1 lemon, cut into 8 slices
- 2 green onions, thinly sliced

Directions

1. Preheat the oven to 375°F (190°C). Grease a baking sheet with 1 tsp. of olive oil.
2. Place the chicken breasts on the baking sheet and rub it with 1/4 tsp. of thyme, 1/2 tsp. of rosemary, 1/4 tsp. of black pepper, and 1 tbsp. of olive oil.
3. Combine the artichoke hearts, chicken broth, garlic, onion, remaining thyme, rosemary, black pepper, and olive oil; toss to coat well.
4. Spread the artichoke around the chicken breasts, then scatter with Parmesan and lemon slices.
5. Place the baking sheet in the preheated oven and roast for 20 minutes or until the internal temperature of the chicken breasts reaches at least 165°F (74°C).
6. Remove the sheet from the oven. Allow to cool for 10 minutes, and serve with green onions on top.

Tip: You can replace the chicken broth with the same amount of white wine.

NutritionCalories: 339 Fats: 9.0 g. Protein: 42.0 g. Carbs: 18.0 g. Fiber: 1.0 g. Sugar: 2.0 g. Sodium: 667 mg.

126. Ritzy Jerked Chicken Breasts

Preparation time: 4 hours 10 minutes
Cooking time: 15 minutes
Servings: 4
Ingredients

- 2 habanero chile peppers, halved lengthwise, seeded
- 1/2 sweet onion, cut into chunks
- 1 tbsp. garlic, minced
- 1 tbsp. ground allspice

- 2 tsp. fresh thyme, chopped
- 1/4 cup lime juice, freshly squeezed
- 1/2 tsp. ground nutmeg
- 1/4 tsp. ground cinnamon
- 1 tsp. freshly ground black pepper
- 2 tbsp. extra-virgin olive oil
- 4 (5 oz./142 g.) chicken breasts, boneless, skinless
- 2 cups fresh arugula
- 1 cup halved cherry tomatoes

Directions

1. Combine the habaneros, onion, garlic, allspice, thyme, lime juice, nutmeg, cinnamon, black pepper, and olive oil in a blender; pulse to blender well.
2. Transfer the mixture into a large bowl or 2 medium bowls, then dunk the chicken in the bowl and press to coat well.
3. Put the bowl in the refrigerator and marinate for at least 4 hours.
4. Preheat the oven to 400°F (205°C).
5. Remove the bowl from the refrigerator, then discard the marinade.
6. Arrange the chicken on a baking sheet, then roast in the preheated oven for 15 minutes or until golden brown and lightly charred. Flip the chicken halfway through the cooking time.
7. Remove the baking sheet from the oven and let sit for 5 minutes. Transfer the chicken to a large plate and serve it with arugula and cherry tomatoes.

Tip: You can use the same amount of blanched spinach to replace the arugula to serve with the chicken.

Nutrition Calories: 226 Fats: 9.0 g. Protein: 33.0 g. Carbs: 3.0 g. Fiber: 0 g. Sugar: 1.0 g. Sodium: 92 mg.

127. Roasted Chicken With Root Vegetables

Preparation time: 20 minutes
Cooking time: 41 minutes
Servings: 6
Ingredients

- 1 tsp. fresh rosemary, minced
- 1 tsp. fresh thyme, minced
- 1 tsp. salt
- 1 tsp. ground black pepper
- 2 tbsp. olive oil, divided

- 6 (6 oz./170 g.) chicken breast halves, boneless, skinless
- 2 medium fennel bulbs, chopped
- 4 medium carrots, peeled and chopped
- 3 medium radishes, peeled and chopped
- 3 tbsp. honey
- 1/2 cup white wine
- 2 cups chicken stock
- 3 bay leaves

Directions

1. Preheat the oven to 375°F (190°C).
2. Mix the rosemary, thyme, salt, and black pepper in a small bowl.
3. Heat 1 tbsp. of olive oil in a non-stick skillet over medium-high heat until shimmering.
4. On a clean work surface, rub the chicken breasts with half of the seasoning mixture.
5. Place the chicken in the skillet and cook for 6 minutes or until lightly browned on both sides. Remove the chicken from the skillet and set it aside.
6. Mix the fennel bulbs, carrots, and radishes in a microwave-safe bowl, then sprinkle with the remaining seasoning mixture and drizzle with honey, white wine, and the remaining olive oil. Toss to combine well.
7. Cover the bowl and microwave the root vegetables for 10 minutes or until soft.
8. Arrange the root vegetables and chicken on a baking sheet, pour the chicken stock, and the honey mixture remains in the bowl. Top them with bay leaves.
9. Place the sheet in the preheated oven and roast for 25 minutes or until the internal temperature of the chicken reaches at least 165°F (74°C).
10. Remove the sheet from the oven and transfer the chicken and vegetables to a large plate. Discard the bay leaves, then allow to cool for a few minutes before serving.

Tip: To make this a complete meal, you can serve it with creamy scallop soup.
Nutrition Calories: 364 Fats: 10.2 g. Protein: 41.8 g. Carbs: 22.2 g. Fiber: 3.8 g. Sugar: 15.1 g. Sodium: 650 mg.

128. Roasted Vegetable and Chicken Tortillas
Preparation time: 10 minutes
Cooking time: 20 minutes
Servings: 4
Ingredients

- 1 red bell pepper, seeded and cut into 1-inch-wide strips
- 1/2 small eggplant, cut into 1/4-inch-thick slices
- 1/2 small red onion, sliced
- 1 medium zucchini, cut lengthwise into strips
- 1 tbsp. extra-virgin olive oil
- Salt and freshly ground black pepper, to taste
- 4 whole-wheat tortilla wraps
- 2 (8 oz./227 g.) chicken breasts, cooked and sliced

Directions

1. Preheat the oven to 400°F (205°C).
2. Line a baking sheet with aluminum foil.
3. Combine the bell pepper, eggplant, red onion, zucchini, and olive oil in a large bowl; toss to coat well.
4. Pour the vegetables into the baking sheet, then sprinkle them with salt and pepper.
5. Roast in the preheated oven for 20 minutes or until tender and charred.
6. Unfold the tortillas on a clean work surface, then divide the vegetables and chicken slices on the tortillas.
7. Wrap and serve immediately.
8. **Tip:** How to cook the chicken breasts
9. Preheat the oven to 400°F (205°C).
10. Grease a baking sheet with 1 tbsp. of olive oil.
11. Place the chicken on the baking sheet and bake in the preheated oven for 24 minutes or until the internal temperature of the chicken reaches at least 165°F (74°C).
12. Allow cooling before using.

Nutrition Calories: 483 Fats: 25.0 g. Protein: 20.0 g. Carbs: 45.0 g. Fiber: 3.0 g. Sugar: 4.0 g. Sodium: 730 mg.

129. Chicken With Carrots and Kale

Preparation time: 15 minutes
Cooking time: 27 minutes
Servings: 2
Ingredients

- 1/2 cup couscous
- 1 cup water, divided
- 1/3 cup basil pesto
- 3 tsp. olive oil, divided
- 3 (2 oz./57 g.) whole carrots, rinsed, thinly sliced
- Salt and ground black pepper, to taste
- 1 (6 oz./170 g.) bunch kale, rinsed, stems removed, chopped
- 2 garlic cloves, minced
- 2 tbsp. currants, dried
- 1 tbsp. red wine vinegar
- 2 (6 oz./170 g.) chicken breasts, boneless, skinless, and rinsed
- 1 tbsp. Italian seasoning

Directions

1. Pour the couscous and 3/4 cup of water into a pot. Bring to a boil on high heat. Reduce the heat to low. Simmer for 7 minutes or until most of the water has been absorbed. Fluffy with a fork and mix in the basil pesto.
2. Heat 1 tsp. of olive oil in a non-stick skillet over medium-high heat until shimmering.
3. Add the carrots, then sprinkle with salt and pepper. Sauté for 3 minutes or until tender.
4. Add the kale and garlic and sauté for 2 minutes or until the kale is lightly wilted.
5. Add the vegetables and the remaining water and sauté for 3 minutes or until most water is soaked.
6. Turn off the heat, then add the red wine vinegar. Transfer them to a large bowl and cover to keep warm.
7. On a clean work surface, rub the chicken with Italian seasoning, salt, and pepper.
8. Clean the skillet and heat 2 tsp. of olive oil over medium-high heat until shimmering.
9. Add the chicken and sear for 12 minutes or until well browned. Flip the chicken halfway through the cooking time.
10. Transfer the chicken to a large plate, then spread with vegetables and couscous. Slice to serve.

Tip: To make this a complete meal, you can serve it with a beef stew or a leafy green salad.
Nutrition Calories: 461 Fats: 14.2 g. Protein: 57.0 g. Carbs: 26.1 g. Fiber: 6.5 g. Sugar: 5.0 g. Sodium: 1210 mg.

130. Turkey Meatball and Vegetable Kabobs

Preparation time: 50 minutes
Cooking time: 20 minutes
Servings: 6
Ingredients

- 20 oz. (567 g.) lean ground turkey, 93% fat-free
- 2 egg whites
- 2 tbsp. Parmesan cheese, grated
- 2 garlic cloves, minced
- 1/2 tsp. salt, or to taste
- 1/4 tsp. ground black pepper
- 1 tbsp. olive oil
- 8 oz. (227 g.) fresh cremini mushrooms, cut in half to make 12 pieces
- 24 cherry tomatoes
- 1 medium onion, cut into 12 pieces
- 1/4 cup balsamic vinegar

Special equipment

- 12 bamboo skewers, soaked in water for at least 30 minutes

Directions

1. Mix the ground turkey, egg whites, Parmesan, garlic, salt, and pepper in a large bowl. Stir to combine well.
2. Shape the mixture into 12 meatballs and place on a baking sheet. Refrigerate for at least 30 minutes.
3. Preheat the oven to 375°F (190°C). Grease another baking sheet with 1 tbsp. of olive oil.
4. Remove the meatballs from the refrigerator. Run the bamboo skewers through 2 meatballs, 1 mushroom, 2 cherry tomatoes, and 1 onion piece alternatively.
5. Arrange the kabobs on the greased baking sheet and brush with balsamic vinegar.
6. Grill in the preheated oven for 20 minutes or until an instant-read

thermometer inserted in the middle of the meatballs reads at least 165°F (74°C). Flip the kabobs halfway through the cooking time.

7. Allow the kabobs to cool for 10 minutes, then serve warm.

Tips: You can use grape tomatoes to replace cherry tomatoes. You can reserve half of the balsamic vinegar when brushing the kabobs, then brush the kabobs with reserved balsamic vinegar and more olive oil when flipping. This will help to grill the kabobs evenly.

Nutrition Calories: 200 Fats: 8.0 g. Protein: 22.0 g. Carbs: 7.0 g. Fiber: 1.0 g. Sugar: 4.0 g. Sodium: 120 mg.

131. Pumpkin, Bean, and Chicken Enchiladas

Preparation time: 35 minutes
Cooking time: 25 minutes
Servings: 4
Ingredients

- 2 tsps. olive oil
- 1/2 cup onion, chopped
- 1 jalapeño, seeded and chopped
- 1 can (15 oz.) pumpkin
- 1 1/2 cups water, more if needed
- 1 tsp. chili powder
- 1/2 tsp. salt
- 1/2 tsp. ground cumin
- 1 cup canned no-salt-added red kidney beans, rinsed and drained
- 1 1/2 cups chicken breast, shredded and cooked
- 1/2 cup part-skim Mozzarella cheese, shredded
- 8 (6-inch) whole-wheat tortillas, softened
- Salsa and lime wedges

Directions

1. Lightly coat a 2-qt. rectangular baking dish with cooking spray and preheat the oven to 400°F.
2. In a saucepan, heat the oil over medium heat.
3. Add the jalapeño and onion and stir-fry until the onion is tender, for 5 minutes.
4. Stir in cumin, salt, chili powder, 1 1/2 cups water, and pumpkin and heat through. Add more water if needed.

5. Place the beans in a bowl and mash slightly with a fork. Stir in 1/4 cup of the cheese, the chicken, and half of the pumpkin mixture.
6. Spoon 1/3 cup bean mixture onto each tortilla. Roll up tortillas and place them in the baking dish (seam sides down). Pour the remaining pumpkin mixture over the enchiladas.
7. Bake, covered, for 15 minutes. Sprinkle with the remaining 1/4 cup cheese. Bake, uncovered until heated through, for about 10 minutes more.
8. Serve with salsa and lime wedges.

Nutrition Calories: 357 Fat: 8 g. Carbs: 44 g. Protein: 28 g.

132. Mu Shu Chicken

Preparation time: 20 minutes
Cooking time: 6 hours
Servings: 6
Ingredients

- 1/2 cup hoisin sauce
- 2 tbsp. water
- 4 tsp. toasted sesame oil
- 1 tbsp. cornstarch
- 1 tbsp. reduced-sodium soy sauce
- 3 garlic cloves, minced
- 1 (16-oz.) pkg. (coleslaw mix) cabbage with carrots, shredded
- 1 cup carrots, coarsely shredded
- 12 oz. chicken thighs, skinless, boneless
- 6 (8-inch) whole wheat flour tortillas
- 1/4 cup green onions

Directions

1. Combine the first 6 ingredients in a bowl (through garlic).
2. In a slow cooker, combine shredded carrots and coleslaw mix.
3. Cut the chicken into 1/8-inch slices, then cut each slice in half lengthwise. Place the chicken on top of the cabbage mix. Drizzle with 1/4 cup of the hoisin mixture.
4. Heat tortillas according to package directions. Fill tortillas with chicken mixture.
5. Top with green onions and serve.

Nutrition Calories: 269 Fat: 8 g. Carbs: 34 g. Protein: 16 g.

133. Stove-Top Chicken, Macaroni, and Cheese

Preparation time: 10 minutes
Cooking time: 30 minutes
Servings: 5
Ingredients

- 1 1/2 cups dried multigrain or elbow macaroni
- 12 oz. chicken breast halves, skinless, boneless, cut into 1-inch pieces
- 1/4 cup onion, chopped
- 1 pkg. (6.5 oz.) light semisoft cheese with garlic and fine herbs
- 1 2/3 cups fat-free milk
- 1 tbsp. all-purpose flour
- 3/4 cup reduced-fat cheddar cheese, shredded
- 2 cups fresh baby spinach
- 1 cup cherry tomatoes, quartered

Directions

1. Cook the macaroni according to package directions. Drain.
2. Meanwhile, coat a skillet with cooking spray; heat the skillet over medium-high heat.
3. Add the onion and chicken and cook until the chicken is no longer pink about 4–6 minutes; stirring frequently. Remove from the heat and stir in semisoft cheese until melted.
4. In a bowl, whisk together flour and milk until smooth. Gradually stir milk mixture into chicken mixture. Cook and stir until bubbly and thickened. Lower heat and gradually add cheddar cheese; stir until melted.
5. Add the cooked macaroni, cook and stir for 1–2 minutes or until heated through.
6. Stir in the spinach. Top with cherry tomatoes and serve.

Nutritio Calories: 369 Fat: 12 g. Carb: 33 g. Protein: 33 g.

134. Chicken Sausage Omelets With Spinach

Preparation time: 20 minutes
Cooking time: 10 minutes
Servings: 2
Ingredients

- 2 cups fresh spinach
- 1/2 pkg. (7 oz.) frozen fully cooked chicken and maple breakfast sausage links thawed and chopped
- 3 eggs, lightly beaten
- 2 tbsp. water
- 1/4 cup part-skim Mozzarella cheese, shredded
- 2 green onions, green tops only, thinly sliced
- 1/2 cup grape tomatoes, quartered
- 1/4 cup fresh basil leaves, thinly sliced
- Non-stick cooking spray

Directions

1. Coat a skillet with non-stick cooking spray. Heat over medium heat.
2. Add the sausage and spinach. Cook until sausage is heated. Remove from the skillet.
3. In a bowl, whisk together the water and eggs. Add the egg mixture to the skillet and cook until the egg is set and shiny.
4. Spoon spinach and sausage mixture over half of the omelet; sprinkle with cheese and green onions. Fold the opposite side of the omelet over the sausage mixture.
5. Cook for 1 minute or until filling is heated and cheese is melted.
6. Transfer to a plate and cut in half; transfer half of the omelet to a second plate.
7. Top with tomatoes and basil and serve.

Nutrition Calories: 252 Fat: 16 g. Carbs: 5 g. Protein: 21 g.

135. Chicken-Broccoli Salad With Buttermilk Dressing

Preparation time: 20 minutes
Cooking time: 0 minutes
Servings: 4
Ingredients

- 3 cups broccoli slaw mix, packaged ,shredded
- 2 cups cooked chicken breast, coarsely chopped
- 1/2 cup cherries, dried
- 1/3 cup celery, sliced
- 1/4 cup red onion, chopped
- 1/3 cup buttermilk
- 1/3 cup light mayonnaise
- 1 tbsp. honey

- 1 tbsp. cider vinegar
- 1 tsp. dry mustard
- 1/2 tsp. salt
- 1/8 tsp. black pepper
- 4 cups fresh baby spinach

Directions

1. Combine the first 5 ingredients in a bowl (through onion).
2. In a small bowl, whisk together the next 7 ingredients (through pepper).
3. Pour the buttermilk mixture over the broccoli mixture. Toss to mix gently.
4. Cover and chill for 2–24 hours.
5. Add baby spinach and serve.

Nutrition Calories: 278 Fat: 7 g. Carbs: 29 g. Protein: 26 g.

136. Country-Style Wedge Salad With Turkey

Preparation time: 10 minutes
Cooking time: 0 minutes
Servings: 4
Ingredients

- 1 head bibb or butterhead lettuce, quartered
- 1 recipe buttermilk-avocado dressing (see below)
- 2 cups cooked turkey breast, shredded
- 1 cup halved grape or cherry tomatoes
- 2 hard-cooked eggs, chopped
- 4 slices less-fat bacon, low-sodium, crisp-cooked, and crumbled
- 1/4 cup red onion, finely chopped
- Cracked black pepper to taste

Directions

1. Arrange a quarter of lettuce on each plate. Drizzle half of the dressing over wedges. Top with the turkey, eggs, and tomatoes. Drizzle with the remaining dressing. Sprinkle with onion, bacon, and pepper.

To make the buttermilk-avocado dressing

2. In a blender, combine 3/4 cup buttermilk, 1/2 avocado, 1 tbsp. of parsley, 1/4 tsp. each salt, onion powder, dry mustard, and black pepper, and 1 garlic clove, minced. Cover and blend until smooth.

Nutrition Calories: 228 Fat: 9 g. Carb: 8 g. Protein: 29 g.

137. Turkey Kabob Pitas

Preparation time: 25 minutes
Cooking time: 15 minutes
Servings: 4
Ingredients

- 1 tsp. whole cumin seeds, lightly crushed
- 1 cup cucumber, shredded
- 1/3 cup Roma tomato, seeded and chopped - 1/4 cup red onion, slivered
- 1/4 cup radishes shredded
- 1/4 cup fresh cilantro, snipped
- 1/4 tsp. black pepper
- 1 lb. turkey breast, cut into thin strips
- 1 recipe curry blend (see below)
- 1/4 cup plain fat-free greek yogurt
- 4 (6-inch) whole-wheat pita bread rounds

Directions

1. Soak the wooden skewers in water for 30 minutes. Toast the cumin seeds for 1 minute and transfer them to a bowl. Add the next 6 ingredients to the bowl (through pepper). Mix well.
2. In another bowl, combine curry blend and turkey. Stir to coat.
3. Thread turkey onto skewers.
4. Grill kabobs, uncovered for 6–8 minutes or until turkey is no longer pink; turning kabobs occasionally.
5. Remove turkey from skewers; spread Greek yogurt on pita bread.
6. Spoon cucumber mixture over yogurt. Top with grilled turkey.
7. Serve and enjoy.

To make the curry blend

8. In a bowl, combine 2 tsp. of olive oil, 1 tsp. of curry powder, 1/2 tsp, each of ground turmeric, ground cumin, and ground coriander, 1/4 tsp. of ground ginger, and 1/8 tsp. of salt and cayenne pepper.

Nutrition Calories: 343 Fat: 6 g. Carbs: 40 g. Protein: 35 g.

138. Chicken With Black Beans and Corn

Preparation time: 10 minutes
Cooking time: 30 minutes
Servings: 4
Ingredients

- 1 tbsp. vegetable oil

- 4 chicken breast halves, skinless, boneless
- 1 can (10 oz.) diced tomatoes with green chile peppers
- 1 can (15 oz.) black beans, rinsed and drained
- 1 can (8.75 oz.) whole kernel corn, drained - Pinch ground cumin

Directions

1. In a large skillet, heat oil over medium-high heat. Brown chicken breasts on both sides.
2. Add tomatoes with green chile peppers, beans, and corn. Reduce heat and let simmer for 25–30 minutes or until chicken is cooked through and juices run clear.
3. Add a dash of cumin and serve.

Nutrition Calories: 310 Fat: 6 g. Carbs: 28 g. Protein: 35 g.

139. Dijon Chicken

Preparation time: 10 minutes
Cooking time: 30 minutes
Servings: 4
Ingredients

- 6 chicken breast halves, skinless, boneless - Salt and pepper to taste
- 1/2 cup honey
- 1/2 cup mustard, prepared
- 1 tsp. basil, dried
- 1 tsp. paprika
- 1/2 tsp. parsley, dried

Directions

1. Preheat oven to 350°F.
2. Sprinkle chicken breasts with salt and pepper to taste, and place them in a lightly greased 9x13-inch baking dish.
3. In a small bowl, combine the honey, mustard, basil, paprika, and parsley. Mix well. Pour 1/2 of this mixture over the chicken, and brush to cover.
4. Bake in the preheated oven for 30 minutes. Turn the chicken pieces over and brush with the remaining 1/2 of the honey mustard mixture.
5. Bake for 10–15 minutes, or until chicken is no longer pink and juices run clear. Let cool 10 minutes before serving.

Nutrition Calories: 232 Fat: 4 g. Carbs: 25 g. Protein: 26 g.

140. Parmesan Chicken Breasts

Preparation time: 10 minutes
Cooking time: 30 minutes
Servings: 4
Ingredients

- 2 tbsp. olive oil
- 1 garlic clove, minced
- 1 cup dry breadcrumbs
- 2/3 cup Parmesan cheese, grated
- 1 tsp. basil leaves, dried
- 1/4 tsp. ground black pepper
- 6 chicken breast halves, skinless, boneless

Directions

1. Preheat the oven to 350°F (175°C). Lightly grease a 9x13-inch baking dish.
2. In a bowl, blend the olive oil and garlic.
3. In a separate bowl, mix the breadcrumbs, Parmesan cheese, basil, and pepper.
4. Dip each chicken breast in the oil mixture, then in the breadcrumb mixture. Arrange the coated chicken breasts in the prepared baking dish, and top with any remaining breadcrumb mixture.
5. Bake for 30 minutes in the preheated oven, or until chicken is no longer pink and juices run clear.

Nutrition Calories: 281 Fat: 11 g. Carbs: 14 g. Protein: 30 g.

141. Greek Lamb Pita Pockets

Preparation time: 15 minutes
Cooking time: 5–7 minutes
Servings: 4
Ingredients
For the dressing

- 1 cup plain Greek yogurt
- 1 tbsp. lemon juice
- 1 tsp. dried dill weed, crushed
- 1 tsp. ground oregano
- 1/2 tsp. salt

For the meatballs

- 1/2 lb. (227 g.) ground lamb
- 1 tbsp. onion, diced
- 1 tsp. parsley, dried
- 1 tsp. dried dill weed, crushed
- 1/4 tsp. oregano
- 1/4 tsp. coriander

- 1/4 tsp. ground cumin
- 1/4 tsp. salt
- 4 pita halves

Suggested toppings

- Red onion, slivered
- Seedless cucumber, thinly sliced
- Crumbled feta cheese
- Sliced black olives
- Chopped fresh peppers

Directions

1. Stir the dressing ingredients together and refrigerate while preparing lamb.
2. Combine all the meatball ingredients in a large bowl and stir to distribute seasonings.
3. Shape the meat mixture into 12 small meatballs, rounded or slightly flattened if you prefer.
4. Air fry at 390°F (199°C) for 5–7 minutes, until well done.
5. Remove and drain on paper towels.
6. To serve, pile meatballs and your choice of toppings in pita pockets and drizzle with dressing.

Nutrition Calories: 270 Fat: 14 g. Protein: 18 g.Carbs: 18 g. Fiber: 2 g. Sugar: 2 g. Sodium: 618 mg.

142. Rosemary Lamb Chops

Preparation time: 30 minutes
Cooking time: 20 minutes
Servings: 2–3
Ingredients

- 2 tsp. oil
- 1/2 tsp. ground rosemary
- 1/2 tsp. lemon juice
- 1 lb. (454 g.) lamb chops, approximately 1-inch thick
- Salt and pepper to taste
- Cooking spray

Directions

1. Mix the oil, rosemary, and lemon juice and rub the lamb chops for all sides; season to taste with salt and pepper.
2. For best flavor, cover the lamb chops and allow them to rest in the fridge for 15–20 minutes.
3. Spray the air fryer basket with cooking spray and place the lamb chops in it.

4. Air fry at 360°F (182°C) for approximately 20 minutes; this will cook chops to medium. The meat will be juicy but have no remaining pink. Air fry for 1–2 minutes longer for well-done chops. For rare chops, stop cooking after about 12 minutes and check for doneness.

Nutrition Calories: 237 Fat: 13 g. Protein: 30 g. Carbs: 0 g. Fiber: 0 g. Sugar: 0 g. Sodium: 116 mg.

143. Herb Butter Lamb Chops

Preparation time: 10 minutes
Cooking time: 5 minutes
Servings: 4
Ingredients

- 4 lamb chops
- 1 tsp. rosemary, diced
- 1 tbsp. butter
- Pepper to taste
- Salt to taste

Directions

1. Season the lamb chops with pepper and salt.
2. Place the dehydrating tray in a multi-level air fryer basket and place the basket in the instant pot.
3. Place the lamb chops on dehydrating tray.
4. Seal the pot with the lid, select AIR FRY mode, set the temperature to 400°F, and the timer for 5 minutes.
5. Mix butter and rosemary and spread overcooked lamb chops.
6. Serve and enjoy.

Nutrition Calories: 278 Fat: 12.8 g.Carbohydrates: 0.2 g.Sugar: 0 g.Protein: 38 g.Cholesterol: 129 mg.

144. Za'atar Lamb Chops

Preparation time: 10 minutes
Cooking time: 10 minutes
Servings: 4
Ingredients

- 4 lamb loin chops
- 1/2 tbsp. Za'atar
- 1 tbsp. fresh lemon juice
- 1 tsp. olive oil
- 2 garlic cloves, minced
- Pepper to taste
- Salt to taste

Directions

1. Coat the lamb chops with oil and lemon juice and rub with Za'atar, garlic, pepper, and salt.
2. Place the dehydrating tray in a multi-level air fryer basket and place the basket in the instant pot.
3. Place the lamb chops on the dehydrating tray.
4. Seal the pot with the lid and select the AIR FRY mode; set the temperature to 400°F and timer for 10 minutes. Turn the lamb chops halfway through.
5. Serve and enjoy.

Nutrition Calories: 266 Fat: 11.2 g.Carbohydrates: 0.6 g.Sugar: 0.1 g.Protein: 38 g.Cholesterol: 122 mg.

145. Greek Lamb Chops

Preparation time: 10 minutes
Cooking time: 10 minutes
Servings: 4
Ingredients

- 2 lbs. lamb chops
- 2 tsp. garlic, minced
- 1 1/2 tsp. oregano, dried
- 1/4 cup fresh lemon juice
- 1/4 cup olive oil
- 1/2 tsp. pepper
- 1 tsp. salt

Directions

1. Add the lamb chops to a mixing bowl. Add the remaining ingredients over the lamb chops and coat well.
2. Arrange the lamb chops on the air fryer oven tray and cook at 400°F for 5 minutes.
3. Turn the lamb chops and cook for 5 more minutes.
4. Serve and enjoy.

Nutrition Calories: 538 Fat: 29.4 g.Carbs: 1.3 g.Protein: 64 g.

146. Herbed Lamb Chops

Preparation time: 1 hour 10 minutes
Cooking time: 13 minutes
Servings: 6
Ingredients

- 1 lb. lamb chops, pastured

For the marinate

- 2 tbsp. lemon juice
- 1 tsp. rosemary, dried

- 1 tsp. salt
- 1 tsp. thyme, dried
- 1 tsp. coriander
- 1 tsp. oregano, dried
- 2 tbsp. olive oil

Directions

1. Prepare the marinade and for this, place all its ingredients in a bowl and whisk until combined.
2. Pour the marinade in a large plastic bag, add the lamb chops, seal the bag, turn it upside down to coat the lamb chops with the marinade, and let it marinate in the refrigerator for at least 1 hour.
3. Then switch on the air fryer, insert the fryer basket, grease it with olive oil, shut with its lid, set the fryer at 390°F, and preheat for 5 minutes.
4. Open the fryer, add the marinated lamb chops in it, close with its lid and cook for 8 minutes until nicely golden and cooked, turning the lamb chops halfway through the frying.
5. When the air fryer beeps, open its lid, transfer lamb chops onto a serving plate and serve.

Nutrition Calories: 177.4 Carbs: 1.7 g.Fat: 8 g.Protein: 23.4 g.Fiber: 0.5 g.

147. Spicy Lamb Sirloin Steak

Preparation time: 40 minutes
Cooking time: 20 minutes
Servings: 4
Ingredients

- 1 lb. lamb sirloin steaks, pastured, boneless

For the marinade

- 1/2 white onion, peeled
- 1 tsp. ground fennel
- 5 garlic cloves, peeled
- 4 slices ginger
- 1 tsp. salt
- 1/2 tsp. ground cardamom
- 1 tsp. garam masala
- 1 tsp. ground cinnamon
- 1 tsp. cayenne pepper

Directions

1. Place all the ingredients for the marinade in a food processor and then pulse until well blended.

2. Make cuts in the lamb chops using a knife, then place them in a large bowl and add the prepared marinade.

3. Mix well until lamb chops are coated with the marinade, and let them marinate in the refrigerator for a minimum of 30 minutes.

4. Switch on the air fryer, insert the fryer basket, grease it with olive oil, then shut with its lid, set the fryer at 330°F, and preheat for 5 minutes.

5. Open the fryer, add the lamb chops in it, close with its lid and cook for 15 minutes until nicely golden and cooked, flipping the steaks halfway through the frying.

6. When the air fryer beeps, open its lid, transfer the lamb steaks onto a serving plate and serve.

Nutrition Calories: 182 Carbs: 3 g.Fat: 7 g.Protein: 24 g.Fiber: 1 g.

148. Garlic Rosemary Lamb Chops

Preparation time: 1 hour 10 minutes
Cooking time: 12 minutes
Servings: 4
Ingredients

- 4 lamb chops, pastured
- 1 tsp. ground black pepper
- 2 tsp. garlic, minced
- 1 1/2 tsp. salt
- 2 tsp. olive oil
- 4 garlic cloves, peeled
- 4 rosemary sprigs

Directions

1. Take the fryer pan, place the lamb chops in it, season the top with 1/2 tsp. of black pepper and 3/4 tsp. of salt, then drizzle evenly with oil and spread with 1 tsp. of minced garlic.

2. Add the garlic cloves and rosemary, and then let the lamb chops marinate in the pan into the refrigerator for at least 1 hour.

3. Switch on the air fryer, insert the fryer pan, then shut with its lid, set the fryer at 360°F, and cook for 6 minutes.

4. Flip the lamb chops, season them with the remaining salt and black pepper, add the remaining minced garlic and continue cooking for 6 minutes or until lamb chops are cooked.

5. When the air fryer beeps, open its lid, transfer the lamb chops onto a serving plate and serve.

Nutrition Calories: 616 Carbs: 1 g.Fat: 28 g.Protein: 83 g.Fiber: 0.3 g.

149. Cherry-Glazed Lamb Chops

Preparation time: 10 minutes
Cooking time: 20 minutes
Servings: 4
Ingredients

- 4 (4 oz./113 g.) lamb chops
- 1 1/2 tsp. fresh rosemary, chopped
- 1/4 tsp. salt
- 1/4 tsp. freshly ground black pepper
- 1 cup frozen cherries, thawed
- 1/4 cup dry red wine
- 2 tbsp. orange juice
- 1 tsp. extra-virgin olive oil

Directions

1. Season the lamb chops with rosemary, salt, and pepper.

2. In a small saucepan over medium-low heat, combine the cherries, red wine, and orange juice; simmer, stirring regularly until the sauce thickens for 8–10 minutes.

3. Heat a large skillet over medium-high heat. When the pan is hot, add the olive oil to coat the bottom lightly.

4. Cook the lamb chops for 3–4 minutes on each side until well-browned yet medium-rare.

5. Serve and topped with the cherry glaze.

Nutrition Calories: 356 Fat: 27 g. Protein: 20 g. Carbs: 6 g. Sugar: 4 g. Fiber: 1 g. Sodium: 199 mg.

150. Lamb and Vegetable Stew

Preparation time: 10 minutes
Cooking time: 3–6 hours
Servings: 6
Ingredients

- 1 lb. (454 g.) boneless lamb stew meat
- 1 lb. (454 g.) turnips, peeled, and chopped
- 1 fennel bulb, trimmed and thinly sliced
- 10 oz. (283 g.) mushrooms, sliced
- 1 onion, diced
- 3 garlic cloves, minced
- 2 cups low-sodium chicken broth

- 2 tbsp. tomato paste
- 1/4 cup dry red wine (optional)
- 1 tsp. fresh thyme
- 1/2 tsp. salt
- 1/4 tsp. freshly ground black pepper
- Chopped fresh parsley, for garnish

Directions

1. In a slow cooker, combine the lamb, turnips, fennel, mushrooms, onion, garlic, chicken broth, tomato paste, red wine (if using), thyme, salt, and pepper.
2. Cover and cook on HIGH for 3 hours or on LOW for 6 hours. When the meat is tender and falling apart, garnish with parsley and serve.
3. If you don't have a slow cooker, in a large pot, heat 2 tsp. of olive oil over medium heat, and sear the lamb on all sides.
4. Remove from the pot and set aside. Add the turnips, fennel, mushrooms, onion, and garlic to the pot, and cook for 3–4 minutes until the vegetables begin to soften.
5. Add the chicken broth, tomato paste, red wine (if using), thyme, salt, pepper, and browned lamb.
6. Bring to a boil, then reduce the heat to low. Simmer for 1 1/2–2 hours until the meat is tender. Garnish with parsley and serve.

Nutrition Calories: 303 Fat: 7 g. Protein: 32 g. Carbs: 27 g. Sugar: 7 g. Fiber: 4 g. Sodium: 310 mg.

151.   Lime-Parsley Lamb Cutlets

Preparation time: 10 minutes
Cooking time: 10 minutes
Servings: 4
Ingredients

- 1/4 cup extra-virgin olive oil
- 1/4 cup lime juice, freshly squeezed
- 2 tbsp. lime zest
- 2 tbsp. fresh parsley, chopped
- Pinch sea salt
- Pinch freshly ground black pepper
- 12 lamb cutlets (about 1 1/2 lb./680 g.)

Directions

1. Whisk together the oil, lime juice, zest, parsley, salt, and pepper in a medium bowl.

2. Transfer the marinade to a resealable plastic bag.
3. Add the cutlets to the bag and remove as much air as possible before sealing.
4. Marinate the lamb in the refrigerator for about 4 hours, turning the bag several times.
5. Preheat the oven to broil.
6. Remove the chops from the bag and arrange them on an aluminum foil-lined baking sheet. Discard the marinade.
7. Broil the chops for 4 minutes per side for medium doneness.
8. Let the chops rest for 5 minutes before serving.

Nutrition Calories: 413 Fat: 29 g. Protein: 31 g. Carbs: 1 g. Sugars: 0 g. Fiber: 0 g. Sodium: 100 mg.

152.   Brine-Soaked Turkey

Preparation time: 10 minutes
Cooking time: 45 minutes
Servings: 8
Ingredients

- 7 lbs. turkey breast, bone-in, skin-on

For the brine

- 1/2 cup salt
- 1 lemon
- 1/2 onion
- 3 garlic cloves, smashed
- 5 sprigs fresh thyme
- 3 bay leaves
- Black pepper

For the turkey breast

- 4 tbsp. butter, softened
- 1/2 tsp. black pepper
- 1/2 tsp. garlic powder
- 1/4 tsp. thyme, dried
- 1/4 tsp. oregano, dried

Directions

1. Mix the turkey brine ingredients in a pot and soak the turkey in the brine overnight. The next day, remove the soaked turkey from the brine.
2. Whisk the butter, black pepper, garlic powder, oregano, and thyme. Brush the butter mixture over the turkey, then place it in a baking tray.
3. Press the POWER button of the air fry oven and turn the dial to select the AIR ROAST mode. Press the TIME button

and again turn the dial to set the cooking time to 45 minutes.

4. Now push the TEMP button and rotate the dial to set the temperature at 370°F. Once preheated, place the turkey baking tray in the oven and close the lid.

5. Slice and serve warm.

Nutrition Calories: 397 Carbohydrates: 59 g.Fat: 16 g.Protein: 8 g.

153. Chicken Tenders and Vegetables

Preparation time: 10 minutes
Cooking time: 18–20 minutes
Servings: 4
Ingredients

- 1 lb. (454 g.) chicken tenders
- 1 tbsp. honey
- Pinch salt
- Freshly ground black pepper, to taste
- 1/2 cup soft fresh breadcrumbs
- 1/2 tsp. thyme, dried
- 1 tbsp. olive oil
- 2 carrots, sliced
- 12 small red potatoes

Directions

1. In a medium bowl, toss the chicken tenders with honey, salt, and pepper.

2. In a shallow bowl, combine the breadcrumbs, thyme, and olive oil, and mix.

3. Coat the tenders in the breadcrumbs, pressing firmly onto the meat.

4. Place the carrots and potatoes in the air fryer basket and top with the chicken tenders.

5. Roast at 380°F (193°C) for 18–20 minutes or until the chicken is cooked and the vegetables are tender; shake the basket halfway during the cooking time.

Nutrition Calories: 379 Fats: 8 g.Protein: 41 g.Carbohydrates: 35 g.Fiber: 3 g.Sugar: 9 g.Sodium: 296 mg.

154. Tandoori Chicken

Preparation time: 5 minutes
Cooking time: 18–23 minutes
Servings: 4
Ingredients

- 2/3 cup plain low-fat yogurt
- 2 tbsp. lemon juice, freshly squeezed
- 2 tsp. curry powder
- 1/2 tsp. ground cinnamon
- 2 garlic cloves, minced
- 2 tsp. olive oil
- 4 (5 oz./142 g.) chicken breasts, boneless, skinless

Directions

1. Whisk the yogurt, lemon juice, curry powder, cinnamon, garlic, and olive oil in a medium bowl.

2. With a sharp knife, cut thin slashes into the chicken. Add it to the yogurt mixture and turn to coat. Let stand for 10 minutes at room temperature. You can also prepare this ahead of time and marinate the chicken in the refrigerator for up to 24 hours.

3. Remove the chicken from the marinade and shake off any excess liquid. Discard any remaining marinade.

4. Roast the chicken at 360°F (182°C) for 10 minutes.

5. With tongs, carefully turn each piece. Roast for 8–13 more minutes, or until the chicken reaches an internal temperature of 165°F (74°C) on a meat thermometer.

6. Serve immediately.

Nutrition Calories: 198 Fat: 5 g. Protein: 33 g. Carbohydrates: 4 g. Fiber: 0 g. Sugar: 3 g. Sodium: 93 mg.

155. Bacon and Chicken Garlic Wrap

Preparation time: 15 minutes
Cooking time: 10 minutes
Servings: 4
Ingredients

- 1 chicken fillet, cut into small cubes
- 8–9 thin slices bacon, cut to fit cubes
- 6 garlic cloves, minced

Directions

1. Preheat your oven to 400°F.

2. Line a baking tray with aluminum foil.

3. Add minced garlic to a bowl and rub each chicken piece with it.

4. Wrap a bacon piece around each garlic chicken bite.

5. Secure with a toothpick.

6. Transfer bites to baking sheet, keeping a little bit of space between them.

7. Bake for about 15–20 minutes until crispy.
8. Serve and enjoy!

Nutrition Calories: 260 Carbohydrates: 5 g.Fat: 19 g.Protein: 22 g.

156. Grilled Lime Chicken

Preparation time: 10 minutes
Cooking time: 25 minutes
Servings: 8
Ingredients

- 8 (4 oz. each) chicken breast halves, boneless and skinless
- 1/2 cup lime juice
- 1/3 cup olive oil
- 4 green onions, chopped
- 4 garlic cloves, minced
- 3 tbsps. chopped fresh dill, divided
- 1/4 tsp. pepper

Directions

1. Flatten the chicken breasts into 1/4-inch. Mix the 2 tbsp. of pepper, dill, garlic, onions, oil, and lime juice in a resealable plastic bag, then add the chicken.
2. Seal the bag securely and flip to coat, then let it chill in the fridge for 2–4 hours.
3. Drain and get rid of the marinade. Grill the chicken for 6–7 minutes per side on medium-hot heat without a cover, or until a thermometer reads 170°F.
4. Sprinkle the leftover dill on top.

Nutrition Calories: 235 Carbohydrates: 3 g.Fats: 12 g.Protein: 27 g. Sodium: 66 mg.Cholesterol: 73 mg.

157. Baked Turkey Spaghetti

Preparation time: 5 minutes
Cooking time: 20 minutes
Servings: 4
Ingredients

- 1 pkg. (10 oz./283 g.) zucchini noodles
- 2 tbsp. extra-virgin olive oil, divided
- 1 lb. (454 g.) lean ground turkey 93%
- 1/2 tsp. oregano, dried
- 2 cups low-sodium spaghetti sauce
- 1/2 cup sharp Cheddar cheese, shredded

Directions

1. Pat zucchini noodles dry between 2 paper towels.

2. In an oven-safe medium skillet, heat 1 tbsp. of olive oil over medium heat. When hot, add the zucchini noodles. Cook for 3 minutes, stirring halfway through.
3. Add the remaining 1 tbsp. of oil, ground turkey, and oregano. Cook for 7–10 minutes, stirring and breaking apart, as needed.
4. Add the spaghetti sauce to the skillet and stir.
5. If your broiler is at the top of your oven, place the oven rack in the center position. Set the broiler on HIGH.
6. Top the mixture with the cheese, and broil for 5 minutes or until the cheese is bubbly.

Nutrition Calories: 335 Fats: 21 g. Protein: 28 g.Carbohydrates: 12 g. Fiber: 3 g. Sugar: 4 g. Sodium: 216 mg.

158. Turkey Scaloppini

Preparation time: 10 minutes
Cooking time: 20 minutes
Servings: 4
Ingredients

- 1/2 cup whole-wheat flour
- 1/2 tsp. sea salt
- 1/4 tsp. freshly ground black pepper
- 3 tbsp. extra-virgin olive oil
- 12 oz. (340 g.) turkey breast, cut into 1/2-inch-thick cutlets and pounded flat
- 1 garlic clove, minced
- 1/2 cup dry white wine
- 2 tbsp. fresh rosemary, chopped
- 1 cup low-sodium chicken broth
- 2 tbsp. salted butter, very cold, cut into small pieces

Directions

1. Preheat the oven to 200°F (93°C).
2. Line a baking sheet with parchment paper.
3. In a medium bowl, whisk together the flour, salt, and pepper.
4. In a large skillet over medium-high heat, heat the olive oil until it shimmers.
5. Working in batches with 1 or 2 pieces of turkey at a time (depending on how much room you have in the pan), dredge the turkey cutlets in the flour and pat off any excess.

6. Cook in the hot oil until the turkey is cooked through, about 3 minutes per side. Add more oil if needed.

7. Place the cooked cutlets on the lined baking sheet and keep them warm in the oven while cooking the remaining turkey and making the pan sauce.

8. Once all the turkey is cooked and warming in the oven, add the garlic to the pan and cook, constantly stirring, for 30 seconds.

9. Add the wine and use a spoon to scrape any browned bits off the pan bottom.

10. Simmer, stirring, for 1 minute. Add the rosemary and chicken broth. Simmer, stirring, until it thickens, 1–2 minutes more.

11. Whisk in the cold butter, one piece at a time, until incorporated. Return the turkey cutlets to the sauce and turn once to coat.

12. Serve with any remaining sauce spooned over the top.

Nutrition Calories: 344 Fats: 20 g.Protein: 24 g.Carbohydrates: 15 g.Fiber: 0 g.Sugar: 2 g.Sodium: 266 mg.

159. Chicken Enchilada Spaghetti Squash

Preparation time: 5 minutes
Cooking time: 40 minutes
Servings: 4
Ingredients

- 1 (3 lb./1.4 kg.) spaghetti squash, halved lengthwise and seeded
- 1 1/2 tsp. ground cumin, divided
- Avocado oil or cooking spray
- 4 (4 oz./113 g.) chicken breasts, boneless and skinless
- 1 large zucchini, diced
- 3/4 cup red enchilada sauce, canned
- 3/4 cup shredded Cheddar or Mozzarella cheese

Directions

1. Preheat the oven to 400°F (205°C).

2. Season both halves of the squash with 1/2 tsp. of cumin, and place them cut-side down on a baking sheet; bake for 25–30 minutes.

3. Meanwhile, heat a large skillet over medium-low heat. When hot, spray the cooking surface with cooking spray and add the chicken breasts, zucchini, and 1 tsp. of cumin. Cook the chicken for 4–5 minutes per side. Stir the zucchini when you flip the chicken.

4. Transfer the zucchini to a medium bowl and set aside. Remove the chicken from the skillet, and let it rest for 10 minutes or until it's cool enough to handle. Shred or dice the cooked chicken.

5. Place the chicken and zucchini in a large bowl, and add the enchilada sauce.

6. Remove the squash from the oven, flip it over, and comb through it with a fork to make thin strands.

7. Scoop the chicken mixture on top of the squash halves and top with the cheese. Return the squash to the oven and broil for 2–5 minutes, or until the cheese is bubbly.

Nutrition Calories: 331 Fat: 11 g. Protein: 35 g.Carbohydrates: 27 g.Fiber: 2 g.Sugars: 4 g.Sodium: 491 mg.

160. Baked Coconut Chicken Tenders

Preparation time: 10 minutes
Cooking time: 20 minutes
Servings: 6
Ingredients

- 4 chicken breasts each cut lengthwise into 3 strips
- 1/2 tsp. salt
- 1/4 tsp. freshly ground black pepper
- 1/2 cup coconut flour
- 2 eggs, beaten
- 2 tbsp. unsweetened plain almond milk
- 1 cup unsweetened coconut flakes

Directions

1. Preheat the oven to 400°F (205°C).

2. Line a baking sheet with parchment paper.

3. Season the chicken pieces with salt and pepper.

4. Place the coconut flour in a small bowl.

5. In another bowl, mix the eggs with the almond milk; spread the coconut flakes on a plate.

6. One by one, roll the chicken pieces in the flour, then dip the floured chicken in the egg mixture and shake off any excess.

7. Roll in the coconut flakes and transfer to the prepared baking sheet.

8. Bake for 15–20 minutes, flipping once halfway through until cooked and browned.

Nutrition Calories: 216 Fat: 13 g.Protein: 20 g.Carbohydrates: 9 g.Fiber: 6 g.Sugar: 2 g.Sodium: 346 mg.

161. Chicken Caesar Salad

Preparation time: 10 minutes
Cooking time: 15 minutes
Servings: 2
Ingredients

- 1 garlic clove
- 1/2 tsp. anchovy paste
- 1/2 lemon juice
- 2 tbsp. extra-virgin olive oil
- 1 (8 oz./227 g.) chicken breast, boneless and skinless
- 1/4 tsp. salt
- Freshly ground black pepper to taste
- 2 romaine lettuce hearts, cored and chopped
- 1 red bell pepper, seeded and cut into thin strips
- 1/4 cup Parmesan cheese, grated

Directions

1. Preheat the broiler to HIGH.
2. In a blender jar, combine the garlic, anchovy paste, lemon juice, and olive oil. Process until smooth and set aside.
3. Cut the chicken breast lengthwise into 2 even cutlets of similar thickness. Season the chicken with salt and pepper, and place it on a baking sheet.
4. Broil the chicken for 5–7 minutes on each side until cooked through and browned. Cut into thin strips.
5. In a medium mixing bowl, toss the lettuce, bell pepper, and cheese. Add the dressing and toss to coat.
6. Divide the salad between 2 plates and top with the chicken.

Nutrition alories: 292 Fats: 18 g.Protein: 28 g.Carbohydrates: 6 g.Fiber: 2 g.Sugar: 3 g.Sodium: 706 mg.

CHAPTER 5:

Beef

162. Meatloaf Slider Wraps

Preparation time: 15 minutes
Cooking time: 10 minutes
Servings: 6
Ingredients

- 1 lb. ground beef, grass-fed
- 1/2 cup almond flour
- 1/4 cup coconut flour
- 1/2 tbsp. minced garlic
- 1/4 cup chopped white onion
- 1 tsp. Italian seasoning
- 1/2 tsp. sea salt - 1/2 tsp. tarragon, dried
- 1/2 tsp. ground black pepper
- 1 tbsp. Worcestershire sauce
- 1/4 cup ketchup
- 2 eggs, pastured, beaten

Directions

1. Place all the ingredients in a bowl, stir well, then shape the mixture into 2-inch diameter and 1-inch-thick patties and refrigerate them for 10 minutes.
2. Meanwhile, switch on the air fryer, insert the fryer basket, and grease it with olive oil. Then close the lid, set the fryer at 360°F, and preheat for 10 minutes.
3. Open the fryer, add the patties in a single layer, close the lid and cook for 10 minutes until nicely golden and cooked; flipping the patties halfway through the frying. When the air fryer beeps, open the lid and transfer patties to a plate.
4. Wrap each patty in lettuce and serve.

Nutrition Calories: 228 Carbs: 6 g.Fat: 16 g.Protein: 13 g.Fiber: 2 g.

163. Double Cheeseburger

Preparation time: 5 minutes
Cooking time: 18 minutes
Servings: 1
Ingredients

- 2 beef patties, pastured

- 1/8 tsp. onion powder
- 2 slices Mozzarella cheese, low fat
- 1/8 tsp. ground black pepper
- 1/8 tsp. salt
- 1/8 cup olive oil

Directions

1. Switch on the air fryer, insert the fryer basket, and grease it with olive oil. Then close the lid, set the fryer at 370°F, and preheat for 5 minutes.
2. Meanwhile, season the patties well with onion powder, black pepper, and salt.
3. Open the fryer, add the beef patties, close the lid and cook for 12 minutes until nicely golden and cooked, flipping the patties halfway through the frying.
4. Then top the patties with a cheese slice and continue cooking for 1 minute or until cheese melts.
5. Serve straight away.

Nutrition Calories: 670 Carbs: 0 g.Fat: 50 g.Protein: 39 g.Fiber: 0 g.

164. Beef Schnitzel

Preparation time: 10 minutes
Cooking time: 15 minutes
Servings: 1
Ingredients

- 1 lean beef schnitzel
- 2 tbsp. olive oil
- 1/4 cup breadcrumbs
- 1 egg
- 1 lemon, to serve

Directions

1. Let the air fryer heat to 180°C.
2. In a big bowl, add breadcrumbs and oil, mix well until it forms a crumbly mixture
3. Dip beef steak in whisked egg and coat in breadcrumbs mixture.
4. Place the breaded beef in the air fryer and cook at 180°C for 15 minutes or more until fully cooked.

5. Take out from the air fryer and serve with the side of salad greens and lemon.

Nutrition Calories: 340 Protein: 20 g. Carbs: 14 g.Fat: 10 g.Fiber: 7 g.

165. Meatloaf

Preparation time: 10 minutes
Cooking time: 40 minutes
Servings: 8
Ingredients

- 4 cups ground lean beef
- 1 cup breadcrumbs, soft and fresh
- 1/2 cup mushrooms, chopped
- 3 garlic cloves, minced
- 1/2 cup carrots, shredded
- 1/4 cup beef broth
- 1/2 cup onions, chopped
- 2 eggs beaten
- 3 tbsp. ketchup
- 1 tbsp. Worcestershire sauce
- 1 tbsp. Dijon mustard

For the glaze

- 1/4 cup honey
- 1/2 cup ketchup
- 2 tsp. Dijon mustard

Directions

1. In a big bowl, add the beef broth and breadcrumbs; stir well. Set it aside in a food processor, add garlic, onions, mushrooms, and carrots, and pulse on HIGH until finely chopped.
2. Add soaked breadcrumbs, Dijon mustard, Worcestershire sauce, eggs, lean ground beef, ketchup, and salt in a separate bowl.
3. With your hands, combine well and make it into a loaf.
4. Let the air fryer preheat to 390°F.
5. Put the meatloaf in the air fryer and let it cook for 45 minutes.
6. In the meantime, add Dijon mustard, ketchup, and brown sugar to a bowl and mix. Glaze this mix over the meatloaf when 5 minutes are left.
7. Rest the meatloaf for 10 minutes before serving.

Nutrition Calories: 330 Protein: 19 g.Carbs: 16 g. Fat: 9.9 g.

166. Steak With Asparagus Bundles

Preparation time: 20 minutes
Cooking time: 30 minutes
Servings: 2
Ingredients

- Olive oil spray
- 2 lb. flank steak, cut into 6 pieces
- Kosher salt and black pepper to taste
- 2 garlic cloves, minced
- 4 cups asparagus
- 1/2 cup tamari sauce
- 3 bell peppers sliced thinly
- 1/3 cup beef broth
- 1 tbsp. unsalted butter
- 1/4 cup balsamic vinegar

Directions

1. Sprinkle salt and pepper on steak and rub.
2. Add the garlic and Tamari sauce, add the steak, toss well, and seal the Ziploc bag.
3. Let it marinate for 1 hour or overnight.
4. Equally, place bell peppers and asparagus in the center of the steak.
5. Roll the steak around the vegetables and secure well with toothpicks.
6. Preheat the air fryer.
7. Spray the steak with olive oil spray. And place steaks in the air fryer.
8. Cook for 15 minutes at 400°F or more until steaks are cooked.
9. Take the steak out from the air fryer and let it rest for 5 minutes.
10. Remove steak bundles and allow them to rest for 5 minutes before serving/slicing.
11. In the meantime, add butter, balsamic vinegar, and broth over medium flame. Mix well and reduce it by half.
12. Add salt and pepper to taste.
13. Pour over steaks right before serving.

Nutrition Calories: 471 Protein: 29 g.Carbs: 20 g.Fat: 15 g.

167. Hamburgers

Preparation time: 5 minutes
Cooking time: 13 minutes
Servings: 4
Ingredients

- 4 buns
- 4 cups lean ground beef chuck
- Salt to taste

- 4 slices any cheese
- Black pepper, to taste
- Ketchup

Directions

1. Let the air fryer preheat to 350°F.
2. In a bowl, add the lean ground beef, pepper, and salt. Mix well and form patties.
3. Put them in the air fryer in a single layer, cook for 6 minutes; turn them over halfway before removing the patties; add the cheese on top.
4. When cheese is melted, take it out from the air fryer.
5. Add ketchup or any dressing to your buns; add the tomatoes, lettuce, and the patties.
6. Serve hot.

Nutrition Calories: 520 Carbohydrates: 22 g.Protein: 31 g.Fat: 34 g.

168. Beef Steak Kabobs With Vegetables

Preparation time: 30 minutes
Cooking time: 10 minutes
Servings: 4
Ingredients

- 2 tbsp. light soy sauce
- 4 cups lean beef chuck ribs, cut into one-inch pieces
- 1/3 cup low-fat sour cream
- 1/2 onion
- 8 (6-inch) skewers
- 1 bell pepper
- Water

Directions

1. In a mixing bowl, add the soy sauce and sour cream, mix well. Add the lean beef chunks, coat well, and let it marinate for 30 minutes or more.
2. Cut the onion and bell pepper into 1-inch pieces. In the water, soak the skewers for 10 minutes.
3. Add the onions, bell peppers, and beef on skewers; alternatively, sprinkle with black pepper.
4. Let it cook for 10 minutes in a preheated air fryer at 400°F, flip halfway through.
5. Serve with yogurt dipping sauce.

Nutrition Calories: 268 Protein: 20 g.Carbs: 15 g.Fat: 10 g.

169. Empanadas

Preparation time: 10 minutes
Cooking time: 20 minutes
Servings: 2
Ingredients:

- 8 square Gyoza® wrappers
- 1 tbsp. olive oil
- 1/4 cup white onion, finely diced
- 1/4 cup mushrooms, finely diced
- 1/2 cup lean ground beef
- 2 tsp. garlic, chopped
- 1/4 tsp. paprika
- 1/4 tsp. ground cumin
- 6 green olives, diced
- 1/8 tsp. ground cinnamon
- 1/2 cup tomatoes, diced
- 1 egg, lightly beaten

Directions

1. Add oil, onions, and beef over a medium flame in a skillet and cook for 3 minutes until the meat turns brown.
2. Add the mushrooms and cook for 6 minutes until it starts to brown. Then add the paprika, cinnamon, olives, cumin, and garlic and cook for 3 minutes or more.
3. Add in the chopped tomatoes, and cook for 1 minute; turn off the heat and let it cool for 5 minutes.
4. Lay the wrappers on a flat surface add 1 1/2 tbsp. of beef filling in each wrapper. Brush edges with water or egg, fold the wrappers, and pinch the edges.
5. Put 4 empanadas in an even layer in an air fryer basket, and cook for 7 minutes at 400°F until nicely browned.
6. Serve with sauce and salad greens.

Nutrition Calories: 343 Fat: 19 g.Protein: 18 g.Carbohydrates: 12.9 g.

170. Rib-Eye Steak

Preparation time: 5 minutes
Cooking time: 14 minutes
Servings: 2
Ingredients

- 2 medium lean rib-eye steaks
- Salt and freshly ground black pepper, to taste

Directions

1. Let the air fryer preheat at 400°F. Pat dry steaks with paper towels.
2. Use any spice blend generously on the steaks or just salt and pepper on both sides of the steaks.
3. Put the steaks in the air fryer basket. Cook according to the rareness you want or cook for 14 minutes and flip after halftime.
4. Take it out from the air fryer and let it rest for 5 minutes.
5. Serve with microgreens salad.

Nutrition Calories: 470 Protein: 45 g.Fat: 31 g.Carbs: 23 g.

171. Bunless Sloppy Joes

Preparation time: 15 minutes
Cooking time: 40 minutes
Servings: 6
Ingredients

- 6 small sweet potatoes
- 1 lb. (454 g.) lean ground beef
- 1 onion, finely chopped
- 1 carrot, finely chopped
- 1/4 cup mushrooms, finely chopped
- 1/4 cup red bell pepper, finely chopped
- 3 garlic cloves, minced
- 2 tsp. Worcestershire sauce
- 1 tbsp. white wine vinegar
- 1 can (15 oz./425 g.) low-sodium tomato sauce
- 2 tbsp. tomato paste

Directions

1. Preheat the oven to 400°F (205°C).
2. Place the sweet potatoes in a single layer on a baking dish. Bake for 25–40 minutes, until they are soft and cooked through, depending on the size.
3. While the sweet potatoes are baking, in a large skillet, cook the beef over medium heat until it's browned, breaking it apart into small pieces as you stir.
4. Add the onion, carrot, mushrooms, bell pepper, garlic, and sauté briefly for 1 minute.
5. Stir in the Worcestershire sauce, vinegar, tomato sauce, and tomato paste. Bring to a simmer, reduce the heat, and cook for 5 minutes for the flavors to meld.

6. Scoop 1/2 cup of the meat mixture on top of each baked potato and serve.

Nutrition Calories: 372 Fat: 19 g.Protein: 16 g.Carbs: 34 g.Sugar: 13 g.Fiber: 6 g.Sodium: 161 mg.

172. Beef Curry

Preparation time: 15 minutes
Cooking time: 10 minutes
Servings: 6
Ingredients

- 1 tbsp. extra-virgin olive oil
- 1 small onion, thinly sliced
- 2 tsp. fresh ginger, minced
- 3 garlic cloves, minced
- 2 tsp. ground coriander
- 1 tsp. ground cumin
- 1 jalapeño or serrano pepper, split lengthwise but not all the way through
- 1/4 tsp. ground turmeric
- 1/4 tsp. salt
- 1 lb. (454 g.) grass-fed sirloin tip steak, top round steak, or top sirloin steak, cut into bite-size pieces
- 2 tbsp. fresh cilantro, chopped
- 1/4 cup water

Directions

1. In a large skillet, heat the oil over medium-high.
2. Add the onion, and cook for 3–5 minutes until browned and softened. Add the ginger and garlic, stirring continuously until fragrant, for 30 seconds.
3. In a small bowl, mix the coriander, cumin, jalapeño, turmeric, and salt. Add the spice mixture to the skillet and stir continuously for 1 minute. Deglaze the skillet with about 1/4 cup of water.
4. Add the beef and stir continuously for 5 minutes until well-browned, but still medium-rare. Remove the jalapeño.
5. Serve topped with cilantro.

Nutrition Calories: 140 Fat: 7 g.Protein: 18 g.Carbs: 3 g.Sugars: 1 g. Fiber: 1 g.Sodium: 141 mg.

173. Asian Grilled Beef Salad

Preparation time: 15 minutes
Cooking time: 15 minutes
Servings: 4
Ingredients
For the dressing

- 1/4 cup lime juice, freshly squeezed
- 1 tbsp. low-sodium tamari or gluten-free soy sauce
- 1 tbsp. extra-virgin olive oil
- 1 garlic clove, minced - 1 tsp. honey
- 1/4 tsp. red pepper flakes

For the salad

- 1 lb. (454 g.) grass-fed flank steak
- 1/4 tsp. salt
- Pinch freshly ground black pepper
- 6 cups leaf lettuce, chopped
- 1 cucumber, halved lengthwise and thinly cut into half-moons
- 1/2 small red onion, sliced
- 1 carrot, cut into ribbons
- 1/4 cup fresh cilantro, chopped

Directions
To make the dressing:

1. Whisk together the lime juice, tamari, olive oil, garlic, honey, and red pepper flakes in a small bowl. Set aside.

To make the salad:

2. Season the beef on both sides with salt and pepper. Heat a skillet over high heat until hot. Cook the beef for 3–6 minutes per side, depending on preferred doneness. Set aside, tented with aluminum foil, for 10 minutes. In a large bowl, toss the lettuce, cucumber, onion, carrot, and cilantro.
3. Slice the beef thinly against the grain and transfer it to the salad bowl.
4. Drizzle with the dressing and toss.
5. Serve.

Nutrition Calories: 231 Fat: 10 g. Protein: 26 g.Carbs: 10 g.Sugars: 4 g.Fiber: 2 g.Sodium: 349 mg.

174. Sunday Pot Roast

Preparation time: 10 minutes
Cooking time: 1 hour 45 minutes
Servings: 10
Ingredients

- 1 (3–4lb./1.4–1.8 kg.) beef rump roast
- 2 tsp. kosher salt, divided
- 2 tbsp. avocado oil
- 1 (about 1 1/2 cups) large onion, coarsely chopped
- 4 large carrots, each cut into 4 pieces
- 1 tbsp. garlic, minced
- 3 cups low-sodium beef broth
- 1 tsp. freshly ground black pepper
- 1 tbsp. parsley, dried
- 2 tbsp. all-purpose flour
- 4 tbsp. water

Directions

1. Rub the roast all over with 1 tsp. of the salt.
2. Set the electric pressure cooker to the SAUTÉ setting. When the pot is hot, pour in the avocado oil.
3. Carefully place the roast in the pot and sear it for 6–9 minutes on each side. (You want a dark caramelized crust.) Hit CANCEL.
4. Transfer the roast from the pot to a plate.
5. Next, put the onion, carrots, and garlic in the pot. Place the roast on top of the vegetables along with any juices that accumulated on the plate.
6. In a medium bowl, whisk together the broth and the remaining 1 tsp. of salt, pepper, and parsley. Pour the broth mixture over the roast.
7. Close and lock the lid of the pressure cooker. Set the valve to sealing.
8. Cook on high pressure for 1 hour and 30 minutes.
9. When the cooking is complete, hit CANCEL and allow the pressure to release naturally.
10. Once the pin drops, unlock and remove the lid.
11. Using large slotted spoons, transfer the roast and vegetables to a serving platter while you make the gravy.
12. Using a large spoon or fat separator, remove the fat from the juices in the pot. Set the electric pressure cooker to the Sauté setting and bring the liquid to a boil.
13. In a small bowl, whisk together the flour and 4 tbsp. of water to make a slurry. Pour the slurry into the pot, occasionally

whisking until the gravy is the thickness you like. Season with salt and pepper, if necessary.

14. Serve the meat and carrots with the gravy.

Nutrition Calories: 245 Fat: 10 g. Protein: 33 g.Carbs: 6 g.Sugar: 2 g.Fiber: 1 g.Sodium: 397 mg.

175. Beef Burrito Bowl

Preparation time: 5 minutes
Cooking time: 15 minutes
Servings: 4
Ingredients

- 1 lb. (454 g.) lean ground beef 93%
- 1 cup canned low-sodium black beans, drained and rinsed
- 1/4 tsp. ground cumin
- 1/4 tsp. chili powder
- 1/4 tsp. garlic powder
- 1/4 tsp. onion powder
- 1/4 tsp. salt
- 1 head romaine or preferred lettuce, shredded
- 2 medium tomatoes, chopped
- 1 cup shredded Cheddar cheese or packaged cheese blend

Directions

1. Heat a large skillet over medium-low heat.
2. Put the beef, beans, cumin, chili powder, garlic powder, onion powder, and salt into the skillet, and cook for 8–10 minutes, until cooked; stir occasionally.
3. Divide the lettuce evenly between 4 bowls. Add 1/4 of the beef mixture to each bowl and top with 1/4 of the tomatoes and cheese.

Nutrition Calories: 351 Fat: 18 g.Protein: 35 g.Carbs: 14 g.Sugar: 4 g.Fiber: 6 g.Sodium: 424 mg.

176. Beef and Pepper Fajita Bowls

Preparation time: 10 minutes
Cooking time: 15 minutes
Servings: 4
Ingredients

- 4 tbsp. extra-virgin olive oil, divided
- 1 head cauliflower, riced

- 1 lb. (454 g.) sirloin steak, cut into 1/4-inch-thick strips
- 1 red bell pepper, seeded and sliced
- 1 onion, thinly sliced
- 2 garlic cloves, minced
- 2 limes juice
- 1 tsp. chili powder

Directions

1. In a large skillet over medium-high heat, heat 2 tbsp. of olive oil until it shimmers. Add the cauliflower. Cook, occasionally stirring, until it softens, for 3 minutes; set aside.
2. Wipe out the skillet with a paper towel. Add the remaining 2 tbsp. of oil to the skillet, and heat it on medium-high until it shimmers.
3. Add the steak and cook, occasionally stirring, until it browns, for 3 minutes. Use a slotted spoon to remove the steak from the oil in the pan and set it aside.
4. Add the bell pepper and onion to the pan. Cook, occasionally stirring, until they start to brown, for 5 minutes.
5. Add the garlic and cook, constantly stirring, for 30 seconds.
6. Return the beef along with any juices that have collected and the cauliflower to the pan. Add the lime juice and chili powder. Cook, stirring until everything is warmed through, about 2–3 minutes.

Nutrition Calories: 310 Fat: 18 g.Protein: 27 g.Carbs: 13 g.Sugar: 2 g.Fiber: 3 g.Sodium: 93 mg.

177. Smothered Sirloin

Preparation time: 15 minutes
Cooking time: 30 minutes
Servings: 5
Ingredients

- 1 lb. (454 g.) beef round sirloin tip
- 1 tsp. freshly ground black pepper
- 1 tsp. celery seeds
- 2 tbsp. extra-virgin olive oil
- 1 medium yellow onion, chopped
- 1/4 cup chickpea flour
- 2 cups chicken broth, divided
- 2 celery stalks, thinly sliced
- 1 medium red bell pepper, chopped
- 2 garlic cloves, minced
- 2 tbsp. whole-wheat flour

- Generous pinch cayenne pepper
- Chopped fresh chives, for garnish (optional)
- Smoked paprika, for garnish (optional)

Directions

1. In a bowl, season the steak on both sides with black pepper and celery seeds.
2. Select the SAUTÉ setting on an electric pressure cooker, and combine the olive oil and onions. Cook for 3–5 minutes, constantly stirring, or until the onions are browned but not burned.
3. Slowly add the chickpea flour, 1 tbsp. at a time, while stirring.
4. Add 1 cup of broth, 1/4 cup at a time, as needed.
5. Stir in the celery, bell pepper, and garlic and cook for 3–5 minutes, or until softened.
6. Lay the beef on top of vegetables, and pour the remaining 1 cup of broth on top.
7. Close and lock the lid and set the pressure valve to seal.
8. Change to the MANUAL setting, and cook for 20 minutes.
9. Once cooking is complete, quick-release the pressure; carefully remove the lid.
10. Remove the steak and vegetables from the pressure cooker, reserving the leftover liquid for the gravy base.
11. To make the gravy, add the whole-wheat flour and cayenne to the liquid in the pressure cooker, mixing continuously until thickened.
12. To serve, spoon the gravy over the steak and garnish with the chives (if using) and paprika (if using).

Nutrition Calories: 253 Fat: 13 g. Protein: 22 g. Carbs: 10 g. Sugar: 3 g. Fiber: 2 g. Sodium: 86 mg.

178. Loaded Cottage Pie

Preparation time: 15 minutes
Cooking time: 1 hour
Servings: 6–8
Ingredients

- 4 large russet potatoes, peeled and halved
- 3 tbsp. extra-virgin olive oil, divided
- 1 small onion, chopped
- 1 bunch collard greens, stemmed and thinly sliced

- 2 carrots, peeled and chopped
- 2 medium tomatoes, chopped
- 1 garlic clove, minced
- 1 lb. (454 g.) lean ground beef 90 %
- 1/2 cup chicken broth
- 1 tsp. Worcestershire sauce
- 1 tsp. celery seeds
- 1 tsp. smoked paprika
- 1/2 tsp. chives, dried
- 1/2 tsp. ground mustard
- 1/2 tsp. cayenne pepper
- Water

Directions

1. Preheat the oven to 400°F (205°C).
2. Bring a large pot of water to a boil.
3. Add the potatoes, and boil for 15–20 minutes, or until fork-tender.
4. Transfer the potatoes to a large bowl and mash them with 1 tbsp. of olive oil.
5. In a large cast-iron skillet, heat the remaining 2 tbsp. of olive oil.
6. Add the onion, collard greens, carrots, tomatoes, and garlic and sauté, often stirring, for 7–10 minutes, or until the vegetables are softened.
7. Add the beef, broth, Worcestershire sauce, celery seeds, and smoked paprika.
8. Spread the meat and vegetable mixture evenly onto the bottom of a casserole dish.
9. Sprinkle the chives, ground mustard, and cayenne on top of the mixture.
10. Spread the mashed potatoes evenly over the top.
11. Transfer the casserole dish to the oven, and bake for 30 minutes, or until the top is light golden brown.

Nutrition Calories: 440 Fat: 17 g. Protein: 27 g. Carbs: 48 g. Sugars: 6 g. Fiber: 9 g. Sodium: 107 mg.

179. Delicious Meatballs

Preparation time: 15 minutes
Cooking time: 25 minutes
Servings: 6
Ingredients

- 200 g. ground beef
- 200 g. ground chicken
- 100 g. ground pork
- 30 g. garlic, minced
- 1 potato

- 1 egg
- 1 tsp. basil
- 1 tsp. cayenne pepper
- 1 tsp. white pepper
- 2 tsp. olive oil

Directions

1. Combine ground beef, chicken meat, and pork in the mixing bowl and stir it gently.
2. Sprinkle it with basil, cayenne pepper, and white pepper.
3. Add minced garlic and egg.
4. Stir the mixture gently; you should get a fluffy mass.
5. Peel the potato and grate it.
6. Add the grated potato to the mixture and stir it again.
7. Preheat the air fryer oven to 180°C.
8. Take a tray and spray it with olive oil.
9. Make the balls from the meat mass and put them on the tray.
10. Lay the tray in the oven and cook it for 25 minutes.

Nutrition Calories: 204 Protein: 26.0 g.Fat: 7.6 g.Carbohydrates: 7.1 g.

180. Low-Fat Steak

Preparation time: 25 minutes
Cooking time: 10 minutes
Servings: 3
Ingredients

- 400 g. beef steak
- 1 tsp. white pepper
- 1 tsp. turmeric
- 1 tsp. cilantro - 1 tsp. olive oil
- 3 tsp. lemon juice
- 1 tsp. oregano
- 1 tsp. salt - 100 g. water

Directions

1. Rub the steaks with white pepper and turmeric, and put them in a large bowl.
2. Sprinkle the meat with salt, oregano, cilantro, and lemon juice.
3. Leave the steaks for 20 minutes.
4. Combine the olive oil and water, and pour it into the bowl with steaks.
5. Grill the steaks in the air fryer for 10 minutes from both sides.
6. Serve it immediately.

Nutrition Calories: 268 Protein: 40.7 g.Fat: 10.1 g.Carbohydrates: 1.4 g.

181. Beef With Mushrooms

Preparation time: 15 minutes
Cooking time: 40 minutes
Servings: 4
Ingredients

- 300 g. beef
- 150 g. mushrooms
- 1 onion
- 1 tsp. olive oil
- 100 g. vegetable broth
- 1 tsp. basil
- 1 tsp. chili
- 30 g. tomato juice

Directions

1. For this recipe, you should take a solid piece of beef. Take the meat and pierce it with a knife.
2. Rub it with olive oil, basil, and chili, and tomato juice. Chop the onion and mushrooms and pour them with vegetable broth. Cook the vegetables for 5 minutes. Take a large tray and put the meat in it. Add vegetable broth to the tray too; it will make the meat juicy.
3. Preheat the air fryer oven to 180°C and cook it for 35 minutes.

Nutrition Calories: 175 Protein: 24.9 g.Fat: 6.2 g.Carbohydrates: 4.4 g.

182. Beef Korma Curry

Preparation time: 10 minutes
Cooking time: 17–20 minutes
Servings: 4
Ingredients

- 1 lb. (454 g.) sirloin steak, sliced
- 1/2 cup yogurt - 1 tbsp. curry powder
- 1 tbsp. olive oil
- 1 onion, chopped
- 2 garlic cloves, minced
- 1 tomato, diced
- 1/2 cup frozen baby peas, thawed

Directions

1. In a medium bowl, combine the steak, yogurt, and curry powder. Stir and set aside.
2. In a metal bowl, combine the olive oil, onion, and garlic. Bake at 350°F (177°C) for 3–4 minutes or until crisp and tender.
3. Add the steak along with the yogurt and the diced tomato. Bake for 12–13

minutes or until the steak is almost tender.

4. Stir in the peas and bake for 2–3 minutes or until hot.

Nutrition Calories: 299 Fat: 11 g.Protein: 38 g.Carbohydrates: 9 g.Fiber: 2 g. Sugar: 3 g.Sodium: 100 mg.

183. Lemon Greek Beef and Vegetables

Preparation time: 10 minutes
Cooking time: 9–19 minutes
Servings: 4
Ingredients

- 1/2 lb. (227 g.) 96% lean ground beef
- 2 medium tomatoes, chopped
- 1 onion, chopped
- 2 garlic cloves, minced
- 2 cups fresh baby spinach
- 2 tbsp. lemon juice, freshly squeezed
- 1/3 cup low-sodium beef broth
- 2 tbsp. low-sodium feta cheese, crumbled

Directions

1. In a baking pan, crumble the beef; place it in the air fryer basket. Air fry at 370°F (188°C) for 3–7 minutes, stirring once during cooking until browned. Drain off any fat or liquid.
2. Swell the tomatoes, onion, and garlic into the pan; air fry for 4–8 minutes more, or until the onion is tender.
3. Add the spinach, lemon juice, and beef broth.
4. Air fry for 2–4 minutes more, or until the spinach is wilted.
5. Sprinkle with the feta cheese and serve immediately.

Nutrition Calories: 98 Fat: 1 g.Protein: 15 g.Carbohydrates: 5 g.Fiber: 1 g.Sugar: 2 g.Sodium: 123 mg.

184. Steak With Mushroom Sauce

Preparation time: 5 minutes
Cooking time: 15 minutes
Servings: 4
Ingredients

- 4 8 oz (225 gram) boneless ribeye steaks, 1-inch thick (or scotch fillet, sirloin, rump, strip or porterhouse steaks)

- Salt and pepper, to season

Gravy:

- 2 tablespoons olive oil
- 1 onion (yellow, white or brown), sliced
- 2 large garlic cloves, minced
- 7 ounces (200 grams) brown mushrooms sliced
- 3 tablespoons unsalted butter
- 3 tablespoons plain flour
- 2 1/2 cups beef broth or stock
- 2 teaspoons Worcestershire sauce
- Salt and pepper to taste

Directions

1. Pat steaks dry with paper towel. Season with salt and pepper to your taste.
2. Heat a lightly oiled skillet or pan (or barbecue) on high heat until just beginning to smoke. Cook steaks for 3 minutes each side or until cooked to your liking. Rest for 5 minutes.
3. Heat remaining oil in the skillet. Add onion and cook for 2-3 minutes until onions are translucent, then add the garlic and cook for a further 30 seconds, or until fragrant.
4. Add the sliced mushrooms into the skillet and cook for 3 minutes until golden and beginning to soften.
5. Reduce heat to medium and melt butter in the skillet. Add flour and cook while stirring for 1 minute, allowing the flour to brown slightly.
6. Slowly and gradually add in the beef broth (or stock), while stirring. Allow to simmer for 4-5 minutes, or until thickened. Stir in the Worcestershire sauce and season with salt and pepper to taste.
7. Add the steaks back into the gravy in the pan along with the juices on the plate OR serve steaks with the onion mushroom gravy on the side.
8. Garnish with chopped thyme, parsley or rosemary if desired.

Nutrition Calories: 226 Fat: 6 g. Protein: 26 g. Carbohydrates: 16 g. Fiber: 5 g. Sugar: 6 g. Sodium: 356 mg.

185. Steak With Tomato and Herbs

Preparation time: 30 minutes
Cooking time: 30 minutes
Servings: 2
Ingredients

- 8 oz. beef loin steak, sliced in half
- Salt and pepper to taste
- Cooking spray
- 1 tsp. fresh basil, snipped
- 1/4 cup green onion, sliced
- 1/2 cup tomato, chopped

Directions

1. Season the steak with salt and pepper.
2. Spray the oil on your pan.
3. Put the pan over medium-high heat.
4. Once hot, add the steaks.
5. Reduce the heat to medium.
6. Cook for 10–13 minutes for medium, turning once.
7. Add the basil and green onion.
8. Cook for 2 minutes.
9. Add the tomato and cook for 1 minute.
10. Let cool a little before slicing.

Nutrition Calories: 170 Fat: 6 g. Protein: 25 g.Carbohydrates: 3 g.Fiber: 1 g.Sugar: 5 g.Sodium: 207 mg.

186. Beef and Asparagus

Preparation time: 15 minutes
Cooking time: 10 minutes
Servings: 4
Ingredients

- 2 tsp. olive oil
- 3 lbs. lean beef sirloin, trimmed and sliced
- 1 carrot, shredded
- Salt and pepper to taste
- 12 oz. asparagus, trimmed and sliced
- 1 tsp. dried herbs de Provence, crushed
- 1/2 cup Marsala
- 1/4 tsp. lemon zest

Directions

1. Pour the oil into a pan over medium heat.
2. Add the beef and carrot.
3. Season with salt and pepper; cook for 3 minutes.
4. Add the asparagus and herbs; cook for 2 minutes.

5. Add the Marsala and lemon zest; cook for 5 minutes, stirring frequently.
6. Serve and enjoy.

Nutrition Calories: 327 Fat: 7 g.Protein: 28 g.Carbohydrates: 29 g.Fiber: 2 g.Sugar: 3 g.Sodium: 209 mg.

187. Italian Beef

Preparation time: 20 minutes
Cooking time: 1 hour 20 minutes
Servings: 4
Ingredients

- Cooking spray
- 2 lb. beef round steak, trimmed and sliced
- 1/2 cup onion, chopped
- 2 garlic cloves, minced
- 1 cup green bell pepper, chopped
- 1/2 cup celery, chopped
- 2 cups mushrooms, sliced
- 14 1/2 oz. tomatoes, canned and diced
- 1/2 tsp. basil, dried
- 1/4 tsp. oregano, dried
- 1/8 tsp. red pepper, crushed
- 2 tbsp. Parmesan cheese, grated

Directions

1. Spray the oil on the pan over medium heat.
2. Cook the meat until brown on both sides.
3. Transfer the meat to a plate.
4. Add the onion, garlic, bell pepper, celery, and mushroom to the pan; cook until tender.
5. Add the tomatoes, herbs, and pepper.
6. Put the meat back in the pan.
7. Simmer while covered for 1 hour 15 minutes; stir occasionally.
8. Sprinkle Parmesan cheese on top of the dish before serving.

Nutrition Calories: 212 Fat: 4 g.Protein: 20 g.Carbohydrates: 15 g.Fiber: 5 g.Sugar: 6 g.Sodium: 296 mg.

188. Barbecue Beef Brisket

Preparation time: 25 minutes
Cooking time: 10 hours
Servings: 10
Ingredients

- 4 lbs. beef brisket, boneless, trimmed, and sliced

- 3 bay leaf
- 2 onions, sliced into rings
- 1/2 tsp. dried thyme, crushed
- 1/4 cup chili sauce
- 1 garlic clove, minced
- Salt and pepper to taste
- 2 tbsp. light brown sugar
- 2 tbsp. cornstarch
- 2 tbsp. cold water

Directions

1. Put the meat in a slow cooker. Add the bay leaf and onion. Mix the thyme, chili sauce, garlic, salt, pepper, and sugar in a bowl.
2. Pour the sauce over the meat. Mix well. Seal the pot and cook on low heat for 10 hours.
3. Discard the bay leaf. Pour cooking liquid into a pan.
4. Add the mixed water and cornstarch.
5. Simmer until the sauce has thickened.
6. Pour the sauce over the meat.

Nutrition Calories: 182 Fat: 6 g. Protein: 20 g. Carbohydrates: 9 g.Fiber: 1 g.Sugar: 4 g.Sodium: 217 mg.

189. Shredded Beef

Preparation time: 10 minutes
Cooking time: 35 minutes
Servings: 2

Ingredients

- 1.5 lbs. lean steak
- 1 cup low-sodium gravy
- 2 tbsp. mixed spices

Directions

1. Mix all the ingredients in your instant pot.
2. Cook on STEW for 35 minutes.
3. Release the pressure naturally.
4. Shred the beef.

Nutrition Calories: 200 Protein: 48 g.Carbohydrates: 2 g.Sugar: 16 g.

190. Classic Mini Meatloaf

Preparation time: 15 minutes
Cooking time: 25 minutes
Servings: 6
Ingredients

- 1 lb. 80/20 ground beef

- 1/4 medium yellow onion, peeled and diced
- 1/2 medium green bell pepper, seeded and diced
- 1 large egg
- 3 tbsp. blanched finely ground almond flour
- 1 tbsp. Worcestershire sauce
- 1/2 tsp. garlic powder
- 1 tsp. parsley, dried
- 2 tbsp. tomato paste
- 1/4 cup water
- 1 tbsp. powdered erythritol

Directions

1. Combine the ground beef, onion, pepper, egg, and almond flour in a large bowl.
2. Pour in the Worcestershire sauce and add the garlic powder and parsley to the bowl. Mix until fully combined.
3. Divide the mixture and place it into 2 (4-inch) loaf baking pans.
4. In a small bowl, mix the tomato paste, water, and erythritol. Spoon half the mixture over each loaf.
5. Working in batches, if necessary, place loaf pans into the air fryer basket.
6. Adjust the temperature to 350°F and set the timer for 25 minutes or until the internal temperature is 180°F.
7. Serve warm.

Nutrition Calories: 170 Fat: 9 g.Protein: 15 g.Carbohydrates: 3 g.Fiber: 1 g.Sugar: 2 g.Sodium: 85 mg.

191. Skirt Steak With Asian Peanut Sauce

Preparation time: 10 minutes
Cooking time: 15 minutes
Servings: 4
Ingredients

- 1/3 cup light coconut milk
- 1 tsp. curry powder
- 1 tsp. coriander powder
- 1 tsp. reduced-sodium soy sauce
- 1 1/4 lb. skirt steak
- Cooking spray
- 1/2 cup Asian Peanut Sauce

Directions

1. Whisk together the coconut milk, curry powder, coriander powder, and soy sauce in a large bowl. Add the steak and turn to coat.
2. Cover the bowl and refrigerate for at least 30 minutes and no longer than 24 hours.
3. Preheat the barbecue or coat a grill pan with cooking spray and place the steak over medium-high heat.
4. Grill the meat until it reaches an internal temperature of 145°F, about 3 minutes per side. Remove the steak from the grill and let it rest for 5 minutes.
5. Slice the steak into 5 oz. pieces and serve each with 2 tbsp. of the Asian Peanut Sauce.

To refrigerate: Store the cooled steak in a resealable container for up to 1 week. Reheat each piece in the microwave for 1 minute.

Nutrition Calories: 361 Fat: 22 g. Protein: 36 g.Carbohydrates: 8 g.Fiber: 5 g.Sodium: 296 mg.

192. Garlic-Braised Short Rib

Preparation time: 5 minutes
Cooking time: 2 hours 20 minutes
Servings: 4
Ingredients

- 4 (4 oz.) beef short ribs
- Sea salt to taste
- Freshly ground black pepper to taste
- 1 tbsp. olive oil
- 2 tsp. garlic, minced
- 1/2 cup dry red wine
- 3 cups Rich Beef Stock

Directions

1. Preheat the oven to 325°F.
2. Season the beef ribs on all sides with salt and pepper. Place a deep ovenproof skillet over medium-high heat and add the olive oil. Sear the ribs on all sides until browned, about 6 minutes in total. Transfer the ribs to a plate. Add the garlic to the skillet and sauté until translucent, about 3 minutes. Whisk in the red wine to deglaze the pan. Be sure to scrape all the browned bits of meat from the bottom of the pan. Simmer the wine until it is slightly reduced, about 2 minutes. Add the beef stock, ribs, and any accumulated juices on the plate back

to the skillet and bring the liquid to a boil.
3. Cover the skillet and place it in the oven to braise the ribs until the meat is fall-off-the-bone tender, about 2 hours.
4. Serve the ribs with a spoonful of the cooking liquid drizzled over each serving.

Nutrition Calories: 481 Fat: 38 g.Protein: 29 g.Carbohydrates: 2 g.Fiber: 3 g.

193. Beef With Barley and Veggies

Preparation time: 10 minutes
Cooking time: 1 hour 5 minutes
Servings: 2
Ingredients

- 3/4 cup filtered water
- 1/4 cup pearl barley - 2 tsp. olive oil
- 7 oz. lean ground beef
- 1 cup fresh mushrooms, sliced
- 3/4 cup onion, chopped
- 2 cups frozen green beans
- 1/4 cup low-sodium beef broth
- 2 tbsp. fresh parsley, chopped
- Pinch salt

Directions

1. In a pan, add water, barley, and a pinch of salt and boil over medium heat.
2. Now, reduce the heat to low and simmer, covered for about 30–40 minutes or until all the liquid is absorbed. Remove from heat and set aside. In a skillet, heat oil over medium-high heat and cook beef for about 8–10 minutes. Add the mushroom and onion and cook for about 6–7 minutes.
3. Add the green beans and cook for about 2–3 minutes. Stir in cooked barley and broth and cook for about 3–5 minutes more. Stir in the parsley and serve hot.

Meal Prep Tip: Transfer the beef mixture into a large bowl and set it aside to cool. Divide the mixture into 2 containers evenly. Cover the containers and refrigerate for 1–2 days. Reheat in the microwave before serving.

Nutrition Calories: 374 Fat: 11 g. Protein: 37 g.Carbohydrates: 33 g.Fiber: 4 g.Sugar: 1 g.Sodium: 136 mg.

194. Taco-Stuffed Peppers

Preparation time: 10 minutes
Cooking time: 15 minutes
Servings: 4
Ingredients

- 1 lb. 80/20 ground beef
- 1 tbsp. chili powder
- 2 tsp. cumin
- 1 tsp. garlic powder
- 1 tsp. salt
- 1/4 tsp. ground black pepper
- 1 can (10 oz.) diced tomatoes and green chiles, drained
- 4 medium green bell peppers
- 1 cup shredded Monterey jack cheese, divided

Directions

1. In a medium skillet over medium heat, brown the ground beef for about 7–10 minutes. When no pink remains, drain the fat from the skillet.
2. Return the skillet to the stovetop and add chili powder, cumin, garlic powder, salt, and black pepper. Add drained can have diced tomatoes and chiles to the skillet. Continue cooking for 3–5 minutes.
3. While the mixture is cooking, cut each bell pepper in half. Remove the seeds and white membrane.
4. Spoon the cooked mixture evenly into each bell pepper and top with a 1/4 cup of cheese. Place the stuffed peppers into the air fryer basket.
5. Adjust the temperature to 350°F and set the timer for 15 minutes.
6. When done, peppers will be fork-tender, and cheese will be browned and bubbling.
7. Serve warm.

Nutrition Calories: 346 Fat: 19 g.Protein: 28 g.Carbohydrates: 111 g.Fibers: 4 g.Sugars: 5 g.Sodium: 991 mg.

195. Asian Beef Stir-Fry

Preparation time: 10 minutes
Cooking time: 15 minutes
Servings: 4
Ingredients

- 3/4 lb. beef top sirloin steak, boneless
- 1/3 tsp. red pepper, crushed
- 1/2 red onion, wedges
- 3 cups napa cabbage, shredded
- 2 cups broccoli florets
- 3 oz. buckwheat noodles or multigrain spaghetti
- 2 tbsp. teriyaki sauce
- 3 tbsp. orange marmalade, low-sugar
- 2 tbsp. water
- 2 tsp. canola oil
- Cooking spray

Directions

1. Bring together the teriyaki sauce, red pepper, marmalade, and water in a bowl; keep aside.
2. Cook the spaghetti according to directions on the pack.
3. In the meantime, apply cooking spray on your skillet. Preheat.
4. Now add the red onion and broccoli to your skillet; cook covered for 3 minutes.
5. Add the cabbage and cook for 3 more minutes.
6. The vegetables should become tender. Take out the vegetables.
7. Now add oil and the beef strips; cook for 3 minutes until the center is slightly pink.
8. Return the vegetables to your skillet with the cabbage and sauce; cook, while stirring, for 1 minute.
9. Serve.

Nutrition Calories: 279 Fats: 4 g.Protein: 25 g.Carbohydrates: 30 g.Fibers: 5 g.Sugars: 1 g. Sodium: 259 mg.

196. Beef With Broccoli

Preparation time: 10 minutes
Cooking time: 14 minutes
Servings: 4
Ingredients

- 2 tbsp. olive oil, divided
- 2 garlic cloves, minced
- 1 lb. beef sirloin steak, trimmed and sliced into thin strips
- 1/4 cup low-sodium chicken broth
- 2 tsp. fresh ginger, grated
- 1 tbsp. ground flax seeds
- 1/2 tsp. red pepper flakes, crushed
- Salt and ground black pepper, as required
- 1 large carrot, peeled and sliced thinly

- 2 cups broccoli florets
- 1 medium scallion, sliced thinly

Directions

1. In a large skillet, heat 1 tbsp. of oil over medium-high heat and sauté the garlic for 1 minute.
2. Add the beef and cook for about 4–5 minutes or until browned.
3. With a slotted spoon, transfer the beef into a bowl.
4. Remove the excess liquid from the skillet.
5. Add the broth, ginger, flax seeds, red pepper flakes, salt, and black pepper in a bowl.
6. In the same skillet, heat the remaining oil over medium heat.
7. Add the carrot, broccoli, and ginger mixture and cook for about 3–4 minutes or until desired doneness.
8. Stir in the beef and scallion and cook for about 3–4 minutes.

Meal Prep Tip: Transfer the beef mixture into a large bowl and set it aside to cool. Divide the mixture into 4 containers evenly. Cover the containers and refrigerate for 1–2 days. Reheat in the microwave before serving.

Nutrition Calories: 211 Fats: 15 g.Protein: 36 g. Carbohydrates: 7 g.Fibers: 2 g.Sugars: 2 g.Sodium: 108 mg.

197. Salisbury Steak in Mushroom Sauce

Preparation time: 10 minutes
Cooking time: 15 minutes
Servings: 4
Ingredients

- 1 lb. 85% lean ground beef
- 1 tsp. Steak seasoning
- 1 egg
- 2 tbsp. butter
- 1/2 onion, sliced
- 1/2 cup button mushrooms, sliced
- 1 cup beef broth
- 2 oz. cream cheese
- 1/4 cup heavy cream
- 1/4 tsp. xanthan gum

Directions

1. Mix egg, steak seasoning, and ground beef in a bowl. Make 4 patties and set them aside.

2. Press the SAUTÉ bottom and melt the butter.
3. Add mushrooms and onion and stir-fry for 3–5 minutes.
4. Press the CANCEL bottom and add beef patties, broth, and cream cheese to the instant pot.
5. Close the lid and press MANUAL.
6. Cook 15 minutes on HIGH.
7. Allow the pressure to release naturally when finished.
8. Remove the patties and set them aside.
9. Add xanthan gum and heavy cream. Whisk to mix.
10. Reduce the sauce on SAUTÉ mode for 5–10 minutes.
11. Press CANCEL and add patties back to the instant pot.
12. Serve.

Nutrition Calories: 420 Fats: 30 g. Protein: 25 g.Carbohydrates: 2 g.

198. Brisket With Cauliflower

Preparation time: 5 minutes
Cooking time: 15 minutes
Servings: 4
Ingredients

- 1 cup water
- 2 cups, fresh cauliflower, chopped
- 3 tbsps. butter
- 1/4 onion, diced
- 1/4 cup pickled jalapeño slices
- 2 cups brisket, cooked
- 2 oz. cream cheese, softened
- 1 cup sharp cheddar cheese, shredded
- 1/4 cup heavy cream
- 1/4 cup crumbled bacon, cooked
- 2 tbsps. green onions, sliced

Directions

1. Add water to the instant pot.
2. Steam the cauliflower on a steamer basket for 1 minute.
3. Release pressure quickly and set aside.
4. Pour out water and press SAUTÉ.
5. Add butter, jalapeño slices, and onion.
6. Sauté for 4 minutes, add cream cheese and cooked brisket.
7. Cook 2 more minutes.
8. Add cauliflower, heavy cream, and sharp cheddar.

9. Press CANCEL and gently mix until mixed well.
10. Sprinkle with green onions and crumbled bacon.
11. Serve.

Nutrition Calories: 574 Fats: 40 g.Protein: 33 g.Carbohydrates: 8 g.

199. Beef and Spaghetti Squash Casserole

Preparation time: 10 minutes
Cooking time: 20 minutes
Servings: 4
Ingredients

- 6 lbs. spaghetti squash cooked and scraped out into long strands with a fork
- 1 cup no sugar added tomato sauce
- 1/2 cup whole-milk ricotta
- 1/4 cup Parmesan cheese, grated
- 3 tbsps. butter
- 1/2 tsp. parsley, dried
- 1/2 tsp. garlic powder
- 1/4 tsp. basil, dried
- 1/2 tsp. salt
- 1/4 tsp. pepper
- 1 lb. 85% lean ground beef cooked
- 1 cup, shredded Mozzarella cheese, divided
- 1 cup water

Directions

1. Place the squash into a bowl.
2. Add the remaining ingredients except for water (reserve 1/2 mozzarella).
3. Mix and pour the mixture into a bowl.
4. Sprinkle the remaining cheese on top and cover with a foil.
5. Pour water into the instant pot and place it on the steam rack.
6. Place bowl on the steam rack and close the lid.
7. Press the MANUAL bottom and cook for 10 minutes.
8. Allow the pressure to release naturally.
9. You can broil the dish in the oven for a few minutes to brown the top.
10. Serve.

Nutrition Calories: 628 Fats: 37 g.Protein: 36 g.Carbohydrates: 9 g.

200. Mini BBQ Meatloaf

Preparation time: 5 minutes
Cooking time: 25 minutes
Servings: 4
Ingredients

- 1 lb. 85% lean ground beef
- 1/2 onion, diced
- 1/2 green pepper, diced
- 1/4 cup almond flour
- 1/4 cup mozzarella cheese, shredded
- 1 egg
- 1 tsp. salt
- 1/4 tsp. pepper
- 1 tsp. garlic powder
- 1/4 cup no sugar added barbecue sauce

Directions

1. Mix all the ingredients in a bowl, except for the barbecue sauce.
2. Make 2 loaves and place them into loaf pans.
3. Pour sauce on top and cover it with foil.
4. Pour 1 cup water into the instant pot and place the steam rack.
5. Place the meatloaf pans on the steam rack.
6. Close the lid and press MANUAL.
7. Cook 25 minutes on HIGH.
8. Serve.

Nutrition Calories: 340 Fats: 20 g.Protein: 26 g.Carbohydrates: 4 g.

201. BBQ Ribs

Preparation time: 5 minutes
Cooking time: 50 minutes
Servings: 4
Ingredients

- 1 (4 lb.) ribs rack
- 1 tbsp. chili powder
- 1 tsp. salt
- 1 tsp. parsley, dried
- 1/2 tsp. pepper
- 1/2 tsp. garlic powder
- 1/2 tsp. onion powder
- 1/2 cup no sugar added barbecue sauce
- 1 cup water
- 1 tbsp. liquid smoke

Directions

1. Rub the ribs with half barbecue sauce and seasonings.
2. Pour the water and liquid smoke into the instant pot, place a steam rack, and close the lid.
3. Press the MEAT bottom and cook 50 minutes on HIGH.
4. When done, place the ribs on a foil-lined baking sheet.
5. Brush with the remaining sauce and serve.
6. If you want a caramelized sauce, then broil it in the oven for a few minutes.

Nutrition Calories: 421 Fats: 24 g.Protein: 40 g.Carbohydrates: 3 g.

202. Cheesy Beef and Broccoli

Preparation time: 5 minutes
Cooking time: 10 minutes
Servings: 4
Ingredients

- 1 lb. 85% lean ground beef
- 1 tsp. salt
- 1/2 tsp. garlic powder
- 1/2 tsp. parsley, dried
- 1/4 tsp. oregano, dried
- 2 tbsp. butter
- 3/4 cup beef broth
- 2 cups broccoli florets
- 1/4 cup heavy cream
- 1 cup cheddar cheese, shredded

Directions

1. Brown the beef on SAUTÉ mode in the instant pot.
2. Press CANCEL and sprinkle seasonings over the meat.
3. Add the broccoli, broth, and butter. Close the lid.

4. Press MANUAL and cook for 2 minutes on HIGH.
5. When done, press CANCEL and stir in the cheddar and heavy cream.
6. Serve.

Nutrition Calories: 476 Fats: 33 g. Protein: 30 g. Carbohydrates: 3 g.

203. Butter Beef and Spinach

Preparation time: 2 minutes
Cooking time: 10 minutes
Servings: 4
Ingredients

- 1 lb. 85% lean ground beef
- 1 cup water
- 4 cups fresh spinach
- 3/4 tsp. salt
- 1/4 cup butter
- 1/4 tsp. pepper
- 1/4 tsp. garlic powder

Directions

1. Brown the beef on SAUTÉ mode in the instant pot.
2. Remove it into a bowl. Drain the grease and clean the pot.
3. Add the water into the pot and place the steam rack.
4. Place the bowl with the beef on top.
5. Add the garlic powder, pepper, butter, salt, and spinach.
6. Cover it with foil and close the lid.
7. Press MANUAL and cook 2 minutes on HIGH.
8. Make a quick release of pressure.
9. Remove foil, stir and serve.

Nutrition Calories: 272 Fats: 19 g. Protein: 18 g. Carbohydrates: 1 g.

CHAPTER 6:

Pork

204. Pork Head Chops With Vegetables

Preparation time: 9 minutes
Cooking time: 24 minutes
Servings: 4
Ingredients

- 4 pork head chops
- 2 red tomatoes
- 1 large green pepper
- 4 mushrooms
- 1 onion
- 4 slices cheese
- Salt to taste
- Ground pepper to taste
- Extra-virgin olive oil

Directions

1. Put the 4 chops on a plate and salt and pepper.
2. Put 2 of the chops in the air fryer basket.
3. Place the tomato slices, cheese slices, pepper slices, onion slices, and mushroom slices. Add some threads of oil.
4. Take the air fryer and cook at 180°C for 20 minutes.
5. Check that the meat is well made and remove it.
6. Repeat the same operation with the other 2 pork chops.

Nutrition Calories: 106 Fat: 3.41 g.Carbohydrates: 0 g.Protein: 20.9 g.

205. Flavored Pork Chops

Preparation time: 9 minutes
Cooking time: 38 minutes
Servings: 2
Ingredients

- 3 garlic cloves, ground
- 2 tbsp. olive oil
- 1 tbsp. marinade
- 4 thawed pork chops

Directions

1. Mix the cloves of ground garlic, marinade, and oil. Then apply this mixture to the chops.
2. Put the chops in the air fryer at 360°F for 35 minutes.
3. Serve.

Nutrition Calories: 118 Fat: 3.41 g.Carbohydrates: 0 g.Protein: 22 g.

206. Pork Trinoza Wrapped in Ham

Preparation time: 8 minutes
Cooking time: 10–15 minutes
Servings: 6
Ingredients

- 6 pieces Serrano ham, thinly sliced
- 454 g. pork, halved, with butter and crushed - 6 g. salt
- 1 g. black pepper
- 227 g. fresh spinach leaves, divided
- 4 slices Mozzarella cheese, divided
- 18 g. sun-dried tomatoes, divided
- 10 ml olive oil, divided

Directions

1. Place 3 pieces of ham on baking paper, slightly overlapping each other. Place 1 half of the pork in the ham. Repeat with the other half.
2. Season the inside of the pork rolls with salt and pepper.
3. Place half of the spinach, cheese, and sun-dried tomatoes on top of the pork loin, leaving a 13 mm. border on all sides.
4. Roll the fillet around the filling well and tie it with a kitchen cord to keep it closed.
5. Repeat the process for the other pork steak and place them in the fridge.
6. Warm in the air fryer and press START/PAUSE.

7. Brush 5 ml. of olive oil on each wrapped steak and place them in the preheated air fryer.
8. Select STEAK. Set the timer to 9 minutes and press START/PAUSE.
9. Let it cool before cutting.

Nutrition Calories: 282 Fat: 23.41 g.Carbohydrates: 0 g.Protein: 16.59 g.

207. Stuffed Cabbage and Pork Loin Rolls

Preparation time: 5 minutes
Cooking time: 28 minutes
Servings: 4
Ingredients

- 500 g. white cabbage
- 1 onion
- 8 pork tenderloin steaks
- 2 carrots
- 4 tbsp. soy sauce
- 50 g. extra virgin olive oil
- Salt to taste
- 8 sheets rice

Directions

1. Put the chopped cabbage in the Thermo mix glass together with the onion and the chopped carrot.
2. Select 5 seconds on the speed 5. Add the extra virgin olive oil. Select 5 minutes, left turn, and spoon speed.
3. Cut the tenderloin steaks into thin strips. Add the meat to the thermo mix glass. Select 5 minutes, room temperature, left turn, spoon speed without beaker.
4. Add the soy sauce. Select 5 minutes, room temperature, left turn, spoon speed. Rectify salt. Let it cold down.
5. Hydrate the rice slices. Extend and distribute the filling between them.
6. Make the rolls, folding so that the edges are completely closed. Set the rolls in the air fryer and paint with the oil.
7. Select 10 minutes, 180ºC.

Nutrition Calories: 120 Fat: 3.41 g.Carbohydrates: 0 g.Protein: 20.99 g.

208. Homemade Flamingos

Preparation time: 8 minutes
Cooking time: 10–15 minutes
Servings: 4
Ingredients

- 400 g. pork fillets, very thin sliced

- 2 eggs, boiled and chopped
- 100 g. Serrano ham, chopped
- 1 egg, beaten
- 1 cup breadcrumbs

Directions

1. Make a roll with the pork fillets. Introduce half-cooked egg and Serrano ham. So that the roll does not lose its shape, fasten with a string or chopsticks.
2. Pass the rolls through the beaten egg and then through the breadcrumbs until it forms a good layer.
3. Warm the air fryer for a few minutes at 180ºC.
4. Insert the rolls in the basket and set the timer for about 8 minutes at 180ºC.

Nutrition Calories: 482 Fat: 23.41 g.Carbohydrates: 0 g.Protein: 16.59 g.

209. Spiced Pork Chops

Preparation time: 8 minutes
Cooking time: 11 minutes
Servings: 2
Ingredients

- 2 pork chops, boneless
- 15 ml. vegetable oil
- 25 g. dark brown sugar, packaged
- 6 g. Hungarian paprika
- 2 g. ground mustard
- 2 g. freshly ground black pepper
- 3 g. onion powder
- 3 g. garlic powder
- Salt and pepper to taste

Directions

1. Warm the air fryer for a few minutes at 180ºC.
2. Cover the pork chops with oil.
3. Put all the spices and season the pork chops abundantly, almost as if you were making them breaded.
4. Place the pork chops in the preheated air fryer.
5. Select STEAK and set the time to 10 minutes.
6. Remove the pork chops when it has finished cooking.
7. Let it stand and serve.

Nutrition Calories: 118 Fat: 6.85 g.Carbohydrates: 0.3 g.Protein: 13.12 g.

210. Pork Rind

Preparation time: 9 minutes
Cooking time: 62 minutes
Servings: 4
Ingredients

- 1 kg pork rinds - Salt to taste
- 1/2 tsp. black pepper

Directions

1. Preheat the air fryer. Set the time to 5 minutes and the temperature to 200°C.
2. Cut the bacon into cubes 1 finger wide.
3. Flavor with salt and a pinch of pepper.
4. Place in the basket of the air fryer. Set the time of 45 minutes and press the POWER button.
5. Shake the basket every 10 minutes so that the pork rinds stay golden brown equally. Once they are ready, drain a little on the paper towel so they stay dry.
6. Transfer to a plate and serve.

Nutrition Calories: 282 Fat: 23.41 g.Carbohydrates: 0.3 g.Protein: 16.59 g.

211. Herbed Pork Ribs

Preparation time: 6 minutes
Cooking time: 20–25 minutes
Servings: 4
Ingredients

- 500 g. pork ribs
- 1 tbsp. provencal herbs
- Salt to taste - Ground pepper to taste
- 1 tsp. oil

Directions

1. Set the ribs in a bowl and add some oil, Provencal herbs, salt, and ground pepper.
2. Stir well and leave in the fridge for at least 1 hour.
3. Put the ribs in the basket of the air fryer and select 200ºC for 20 minutes.
4. From time to time, shake the basket and remove the ribs.

Nutrition Calories: 296 Fat: 3.41 g.Carbohydrates: 6 g.Protein: 29 g.

212. Country-Style Pork Ribs

Preparation time: 5 minutes
Cooking time: 20–25 minutes
Servings: 4
Ingredients

- 12 country-style pork ribs, trimmed of excess fat

- 2 tbsp. cornstarch
- 2 tbsp. olive oil
- 1 tsp. dry mustard
- 1/2 tsp. thyme
- 1/2 tsp. garlic powder
- 1 tsp. marjoram, dried
- Pinch salt
- Freshly ground black pepper, to taste

Directions

1. Place the ribs on a clean work surface.
2. In a small bowl, combine the cornstarch, olive oil, mustard, thyme, garlic powder, marjoram, salt, and pepper, and rub into the ribs.
3. Place the ribs in the air fryer basket and roast at 400°F (204°C) for 10 minutes.
4. Carefully turn the ribs using tongs and roast for 10–15 minutes or until the ribs are crisp and register an internal temperature of at least 150°F (66°C).

Nutrition Calories: 579 Fats: 44 g. Protein: 40 g. Carbohydrates: 4 g. Fibers: 0 g. Sugars: 0 g. Sodium: 155 mg.

213. Lemon and Honey Pork Tenderloin

Preparation time: 5 minutes
Cooking time: 10 minutes
Servings: 4
Ingredients

- 1 (1 lb./454 g.) pork tenderloin, cut into 1/2-inch slices
- 1 tbsp. olive oil
- 1 tbsp. lemon juice, freshly squeezed
- 1 tbsp. honey
- 1/2 tsp. lemon zest, grated
- 1/2 tsp. marjoram, dried
- Pinch salt
- Freshly ground black pepper, to taste

Directions

1. Put the pork tenderloin slices in a medium bowl.
2. Combine the olive oil, lemon juice, honey, lemon zest, marjoram, salt, and pepper in a small bowl. Mix well.
3. Pour this marinade over the tenderloin slices and massage gently with your hand so that it integrates into the pork.

4. Place the pork in the air fryer basket and roast at 400°F (204°C) for 10 minutes or until the pork registers at least 145°F (63°C) in a meat thermometer.

Nutrition Calories: 208 Fats: 8 g. Protein: 30 g. Carbohydrates: 5 g. Fibers: 0 g. Sugars: 4 g. Sodium: 104 mg.

214. Dijon Pork Tenderloin
Preparation time: 10 minutes
Cooking time: 12–14 minutes
Servings: 4
Ingredients

- 1 lb. (454 g.) pork tenderloin, cut into 1-inch slices
- Pinch salt
- Freshly ground black pepper, to taste
- 2 tbsp. Dijon mustard
- 1 garlic clove, minced
- 1/2 tsp. basil, dried
- 1 cup soft breadcrumbs
- 2 tbsp. olive oil

Directions

1. Slightly pound the pork slices until they are about 3/4-inch thick. Sprinkle with salt and pepper on both sides.
2. Coat the pork with the Dijon mustard and sprinkle with the garlic and basil.
3. On a plate, combine the breadcrumbs and olive oil and mix well. Coat the pork slices with the breadcrumb mixture, patting, so the crumbs adhere.
4. Place the pork in the air fryer basket, leaving a little space between each piece. Air fry at 390°F (199°C) for 12–14 minutes or until the pork reaches at least 145°F (63°C) on a meat thermometer and the coating is crisp and brown.
5. Serve immediately.

Nutrition Calories: 336 Fats: 13 g. Protein: 34 g. Carbohydrates: 20 g. Fibers: 2 g. Sugars: 2 g. Sodium: 390 mg.

215. Air Fryer Pork Satay
Preparation time: 15 minutes
Cooking time: 9–14 minutes
Servings: 4
Ingredients

- 1 (1 lb./454 g.) pork tenderloin, cut into 1 1/2-inch cubes
- 1/4 cup onion, minced
- 2 garlic cloves, minced

- 1 jalapeño pepper, minced
- 2 tbsp. lime juice, freshly squeezed
- 2 tbsp. coconut milk
- 2 tbsp. unsalted peanut butter
- 2 tsp. curry powder

Directions

1. In a medium bowl, mix the pork, onion, garlic, jalapeño, lime juice, coconut milk, peanut butter, and curry powder until well combined. Let position for 10 minutes at room temperature.
2. With a slotted spoon, remove the pork from the marinade. Reserve the marinade.
3. Thread the pork onto about 8 bamboo or metal skewers. Air fry at 380°F (193°C) for 9–14 minutes, brushing once with the reserved marinade until the pork reaches at least 145°F (63°C) on a meat thermometer.
4. Discard any remaining marinade.
5. Serve immediately.

Nutrition Calories: 195 Fats: 25 g. Protein: 7 g. Carbohydrates: 1 g. Fibers: 1 g. Sugars: 3 g. Sodium: 65 mg.

216. Pork Burgers With Red Cabbage Slaw
Preparation time: 20 minutes
Cooking time: 7–9 minutes
Servings: 4
Ingredients

- 1/2 cup Greek yogurt
- 2 tbsp. low-sodium mustard, divided
- 1 tbsp. lemon juice, freshly squeezed
- 1/4 cup red cabbage, sliced
- 1/4 cup carrots, grated
- 1 lb. (454 g.) lean ground pork
- 1/2 tsp. paprika
- 1 cup baby lettuce greens, mixed
- 2 small tomatoes, sliced
- 8 small low-sodium whole-wheat sandwich buns, cut in half

Directions

1. In a lesser bowl, syndicate the yogurt, 1 tbsp. mustard, lemon juice, cabbage, and carrots; mix and refrigerate.
2. In a medium bowl, combine the pork, the remaining 1 tbsp. mustard, and paprika. Form into 8 small patties.

3. Lay the patties into the air fryer basket. Air fry at 400°F (204°C) for 7–9 minutes, or until the patties register 165°F (74°C) as tested with a meat thermometer.
4. Assemble the burgers by placing some of the lettuce greens on a bun bottom. Top with a tomato slice, the patties, and the cabbage mixture. Add the bun top and serve immediately.

Nutrition Calories: 473 Fats: 15 g. Protein: 35 g. Carbohydrates: 51 g. Fibers: 8 g. Sugars: 8 g. Sodium: 138 mg.

217. Diet Boiled Ribs

Preparation time: 10 minutes
Cooking time: 30 minutes
Servings: 4
Ingredients

- 400 g. pork ribs
- 1 tsp. black pepper
- 1 g. bay leaf
- 1 tsp. basil
- 1 white onion
- 1 carrot
- 1 tsp. cumin
- 700 ml. water

Directions

1. Cut the ribs on the portions and sprinkle them with black pepper.
2. Take a large saucepan and pour water into it.
3. Add the ribs and bay leaf.
4. Peel the onion and carrot and add them to the water with meat.
5. Sprinkle it with cumin and basil.
6. Cook it on medium heat in the air fryer for 30 minutes.

Nutrition Calories: 294 Fats: 18 g. Protein: 27 g. Carbohydrates: 5 g.

218. Quick and Juicy Pork Chops

Preparation time: 10 minutes
Cooking time: 12 minutes
Servings: 4
Ingredients

- 4 pork chops
- 1 tsp. olive oil
- 1 tsp. onion powder
- 1 tsp. paprika
- Pepper and salt to taste

Directions

1. Cover the pork chops with olive oil and season with paprika, onion powder, pepper, and salt.
2. Place the dehydrating tray in a multi-level air fryer basket and place the basket in the instant pot.
3. Place pork chops on dehydrating tray.
4. Seal the pot with an air fryer lid, select AIR FRY mode, then set the temperature to 380°F and timer for 12 minutes. Turn pork chops halfway through.
5. Serve and enjoy.

Nutrition Calories: 270 Fats: 21 g. Protein: 18 g. Carbohydrates: 1 g. Sugars: 0.3 g.

219. Delicious and Tender Pork Chops

Preparation time: 10 minutes
Cooking time: 12 minutes
Servings: 2

Ingredients

- 2 pork chops
- 1 tbsp. olive oil
- 1/4 tsp. garlic powder
- 1/2 tsp. onion powder
- 1 tsp. ground mustard
- 1 1/2 tsp. pepper
- 1 tbsp. paprika
- 2 tbsp. brown sugar
- 1 1/2 tsp. salt

Directions

1. Mix garlic powder, onion powder, mustard, paprika, pepper, brown sugar, and salt in a small container.
2. Cover the pork chops with olive oil and rub with spice mixture.
3. Place the dehydrating tray in a multi-level air fryer basket and place the basket in the instant pot.
4. Place the pork chops on dehydrating tray.
5. Seal the pot with an air fryer lid; select AIR FRY mode, then set the temperature to 400°F and timer for 12 minutes. Turn pork chops halfway through. Serve and enjoy.

Nutrition Calories: 375 Fats: 28 g. Protein: 19 g. Carbohydrates: 13 g. Sugars: 9 g.

220. Perfect Pork Chops

Preparation time: 10 minutes
Cooking time: 15 minutes
Servings: 4
Ingredients

- 4 pork chops
- Pepper to taste
- Salt to taste

Directions

1. Season pork chops with pepper and salt.
2. Place the dehydrating tray in a multi-level air fryer basket and place the basket in the instant pot.
3. Place the pork chops on a dehydrating tray.
4. Seal the pot with an air fryer lid, select air fry mode, then set the temperature to 400°F and timer for 15 minutes. Turn pork chops halfway through.
5. Serve and enjoy.

Nutrition Calories: 256 Fats: 20 g. Protein: 18 g. Carbohydrates: 0 g. Sugars: 0 g.

221. Pork Chops With Grape Sauce

Preparation time: 15 minutes
Cooking time: 25 minutes
Servings: 4
Ingredients

- Cooking spray
- 4 pork chops
- 1/4 cup onion, sliced
- 1 garlic clove, minced
- 1/2 cup low-sodium chicken broth
- 3/4 cup apple juice
- 1 tbsp. cornstarch
- 1 tbsp. balsamic vinegar
- 1 tsp. honey
- 1 cup seedless red grapes, sliced in half

Directions

1. Spray oil on your pan.
2. Put it over medium heat.
3. Add the pork chops to the pan.
4. Cook for 5 minutes per side.
5. Remove and set aside.
6. Add the onion and garlic.
7. Cook for 2 minutes.
8. Pour in the broth and apple juice.
9. Bring to a boil.
10. Reduce the heat to simmer.
11. Put the pork chops back to the skillet.

12. Simmer for 4 minutes.
13. In a bowl, mix the cornstarch, vinegar, and honey; add to the pan.
14. Cook until the sauce has thickened.
15. Add the grapes.
16. Pour sauce over the pork chops before serving.

Nutrition Calories: 188 Fats: 4 g. Protein: 19 g. Carbohydrates: 18 g. Fibers: 1 g. Sugars: 13 g. Sodium: 117 mg.

222. Roasted Pork and Apples

Preparation time: 15 minutes
Cooking time: 30 minutes
Servings: 4
Ingredients

- Salt and pepper to taste
- 1/2 tsp. sage dried, crushed
- 1 lb. pork tenderloin
- 1 tbsp. canola oil
- 1 onion, sliced into wedges
- 3 cooking apples, sliced into wedges
- 2/3 cup apple cider
- Sprigs fresh sage

Directions

1. In a bowl, mix salt, pepper, and sage.
2. Season both sides of pork with this mixture.
3. Place a pan over medium heat.
4. Brown both sides.
5. Transfer to a roasting pan.
6. Add the onion on top and around the pork. Drizzle oil on top of the pork and apples. Roast in the oven at 425°F for 10 minutes.
7. Add the apples, roast for another 15 minutes. In a pan, boil the apple cider and then simmer for 10 minutes.
8. Pour the apple cider sauce over the pork before serving.

Nutrition Calories: 239 Fats: 6 g. Protein: 24 g. Carbohydrates: 22 g. Fibers: 3 g. Sugars: 16 g. Sodium: 209 mg.

223. Pork With Cranberry Relish

Preparation time: 30 minutes
Cooking time: 30 minutes
Servings: 4
Ingredients

- 12 oz. pork tenderloin, fat trimmed and sliced crosswise

- Salt and pepper to taste
- 1/4 cup all-purpose flour
- 2 tbsp. olive oil
- 1 onion, sliced thinly
- 1/4 cup cranberries, dried
- 1/4 cup low-sodium chicken broth
- 1 tbsp. balsamic vinegar

Directions

1. Flatten each slice of pork using a mallet.
2. In a dish, mix the salt, pepper, and flour.
3. Dip each pork slice into the flour mixture.
4. Add oil to a pan over medium-high heat.
5. Cook the pork for 3 minutes per side or until golden crispy.
6. Transfer to a serving plate and cover with foil.
7. Cook the onion in the pan for 4 minutes.
8. Stir in the rest of the ingredients.
9. Simmer until the sauce has thickened.

Nutrition Calories: 211 Fats: 9 g. Protein: 18 g. Carbohydrates: 15 g. Fibers: 1 g. Sugars: 6 g. Sodium: 116 mg.

224. Sesame Pork With Mustard Sauce

Preparation time: 25 minutes
Cooking time: 25 minutes
Servings: 4
Ingredients

- 2 tbsp. low-sodium teriyaki sauce
- 1/4 cup chili sauce
- 2 garlic cloves, minced
- 2 tsp. ginger, grated
- 2 pork tenderloins
- 2 tsp. sesame seeds
- 1/4 cup low-fat sour cream
- 1 tsp. Dijon mustard
- Salt to taste
- Scallion, chopped

Directions

1. Preheat your oven to 425°F.
2. Mix the teriyaki sauce, chili sauce, garlic, and ginger.
3. Put the pork on a roasting pan.
4. Brush the sauce on both sides of the pork.
5. Bake in the oven for 15 minutes.
6. Brush with more sauce.
7. Top with sesame seeds.

8. Roast for 10 more minutes.
9. Mix the rest of the ingredients.
10. Serve the pork with mustard sauce.

Nutrition Calories: 135 Fats: 3 g. Protein: 20 g. Carbohydrates: 7 g. Fibers: 1 g. Sugars: 15 g. Sodium: 302 mg.

225. Irish Pork Roast

Preparation time: 40 minutes
Cooking time: 1 hour
Servings: 8
Ingredients

- 1/2 lb. parsnips, peeled and sliced into small pieces
- 1/2 lb. carrots, sliced into small pieces
- 3 tbsp. olive oil, divided
- 2 tsp. fresh thyme leaves, divided
- Salt and pepper to taste
- 2 lb. pork loin roast
- 1 tsp. honey
- 1 cup dry hard cider Applesauce

Directions

1. Preheat the oven to 400°F.
2. Drizzle half of the oil over the parsnips and carrots. Season with half of the thyme, salt, and pepper.
3. Arrange on a roasting pan. Rub the pork with the remaining oil.
4. Season with the remaining thyme, salt, and pepper. Put it on the roasting pan on top of the vegetables.
5. Roast for 60 minutes.
6. Let cool before slicing.
7. Transfer the carrots and parsnips to a bowl and mix with honey.
8. Add the cider. Place in a pan and simmer over low heat until the sauce has thickened.
9. Serve the pork with the vegetables and the applesauce.

Nutrition Calories: 272 Fats: 8 g. Protein: 24 g. Carbohydrates: 23 g. Fibers: 6 g.Sugars: 10 g.

226. Roasted Pork Loin With Grainy Mustard Sauce

Preparation time: 10 minutes
Cooking time: 70 minutes
Servings: 8
Ingredients

- 1 (2 lbs.) pork loin roast, boneless
- Sea salt to taste

- Freshly ground black pepper to taste
- 3 tbsp. olive oil
- 1 1/2 cups heavy (whipping) cream
- 3 tbsp. grainy mustard, such as Pommery

Directions

1. Preheat the oven to 375°F.
2. Season the pork roast all over with sea salt and pepper.
3. Place a large skillet over medium-high heat and add the olive oil.
4. Brown the roast for all sides for 6 minutes and place it in a baking dish.
5. Roast until a meat thermometer inserted in the thickest part of the roast reads 155°F, about 1 hour.
6. When there are approximately 15 minutes of roasting time left, place a small saucepan over medium heat and add the heavy cream and mustard.
7. Stir the sauce until it simmers, then reduce the heat to low. Simmer the sauce until it is very rich and thick, about 5 minutes. Remove the pan from the heat and set it aside.
8. Let the pork rest for 10 minutes before slicing and serve with the sauce.

Nutrition Calories: 368 Fats: 29 g. Protein: 25 g. Carbohydrates: 2 g. Fibers: 0 g.

227. **Pulled Pork**

Preparation time: 10 minutes
Cooking time: 2 1/2 hours
Servings: 8
Ingredients

- 2 tbsp. chili powder
- 1 tsp. garlic powder
- 1/2 tsp. onion powder
- 1/2 tsp. ground black pepper
- 1/2 tsp. cumin
- 4 lbs. pork shoulder

Directions

1. Mix the chili powder, garlic powder, onion powder, pepper, and cumin in a small bowl.
2. Rub the spice mixture over the pork shoulder, patting it into the skin.
3. Place the pork shoulder into the air fryer basket.
4. Adjust the temperature to 350°F and set the timer for 2 1/2 hours.

5. Pork skin will be crispy and meat easily shredded with 2 forks when done. The internal temperature should be at least 145°F.

Nutrition Calories: 537 Fats: 35 g. Protein: 43 g. Carbohydrates: 1 g. Fibers: 1 g. Sodium: 180 mg.

228. **Pork Chops in Peach Glaze**

Preparation time: 10 minutes
Cooking time: 16 minutes
Servings: 2
Ingredients

- 2 (6 oz.) boneless pork chops, trimmed
- Sea salt and ground black pepper, as required
- 1/2 ripe yellow peach, peeled, pitted, and chopped
- 1 tbsp. olive oil
- 2 tbsp. shallot, minced
- 2 tbsp. garlic, minced
- 2 tbsp. fresh ginger, minced
- 4–6 drops liquid stevia
- 1 tbsp. balsamic vinegar
- 1/4 tsp. red pepper flakes, crushed
- 1/4 cup filtered water

Directions

1. Season the pork chops with sea salt and black pepper generously.
2. In a blender, add the peach pieces and pulse until a puree forms.
3. Reserve the remaining peach pieces.
4. Heat the oil over medium heat in a skillet and sauté the shallots for about 1–2 minutes.
5. Add the garlic and ginger and sauté for about 1 minute.
6. Stir in the remaining ingredients and bring to a boil.
7. Now, reduce the heat to medium-low and simmer for about 4–5 minutes or until a sticky glaze forms.
8. Remove from the heat, reserve 1/3 of the glaze, and set aside.
9. Coat the chops with the remaining glaze.
10. Heat a non-stick skillet over medium-high heat and sear the chops for about 4 minutes per side.
11. Transfer the chops onto a plate and coat with the remaining glaze evenly.
12. Serve immediately.

Meal Prep Tip: Transfer the pork chops into a large bowl and set them aside to cool. Divide the chops into 2 containers evenly. Cover the containers and refrigerate for 1–2 days. Reheat in the microwave before serving.

Nutrition Calories: 359 Fats: 3 g. Protein: 46 g. Carbohydrates: 12 g. Fibers: 2 g. Sugars: 4 g. Sodium: 102 mg.

229. Pork Loin

Preparation time: 10 minutes
Cooking time: 20 minutes
Servings: 6
Ingredients

- 1/2 lb. pork tenderloin patted dry
- Non-stick cooking spray
- 2 tbsps. garlic scape pesto
- Salt to taste
- Pepper to taste

Directions

1. Adjust the temperature of the air fryer to 375°F.
2. Rub all sides of the tenderloin with the non-stick cooking spray
3. Add pepper, garlic scape pesto, and salt.
4. Sprinkle the air fryer basket with cooking spray.
5. Place the tenderloin on the air fryer.
6. Cook the meal at 400°F for 10 minutes.
7. Flip over to the other side and cook for another 10 minutes on the first side.
8. Remove the food from the air fryer.
9. Serve.

Nutrition Calories: 379 Fats: 2 g. Protein: 8 g. Carbohydrates: 0 g.

230. Nut-Stuffed Pork Chops

Preparation time: 10 minutes
Cooking time: 30 minutes
Servings: 4
Ingredients

- 3 oz. goat cheese
- 1/2 cup walnuts, chopped
- 1/4 cup almonds, toasted and chopped
- 1 tsp. fresh thyme, chopped
- 4 center-cut pork chops, butterflied
- Sea salt to taste
- Freshly ground black pepper
- 2 tbsp. olive oil

Directions

1. Preheat the oven to 400°F.

2. In a small bowl, make the filling by stirring together the goat cheese, walnuts, almonds, and thyme until well mixed.
3. Season the pork chops inside and outside with salt and pepper. Stuff each chop, pushing the filling to the bottom of the cut section. Secure the stuffing with toothpicks through the meat.
4. Place a large skillet over medium-high heat and add the olive oil. Pan sear the pork chops until they're browned on each side, about 10 minutes in total.
5. Transfer the pork chops to a baking dish and roast the chops in the oven until cooked through about 20 minutes.
6. Serve after removing the toothpicks.

Nutrition Calories: 481 Fats: 38 g. Protein: 29 g. Carbohydrates: 5 g. Fibers: 3 g.

231. Blackberry Pulled Pork Shoulder

Preparation time: 15 minutes
Cooking time: 8–10 hours
Servings: 10–12
Ingredients

- 1/4 cup brown sugar
- 1/2 tsp. red pepper
- 1 big onion, chopped
- 1 tsp. apple cider vinegar
- 1 tsp. salt
- 2 pints fresh blackberries
- 2 tsp. garlic powder
- 2–3-lb. pork shoulder

Directions

1. Put the pork shoulder in the slow cooker and layer the onion on top.
2. Puree the blackberries and pass them through a sieve or strainer to separate the puree from the seeds.
3. Combine the rest of the ingredients with the blackberry puree.
4. Pour the blackberry puree over the contents of the slow cooker.
5. Cover and cook on LOW for approximately 8–10 hours.
6. Take out the roast and shred by pulling using 2 forks. Mix back into the liquid in the Slow Cooker. Serve on buns.

Nutrition Calories: 218 Fats: 12 g. Protein: 6 g. Carbohydrates: 8 g. Fibers: 3 g. Sugars: 6 g. Sodium: 241 mg.

232. Cranberry Pork Roast

Preparation time: 20 minutes
Cooking time: 8–10 hours
Servings: 9
Ingredients

- 1/8 tsp. ground cloves
- 1/8 tsp. ground nutmeg
- 1 cup ground, or finely chopped, cranberries - 1 tsp. orange peel, grated
- 2 3/4 lbs. boneless pork roast, trimmed of fat - 3 tbsp. honey

Directions

1. Place the roast in a crockpot.
2. Mix the rest of the ingredients and pour over the roast.
3. Cover and cook on LOW for approximately 8–10 hours.

Nutrition Calories: 214 Fats: 9 g. Protein: 25 g. Fibers: 1 g. Carbohydrates: 7 g. Sugars: 7 g.

233. Crock Pork Tenderloin

Preparation time: 5–15 minutes
Cooking time: 4 hours
Servings: 6
Ingredients

- 3/4 cup red wine - 1 cup water
- 1 envelope salt-free onion soup mix
- 2 lbs. soft pork loin, cut in half lengthwise, visible fat removed
- 3 tbsp. light soy sauce
- 6 garlic cloves, peeled and chopped
- Freshly ground pepper to taste

Directions

1. Place the soft pork loin pieces in a crockpot. Pour water, wine, and soy sauce over the pork.
2. Turn the pork over in liquid several times to moisten.
3. Drizzle with dry onion soup mix. Top with chopped garlic and pepper.
4. Cover and cook on LOW for approximately 4 hours.

Nutrition Calories: 220 Fats: 4 g. Protein: 37 g. Fibers: 0 g. Carbohydrates: 6 g. Sugars: 2 g.

234. Epicurean Pork Chops

Preparation time: 15–20 minutes
Cooking time: 60–75 minutes
Servings: 6
Ingredients

- 1/4 tsp. salt

- 1/2 cup whole wheat panko breadcrumbs
- 3/4 cup water
- 1 tsp. dried rosemary, crushed
- 1 tsp. ground ginger
- 1 can (10 1/2 oz.) lower-sodium, lower-fat cream of chicken soup
- 2 tbsp. flour
- 2 tbsp. vegetable oil
- 6 loin pork chops, 1/2-inch thick
- Dash pepper to taste

Directions

1. Place the oil in a large frying pan.
2. Mix the flour, salt, and pepper in a shallow but wide dish.
3. Dredge chops in the mixture one at a time.
4. Place 2 or 3 chops in oil in a frying pan at a time, being cautious not crowd the frying pan. Brown the chops over moderate to high heat, 3–4 minutes on each side, until a browned crust forms.
5. As chops brown, place in thoroughly-oil-coated 7×11-inch baking dish.
6. In a vessel, mix soup, water, ginger, and rosemary; pour over the chops.
7. Drizzle with half the panko breadcrumbs.
8. Cover and bake at 350°F for 50–60 minutes, or until chops are soft but not dry.
9. Remove the cover. Drizzle with residual panko breadcrumbs.
10. Bake with an open lid 10–15 minutes. Take out from the oven and serve.

Nutrition Calories: 215 Fats: 10 g. Protein: 18 g. Fibers: 1 g. Carbohydrates: 11 g.Sugars: 1 g. Sodium: 315 mg.

235. Flawless Pork Chops

Preparation time: 20 minutes
Cooking time: 3–4 hours
Servings: 2
Ingredients

- 1/4 cup hot water
- 1/2 lb. boneless, center loin pork chops, frozen, trimmed of fat
- 3/4 tsp. bouillon granules, reduced-sodium
- 2 small onions

- 2 tbsp. mustard with white wine, prepared
- Fresh ground pepper, to taste
- Fresh parsley sprigs, or lemon slices, optional

Directions

1. Cut off the ends of the onions and peel them. Chop the onions in half crosswise to make 4 thick wheels. Place in the bottom of the crockpot.
2. Sear both sides of the frozen chops in the heavy frying pan. Place the onions in the pot. Drizzle with pepper.
3. Dissolve the bouillon in hot water. Mix in mustard and pour into the crockpot.
4. Cover and cook on high heat for approximately 3–4 hours.
5. Serve topped with fresh parsley sprigs or lemon slices, if desired.

Nutrition Calories: 204 Fats: 8 g. Protein: 22 g. Fibers: 2 g. Carbohydrates: 11 g. Sugars: 7 g.

236. Pork and Cabbage Dinner

Preparation time: 25 minutes
Cooking time: 5–6 hours
Servings: 8
Ingredients

- 1/8 tsp. allspice - 1/8 tsp. pepper
- 1/4 cup chopped fresh parsley, or 2 tbsp. dried parsley
- 1/2 cup beef broth
- 1/2 tsp. caraway seeds
- 3/4 cup onions, chopped
- 1 tsp. salt
- 2 moderate cooking apples, cored and sliced 1/4-inch thick
- 2 lbs. pork steaks, or chops, or shoulder, bone-in, trimmed of fat
- 4 cups cabbage, shredded

Directions

1. Place the pork in the crockpot; layer onions, parsley, and cabbage over pork.
2. Mix salt, pepper, caraway seeds, and allspice; drizzle over the cabbage. Pour broth over cabbage.
3. Cover and cook on LOW for approximately 5–6 hours.
4. Put in the apple slices approximately 30 minutes before serving.

Nutrition Calories: 149 Fats: 5 g. Protein: 18 g. Fibers: 2 g. Carbohydrates: 9 g. Sugars: 6 g.

237. Pork Chops With Apple Stuffing

Preparation time: 20 minutes
Cooking time: 45–60 minutes
Servings: 6
Ingredients

- 1/4 cup celery, chopped
- 1/4 cup onion, chopped
- 1/4 cup sugar
- 1/4 tsp. pepper - 1/4 tsp. salt
- 1/2 cup breadcrumbs, or cracker crumbs
- 1 tbsp. canola oil
- 2 tsp. parsley, chopped
- 3 apples, peeled, cored, and diced
- 6 bone-in pork chops, at least 1-inch thick, and Approximately 2 lbs. total

Directions

1. Chop a pocket approximately 1 1/2-inch deep into the side of each chop for stuffing.
2. Heat the oil in a frying pan.
3. Stir celery and onion into the oil in a frying pan. Cook over moderate until soft, stirring regularly.
4. Mix in diced apples. Drizzle with sugar.
5. Cover the frying pan and cook the apples over low heat until soft and glazed.
6. Mix in the breadcrumbs.
7. Mix in salt, pepper, and parsley.
8. Open the pocket of each chop with your fingers, stuff it with the mixture.
9. Place half of the stuffed chops in a frying pan. Brown on both sides over moderate to high heat. Take out browned chops to the platter. Cover to keep warm.
10. Repeat Step 9 with the rest of the chops.
11. Return the other chops to the frying pan.
12. Reduce the heat. Put in a few tbsp. of water. Cover and cook slowly over low heat until done, approximately 20–25 minutes.

Nutrition Calories: 270 Fats: 9 g. Protein: 24 g. Fibers: 1 g. Carbohydrates: 24 g. Sugars: 16 g.

238. Simple Barbecue Pork Chops

Preparation time: 5 minutes
Cooking time: 5 hours
Servings: 4
Ingredients

- 3 lbs. bone-in thick-cut pork chops

- 2–3 tbsp. barbecue seasoning
- 1/4 cup water

Directions

1. Cover each side of each pork chop with barbecue seasoning. Put them in the slow cooker.
2. Pour the water around the outside of the pork chops.
3. Close the lid and cook on LOW for approximately 5 hours.

Nutrition Calories: 507 Fats: 20 g. Protein: 72 g. Fibers: 0 g. Carbohydrates: 4 g. Sugars: 0 g.

239. Sweet-Sour Pork

Preparation time: 30 minutes
Cooking time: 5–7 hours
Servings: 6
Ingredients

- 1/4 cup cider vinegar
- 1/4 cup water
- 1/2 moderate onion, thinly sliced
- 3/4 cup carrots, shredded
- 1 cup pineapple juice (reserved from pineapple chunks)
- 1 green bell pepper, cut into strips
- 1 tbsp. soy sauce
- 2 lbs. boneless pork shoulder, cut in strips, trimmed of fat
- 2 tbsp. brown sugar substitute to equal 1 tbsp. sugar
- 2 tbsp. sweet pickles, coarsely chopped
- 2 tbsp. cornstarch
- 1 can (20 oz.) pineapple chunks canned in juice

Directions

1. Place the pork strips in the crockpot.
2. Put in the green pepper, onion, carrots, and pickles. In a container, combine brown sugar and cornstarch.
3. Put in the water, pineapple juice, vinegar, and soy sauce. Stir until smooth.
4. Pour over the ingredients in the crockpot.
5. Cover and cook on LOW for approximately 5–7 hours. One hour before serving, add the pineapple chunks. Stir.
6. Serve.

Nutrition Calories: 270 Fats: 8 g. Protein: 22 g. Fibers: 2 g. Carbohydrates: 27 g. Sugars: 21 g. Sodium: 285 mg.

240. Yummy Pulled Pork

Preparation time: 20 minutes
Cooking time: 2–4 hours
Servings: 10
Ingredients

- 1/2 cup water
- 1 cup barbecue sauce of your choice
- 1 tsp. cumin
- 2 tbsp. Worcestershire sauce
- 2 1/2 lbs. boneless pork shoulder roast, or pork sirloin roast
- 3 tbsp. cider vinegar
- Salt and pepper, to taste

Directions

1. Remove the fat from the roast. Fit roast into the crockpot.
2. Sprinkle meat with salt and pepper.
3. In a small container, mix water, vinegar, Worcestershire sauce, and cumin. Spoon over the roast, being cautious not to wash off the seasonings.
4. Cover and cook on LOW for approximately 8–10 hours, or on HIGH 4–5 hours, just until pork is very soft but not dry.
5. Take out the meat onto a platter. Discard liquid.
6. Shred meat using 2 forks. Put back into the crockpot.
7. Mix in the barbecue sauce.
8. Cover and cook on high heat for approximately 30–45 minutes.
9. Serve.

Nutrition Calories: 190 Fats: 3 g. Protein: 26 g. Fibers: 0 g. Carbohydrates: 12 g. Sugars: 10 g. Sodium: 280 mg.

241. Lime Pulled Pork

Preparation time: 5 minutes
Cooking time: 30 minutes
Servings: 4
Ingredients

- 1 tbsp. chili adobo sauce
- 1 tbsp. chili powder
- 2 tsp. salt
- 1 tsp. garlic powder
- 1 tsp. cumin
- 1/2 tsp. pepper
- 1 lb. pork butt, cubed
- 1 tbsp. coconut oil

- 2 cups beef broth
- 1 lime, cut into wedges
- 1/4 cup cilantro, chopped

Directions

1. Mix the pepper, cumin, garlic powder, salt, chili powder, and sauce in a bowl.
2. Melt the oil on SAUTÉ in the instant pot.
3. Rub the pork with the spice mixture.
4. Place the pork and sear for 3–5 minutes per side.
5. Add broth and close the lid.
6. Press MANUAL and cook for 30 minutes.
7. Allow the natural release and open it.
8. Shred the pork.
9. If you want crispy pork, then heat in a skillet.
10. Serve warm with cilantro garnish and fresh lime wedges.

Nutrition Calories: 570 Fats: 35 g. Protein: 55 g. Carbohydrates: 2 g.

242. Chipotle Pork Chops

Preparation time: 7 minutes
Cooking time: 15 minutes
Servings: 4
Ingredients

- 2 tbsp. coconut oil
- 3 chipotle chilies
- 2 tbsp. adobo sauce
- 2 tsp. cumin
- 1 tsp. thyme, dried
- 1 tsp. salt
- 4 (5 oz.) pork chops, boneless
- 1/2 onion, chopped
- 2 bay leaves
- 1 cup chicken broth
- 1/2 (7 oz.) diced tomatoes, fire-roasted
- 1/3 cup cilantro, chopped

Directions

1. Melt the oil on SAUTÉ mode in the instant pot.
2. In a food processor, add salt, thyme, cumin, adobo sauce, and chilies. Pulse to make a paste.
3. Rub the paste into the pork chops.
4. Sear the chops for 5 minutes on each side.

5. Add cilantro, tomatoes, broth, bay leaves, and onion to the instant pot.
6. Close the lid and press MANUAL.
7. Cook 15 minutes on HIGH.
8. Do a natural release when done.
9. Serve warm with cilantro garnish.

Nutrition Calories: 375 Fats: 24 g. Protein: 31 g. Carbohydrates: 3 g.

243. Buttery Pot Roast

Preparation time: 5 minutes
Cooking time: 90 minutes
Servings: 4
Ingredients

- 4 tsp. onion powder
- 2 tsp. parsley, dried
- 1 tsp. salt
- 1 tsp. garlic powder
- 1/2 tsp. oregano, dried
- 1/2 tsp. pepper
- 1 (2 lbs.) chuck roast
- 1 tbsp. coconut oil
- 1 cup beef broth
- 1/2 packet dry ranch seasoning
- 1 stick butter
- 10 pepperoncini

Directions

1. Press SAUTÉ and heat the Pot.
2. Mix the pepper, oregano, garlic powder, salt, parsley, and onion powder in a bowl.
3. Rub the seasoning onto the roast.
4. Add oil to the pot and place the roast.
5. Sear for 5 minutes on each side.
6. Remove the roast and set aside.
7. Add the broth and deglaze.
8. Place the roast back into the instant pot.
9. Sprinkle with ranch powder.
10. Place butter on top and add pepperoncini.
11. Close the lid and press MANUAL.
12. Cook for 90 minutes.
13. Make a natural release.
14. Open the lid and remove the roast.
15. Slice and serve.

Nutrition Calories: 561 Fats: 33 g. Protein: 51 g. Carbohydrates: 5 g.

CHAPTER 7:

Fish And Seafood

244. Salmon Cakes in Air Fryer

Preparation time: 10 minutes
Cooking time: 10 minutes
Servings: 2
Ingredients

- 8 oz. Fresh salmon fillet
- 1 egg
- 1/8 tsp. salt
- 1/4 tsp. garlic powder
- 1 lemon, sliced

Directions

1. In the bowl, chop the salmon, add the egg and spices.
2. Form tiny cakes.
3. Let the air fryer preheat to 390°F.
4. On the bottom of the air fryer bowl lay sliced lemons—place cakes on top.
5. Cook them for 7 minutes.
6. Based on your diet preferences, eat with your chosen dip.

Nutrition Calories: 194 Fat: 9 g. Protein: 25 g. Carbohydrates: 2.45 g.

245. Coconut Shrimp

Preparation time: 10 minutes
Cooking time: 30 minutes
Servings: 4
Ingredients

- 1/2 cup pork rinds, crushed
- 4 cups. jumbo shrimp, deveined
- 1/2 cup coconut flakes preferably
- 2 eggs
- 1/2 cup coconut flour
- Any oil of your choice for frying at least half-inch in pan
- Freshly ground black pepper and kosher salt to taste

For the dipping sauce (Piña colada flavor)

- 2–3 tbsp. powdered Sugar as Substitute
- 3 tbsp. mayonnaise
- 1/2 cup sour cream

- 1/4 tsp. coconut extract or to taste
- 3 tbsp. coconut cream
- 1/4 tsp. pineapple flavoring as much to taste
- 3 tbsp. coconut flakes preferably unsweetened this is optional

Directions

To make the piña colada (Sauce)

1. Mix all the ingredients into a tiny bowl for the Dipping sauce (Pina colada flavor). Combine well and put in the fridge until ready to serve.

To make the shrimps

1. Whip all eggs in a deep bowl. Add the crushed pork rinds, coconut flour, sea salt, coconut flakes, and freshly ground black pepper in another small shallow bowl.
2. Put the shrimp one by one in the mixed eggs for dipping, then in the coconut flour blend. Put them on a clean plate or the air fryer's basket.
3. Place the shrimp battered in a single layer on your air fryer basket. Spritz the shrimp with oil and cook for 8–10 minutes at 360°F, flipping them through halfway.
4. Enjoy hot with the dipping sauce.

Nutrition Calories: 340 Protein: 25 g. Fat: 16 g. Carbohydrates: 20.67 g.

246. Crispy Fish Sticks in Air Fryer

Preparation time: 10 minutes
Cooking time: 15 minutes
Servings: 4
Ingredients

- 1 lb. whitefish such as cod
- 1/4 cup mayonnaise
- 1 tbsp. Dijon mustard
- 2 tbsp. water
- 1 1/2 cup pork rind

- 3/4 tsp. Cajun seasoning
- Kosher salt and pepper to taste
- Non-stick cooking spray

Directions

1. Spray a non-stick cooking spray on the air fryer rack.
2. Pat the fish dry and cut into sticks about 1x2-inches broad.
3. Stir together the mayo, mustard, and water in a tiny small dish.
4. Mix the pork rinds and Cajun seasoning into another small container.
5. Adding the kosher salt and pepper to taste (both pork rinds and seasoning can have a decent amount of kosher salt, so you can dip a finger to see how salty it is).
6. Working with 1 slice of fish at a time, dip to cover in the mayo, mix and then tap off the excess. Dip into the mixture of pork rind, then flip to cover. Place on the rack of an air fryer.
7. Set at 400°F to air fry and bake for 5 minutes, then turn the fish with tongs and bake for another 5 minutes.
8. Serve.

Nutrition Calories: 263 Fat: 16 g. Protein: 26.4 g. Carbohydrates: 22.58 g.

247. Honey-Glazed Salmon

Preparation time: 10 minutes
Cooking time: 15 minutes
Servings: 2
Ingredients

- 6 tsp. gluten-free soy sauce
- 2 pcs. salmon Fillets
- 3 tsp. sweet rice wine
- 1 tsp. water
- 6 tbsp. honey

Directions

1. In a bowl, mix sweet rice wine, soy sauce, honey, and water.
2. Set half of it aside.
3. In half of it, marinate the fish and let it rest for 2 hours.
4. Let the air fryer preheat to 180°C.
5. Cook the fish for 8 minutes, flip halfway through and cook for another 5 minutes.
6. Baste the salmon with the marinade mixture after 3 or 4 minutes.

7. Pour half of the marinade into a saucepan, reduce by half and serve with the salmon.

Nutrition Calories: 254 Protein: 20 g. Fat: 12 g. Carbohydrates: 52.67 g.

248. Basil-Parmesan Crusted Salmon

Preparation time: 5 minutes
Cooking time: 15 minutes
Servings: 4
Ingredients

- 3 tbsp. Parmesan cheese, grated
- 4 salmon fillets, skinless
- 1/4 tsp. salt
- Freshly ground black pepper
- 3 tbsp. low-fat mayonnaise basil leaves, chopped
- 1/2 lemon juice
- Olive oil

Directions

1. Let the air fryer preheat to 400°F.
2. Spray the basket with olive oil.
3. Season the salmon with salt, pepper, and lemon juice.
4. In a bowl, mix 2 tbsp. of Parmesan cheese, mayonnaise, and basil leaves.
5. Add this mix and more parmesan on the top of salmon and cook for 7 minutes or until fully cooked.
6. Serve hot.

Nutrition Calories: 289 Protein: 30 g. Fat: 18.5 g. Carbohydrates: 3.77 g.

249. Cajun Shrimp in Air Fryer

Preparation time: 10 minutes
Cooking time: 21 minutes
Servings: 4
Ingredients

- 24 extra-jumbo shrimp, peeled
- 2 tbsp. olive oil
- 1 tbsp. Cajun seasoning
- 1 zucchini, thick slices(half-moons)
- 1/4 cup cooked Turkey
- 1 Yellow squash, sliced half-moons
- 1/4 tsp. kosher salt

Directions

1. In a bowl, mix the shrimp with Cajun seasoning.
2. In another bowl, add zucchini, turkey, salt, squash, and coat with oil.

3. Let the air fryer preheat to 400°F.
4. Move the shrimp and vegetable mix to the fryer basket and cook for 3 minutes.
5. Serve hot.

Nutrition Calories: 284 Protein: 31 g. Fat: 14 g. Carbohydrates: 4.21 g.

250. Crispy Air Fryer Fish

Preparation time: 10 minutes
Cooking time: 17 minutes
Servings: 4
Ingredients

- 1 tsp. old bay
- 4–6 whiting fish fillets, cut in half,
- 3/4 cup fine cornmeal
- 1/4 cup flour
- 1 tsp. paprika
- 1/2 tsp. garlic powder
- 1 1/2 tsp. salt
- 1/2 tsp. freshly ground black pepper

Directions

1. In a Ziploc® bag, add all the ingredients and coat the fish fillets with it.
2. Spray oil on the basket of the air fryer and put the fish in it.
3. Cook for 10 minutes at 400°F. Flip the fish if necessary, coat with oil spray, and cook for another 7-minutes.
4. Serve with salad green.

Nutrition Calories: 254 Fat: 12.7 g. Protein: 17.5 g. Carbohydrates: 30.08 g.

251. Air Fryer Lemon Cod

Preparation time: 5 minutes
Cooking time: 10 minutes
Servings: 1
Ingredients

- 1 cod fillet
- 1/2 tsp. parsley, dried
- Kosher salt and pepper to taste
- 1/8 tsp. garlic powder
- 1 lemon

Directions

1. In a bowl, mix all the ingredients and coat the fish fillet with spices.
2. Slice the lemon and lay it at the bottom of the air fryer basket.
3. Put spiced fish on top. Cover the fish with lemon slices.

4. Cook for 10 minutes at 375°F; the internal temperature of the fish should be 145°F.
5. Serve with a microgreen salad.

Nutrition Calories: 101 Protein: 16 g. Fat: 1 g. Carbohydrates: 7.9 g.

252. Air Fryer Salmon Fillets

Preparation time: 5 minutes
Cooking time: 15 minutes
Servings: 2
Ingredients

- 1/4 cup low-fat Greek yogurt
- 2 salmon fillets
- 1 tbsp. fresh dill, chopped
- 1 lemon and lemon juice
- 1/2 tsp. garlic powder
- Kosher salt and pepper to taste

Directions

1. Cut the lemon into slices and lay it at the bottom of the air fryer basket.
2. Season the salmon with kosher salt and pepper. Put the salmon on top of lemons.
3. Let it cook at 330°F for 15 minutes.
4. In the meantime, mix garlic powder, lemon juice, salt, pepper with yogurt and dill.
5. Serve the fish with sauce.

Nutrition Calories: 194 Protein: 25 g. Fat: 7 g. Carbohydrates: 8.45 g.Sugars: 4.38 g.

253. Air Fryer Fish and Chips

Preparation time: 10 minutes
Cooking time: 35 minutes
Servings: 4
Ingredients

- 4 cups any fish fillet
- 1/4 cup flour
- 1 cup whole-wheat breadcrumbs
- 1 egg
- 1 tbsp. oil
- 1 lb. potatoes
- 1 tsp. salt

Directions

1. Cut the potatoes in fries. Then coat with oil and salt.
2. Cook in the air fryer for 20 minutes at 400°F, toss the fries halfway through.

3. In the meantime, coat the fish in flour, then in the whisked egg, and finally in the breadcrumbs mix.
4. Place the fish in the air fryer and let it cook at 330°F for 15 minutes.
5. Flip it halfway through, if needed.
6. Serve with tartar sauce and salad green.

Nutrition Calories: 409 Protein: 30 g. Fat: 11 g. Carbohydrates: 6.23 g.Sugars: 0.18 g.

254. Grilled Salmon With Lemon

Preparation time: 10 minutes
Cooking time: 21 minutes
Servings: 4
Ingredients

- 2 tbsp. olive oil
- 2 salmon fillets
- 1 lemon juice
- 1/3 cup water
- 1/3 cup gluten-free light soy sauce
- 1/3 cup honey
- 2 scallion slices
- 1 cherry tomato
- Freshly ground black pepper, garlic powder, and Kosher salt to taste

Directions

1. Season salmon with pepper, garlic powder and salt
2. In a bowl, mix honey, soy sauce, lemon juice, water, oil. Add salmon to this marinade and let it rest for at least 2 hours.
3. Let the air fryer preheat at 180°C.
4. Place fish in the air fryer and cook for 8 minutes.
5. Move to a dish and top with scallion slices and cherry tomato.

Nutrition Calories: 211 Protein: 15 g. Fat: 9 g. Carbohydrates: 26.76 g.Sugars: 4.12 g.

255. Air-Fried Fish Nuggets

Preparation time: 15 minutes
Cooking time: 10 minutes
Servings: 4
Ingredients

- 2 cups fish fillets in cubes, skinless
- 1 egg, beaten
- 5 tbsp. flour
- 5 tbsp. water

- Kosher salt and pepper to taste breadcrumbs mix
- 1 tbsp. smoked paprika
- 1/4 cup whole-wheat breadcrumbs
- 1 tbsp. garlic powder
- Non-stick cooking spray

Directions

1. Season the fish cubes with kosher salt and pepper.
2. In a bowl, add flour and gradually add water, mixing as you add.
3. Then mix in the egg and keep mixing but do not overmix.
4. Coat the cubes in batter, then in the breadcrumb mix; coat well.
5. Place the cubes in a baking tray and spray with oil.
6. Let the air fryer preheat to 200°C.
7. Place the cubes in the air fryer and cook for 12 minutes or until well cooked and golden brown.
8. Serve with salad greens.

Nutrition Calories: 184 Protein: 19 g. Fat: 3.3 g. Carbohydrates: 13.78 g.Sugars: 1.07 g.

256. Garlic Rosemary Grilled Prawns

Preparation time: 6 minutes
Cooking time: 11 minutes
Servings: 2
Ingredients

- 1/2 tbsp. melted butter
- 1 green capsicum, sliced
- 8 prawns
- 1/4 cup rosemary leaves
- Kosher salt and freshly ground black pepper - 3–4 garlic cloves, minced

Directions

1. In a bowl, mix all the ingredients and marinate the prawns in it for at least 60 minutes or more
2. Add 2 prawns and 2 slices of capsicum on each skewer.
3. Let the air fryer preheat to 180°C.
4. Cook for 5–6 minutes. Then change the temperature to 200°C and cook for another minute. Serve with lemon wedges.

Nutrition Calories: 194 Fat: 10 g. Carbohydrates: 12 g. Protein: 4.6 g.Sugars: 0.05 g.

257. Air-Fried Crumbed Fish

Preparation time: 10 minutes
Cooking time: 13 minutes
Servings: 2
Ingredients

- 4 fish fillets - 4 tbsp. olive oil
- 1 egg beaten
- 1/4 cup whole-wheat breadcrumbs

Directions

1. Let the air fryer preheat to 180°C.
2. In a bowl, mix breadcrumbs with oil. Mix well.
3. First, coat the fish in the egg mix (egg beaten with water) than in the breadcrumb mix. Coat well.
4. Place in the air fryer and let it cook for 10–12 minutes. Serve hot with salad green and lemon.

Nutrition Calories: 254 Fat: 12.7 g. Protein: 15.5 g. Carbohydrates: 18.02 g.Sugars: 0.23 g.

258. Parmesan Garlic Crusted Salmon

Preparation time: 5 minutes
Cooking time: 15 minutes
Servings: 2
Ingredients

- 1/4 cup whole-wheat breadcrumbs
- 4 cups salmon - 1 tbsp. butter, melted
- 1/4 tsp. freshly ground black pepper
- 1/4 cup Parmesan cheese, grated
- 2 tsp. garlic, minced
- 1/2 tsp. Italian seasoning

Directions

1. Let the air fryer preheat to 400°F, spray the oil over the air fryer basket.
2. Pat the salmon dry.
3. In a bowl, mix Parmesan cheese, Italian seasoning, and breadcrumbs. In another pan, mix melted butter with garlic and add to the breadcrumbs mix. Mix well.
4. Add kosher salt and freshly ground black pepper to salmon. On top of every salmon piece, add the crust mix and press gently.
5. Let the air fryer preheat to 400°F and add salmon to it. Cook until done to your liking.
6. Serve hot with vegetable side dishes.

Nutrition Calories: 330 Fat: 19 g. Protein: 31 g. Carbohydrates: 7.72 g.Sugars: 0.26 g.

259. Air Fryer Salmon With Maple Soy Glaze

Preparation time: 6 minutes
Cooking time: 8 minutes
Servings: 4
Ingredients

- 1 tbsp. pure maple syrup
- 3 tbsp. gluten-free soy sauce
- 1 tbsp. sriracha hot sauce
- 2 garlic cloves, minced
- 4 fillets salmon, skinless

Directions

1. In a Ziploc® bag, mix sriracha, maple syrup, garlic, and soy sauce with salmon.
2. Mix well and let it marinate for at least 30 minutes. Let the air fryer preheat to 400°F and spray the basket with oil.
3. Take fish out from the marinade, pat dry.
4. Put the salmon in the air fryer, cook for 7–8 minutes or longer.
5. In the meantime, in a saucepan, add the marinade, let it simmer until reduced to half. Add the glaze over the salmon and serve.

Nutrition Calories: 292 Protein: 35 g. Fat: 11 g. Carbohydrates: 4.75 g.Sugars: 3.27 g.

260. Air Fried Cajun Salmon

Preparation time: 10 minutes
Cooking time: 21 minutes
Servings: 1
Ingredients

- 1 fresh salmon
- 1 tbsp. Cajun seasoning
- 1 lemon juice

Directions

1. Let the air fryer preheat to 180°C.
2. Pat dries the salmon fillet. Rub lemon juice and Cajun seasoning over the fish fillet. Place in the air fryer and cook for 7 minutes.
3. Serve with salad greens and lime wedges.

Nutrition Calories: 216 Fat: 19 g. Protein: 19.2 g. Carbohydrates: 1.06 g.Sugars: 0.39 g.

261. Air Fryer Shrimp Scampi

Preparation time: 5 minutes
Cooking time: 11 minutes
Servings: 2
Ingredients

- 4 cups raw shrimp

- 1 tbsp. lemon juice
- 1/2 tsp. fresh basil, chopped
- 2 tsp. red pepper flakes
- 4 tbsp. butter
- 1/4 cup chives, chopped
- 1 tbsp. chicken stock
- 1 tbsp. garlic, minced

Directions

1. Let the air fryer preheat with a metal pan to 330°F.
2. In the hot pan, add the garlic, red pepper flakes, and half of the butter. Let it cook for 2 minutes.
3. Add the butter, shrimp, chicken stock, minced garlic, chives, lemon juice, basil to the pan. Let it cook for 5 minutes. Bathe the shrimp in melted butter.
4. Take it out from the air fryer and let it rest for 1 minute.
5. Add the fresh basil leaves and chives and serve.

Nutrition Calories: 287 Fat: 5.5 g. Protein: 18 g. Carbohydrates: 6.82 g.Sugar: 2.66 g.

262. Sesame Seeds Fish Fillet

Preparation time: 10 minutes
Cooking time: 22 minutes
Servings: 2
Ingredients

- 1 tbsp. plain flour
- 1 egg, beaten
- 5 frozen fish fillets

For the coating

- 2 tbsp. oil
- 1/2 cup sesame seeds
- 1/2 tsp. Rosemary herbs
- 5–6 biscuits crumbs
- Kosher salt and pepper to taste

Directions

1. Sauté the sesame seeds in a pan for 2 minutes, without oil. Brown them and set it aside.
2. On a plate, mix all coating ingredients.
3. Place the aluminum foil on the air fryer basket and let it preheat at 200°C.
4. First, coat the fish in flour. Then in egg, then in the coating mix.

5. Place in the air fryer. If fillets are frozen, cook for 10 minutes, then turn the fillet and cook for another 4 minutes.
6. If not frozen, then cook for 8 minutes and 2 minutes.

Nutrition Calories: 250 Fat: 8 g. Protein: 20 g. Carbohydrates: 57.19 g.Sugar: 4.71 g.

263. Lemon Pepper Shrimp in Air Fryer

Preparation time: 6 minutes
Cooking time: 11 minutes
Servings: 2
Ingredients

- 1 1/2 cup peeled raw shrimp, deveined
- 1/2 tbsp. olive oil
- 1/4 tsp. garlic powder
- 1 tsp. lemon pepper
- 1/4 tsp. paprika
- 1 lemon, juiced

Directions

1. Let the air fryer preheat to 400°F.
2. Mix lemon pepper, olive oil, paprika, garlic powder, and lemon juice in a bowl. Mix well. Add the shrimps and coat well.
3. Add the shrimps to the air fryer, cook for 8 minutes and top with lemon slices and serve.

Nutrition Calories: 237 Fat: 6 g. Protein: 36 g.Carbohydrates: 2.11 g.Sugars 0.65 g.

264. Shrimp and Okra

Preparation time: 15 minutes
Cooking time: 0
Servings: 4
Ingredients

- 1 lb. shrimp; peeled and deveined
- 1 1/2 cups okra
- 1/2 cup chicken stock
- 2 tbsp. coconut aminos
- 3 tbsp. balsamic vinegar
- 1 tbsp. parsley; chopped.
- A pinch salt and black pepper

Directions

1. In a pan that fits your air fryer, mix all the ingredients, toss, introduce in the fryer and cook at 380°F for 10 minutes.
2. Divide into bowls and serve.

Nutrition Calories: 251 Fat: 10 g. Fiber: 3 g. Carbs: 4 g. Protein: 8 g.

265. Swordfish Steaks and Tomatoes

Preparation time: 15 minutes
Cooking time: 0
Servings: 2
Ingredients

- 30 oz. canned tomatoes; chopped.
- 2 (1-inch thick) swordfish steaks
- 2 tbsp. capers, drained
- 1 tbsp. red vinegar
- 2 tbsp. oregano, chopped.
- Pinch salt and black pepper

Directions

1. In a pan that fits the air fryer, combine all the ingredients, toss, put the pan in the fryer and cook at 390°F for 10 minutes; flipping the fish halfway.
2. Divide the mix between plates and serve.

Nutrition Calories: 280 Fat: 12 g. Fiber: 4 g. Carbs: 6 g. Protein: 11 g.

266. Buttery Cod

Preparation time: 13 minutes
Cooking time: 0
Servings: 2
Ingredients

- 2 (4 oz.) cod fillets
- 1/2 medium lemon, sliced
- 2 tbsp. salted butter; melted.
- 1 tsp. Old Bay seasoning

Directions

1. Place cod fillets into a 6-inch round baking dish. Brush each fillet with butter and sprinkle with Old Bay seasoning. Lay 2 lemon slices on each fillet.
2. Secure the dish with foil and place it into the air fryer basket. Adjust the temperature to 350°F and set the timer for 8 minutes; flip halfway through the cooking time.
3. When cooked, the internal temperature should be at least 145°F. Serve warm.

Nutrition Calories: 179 Protein: 14 g. Fiber: 0 g. Fat: 11 g. Carbs: 0 g.

267. Lime Baked Salmon

Preparation time: 22 minutes
Cooking time: 0
Servings: 2
Ingredients

- 2 (3 oz.) salmon fillets, skin removed

- 1/4 cup jalapeños, sliced and pickled
- 1/2 medium lime, juiced
- 2 tbsp. cilantro, chopped
- 1 tbsp. salted butter; melted.
- 1/2 tsp. garlic, finely minced
- 1 tsp. chili powder

Directions

1. Place the salmon fillets into a 6-inch round baking pan.
2. Brush each with butter and sprinkle with chili powder and garlic.
3. Place the jalapeño slices on top and around salmon.
4. Pour half of the lime juice over the salmon and cover with foil.
5. Place pan into the air fryer basket.
6. Adjust the temperature to 370°F and set the timer for 12 minutes.
7. When fully cooked, salmon should flake easily with a fork and reach an internal temperature of at least 145°F.
8. To serve, spritz with the remaining lime juice and garnish with cilantro.

Nutrition Calories: 167 Protein: 18 g. Fiber: 7 g. Fat: 9 g. Carbs: 6 g.

268. Lime Trout and Shallots

Preparation time: 17 minutes
Cooking time: 0
Servings: 4
Ingredients

- 4 trout fillets, boneless
- 3 garlic cloves, minced
- 6 shallots, chopped.
- 1/2 cup butter, melted
- 1/2 cup olive oil
- 1 lime juice
- A pinch salt and black pepper

Directions

1. In a pan that fits in the air fryer. Combines the fish with the shallots and the rest of the ingredients; stir gently.
2. Put the pan in the machine and cook at 390°F for 12 minutes; flipping the fish halfway.
3. Cut between plates and serve with a side salad.

Nutrition Calories: 270 Fat: 12 g. Fiber: 4 g. Carbs: 6 g. Protein: 12 g.

269. Crab Legs

Preparation time: 20 minutes
Cooking time: 0
Servings: 4
Ingredients

- 3 lb. crab legs
- 1/4 cup salted butter, melted and divided - 1/2 medium lemon juice
- 1/4 tsp. garlic powder.

Directions

1. Take a large bowl, drizzle 2 tbsp. of butter over crab legs. Set the crab legs into the air fryer basket.
2. Adjust the temperature to 400°F and set the timer for 15 minutes.
3. In a small bowl, mix the remaining butter, garlic powder, and lemon juice
4. To serve, crack open the crab legs and detach meat. Dip in the lemon butter.

Nutrition Calories: 123 Protein: 17 g. Fiber: 0 g. Fat: 6 g. Carbs: 4 g.

270. Cajun Salmon

Preparation time: 12 minutes
Cooking time: 0
Servings: 2
Ingredients

- 2 (4 oz.) salmon fillets, skin removed
- 2 tbsp. unsalted butter, melted.
- 1 tsp. paprika
- 1/4 tsp. ground black pepper
- 1/8 tsp. ground cayenne pepper
- 1/2 tsp. garlic powder.

Directions

1. Brush each fillet with butter.
2. Combine the remaining ingredients in a small bowl and then rub them onto the fish. Place the fillets into the air fryer basket. Bring the temperature to 390°F and set the timer for 7 minutes. When fully cooked, the internal temperature will be 145°F. Serve immediately.

Nutrition Calories: 253 Protein: 29 g. Fiber: 4 g. Fat: 16 g. Carbs: 4 g.

271. Trout and Zucchinis

Preparation time: 20 minutes
Cooking time: 0
Servings: 4
Ingredients

- 3 zucchinis, cut in medium chunks

- 4 trout fillets; boneless
- 1/4 cup tomato sauce
- 1 garlic clove; minced
- 1/2 cup cilantro; chopped.
- 1 tbsp. lemon juice
- 2 tbsp. olive oil
- Salt and black pepper to taste.

Directions

1. In a pan that fits in the air fryer, mix the fish with the other ingredients, toss, introduce it in the fryer, and cook at 380°F for 15 minutes.
2. Divide everything between plates and serve right away.

Nutrition Calories: 220 Fat: 12 g. Fiber: 4 g. Carbs: 6 g. Protein: 9 g.

272. Crab Cakes

Preparation time: 20 minutes
Cooking time: 0
Servings: 4
Ingredients

- 1/2 medium green bell pepper; seeded and chopped
- 1/4 cup green onion, chopped
- 1 large egg.
- 2 cans (6 oz.) lump crabmeat
- 1/4 cup ground almond flour, blanched finely
- 1/2 tbsp. lemon juice
- 2 tbsp. full-fat mayonnaise
- 1/2 tsp. Old Bay seasoning
- 1/2 tsp. Dijon mustard

Directions

1. Take a large bowl, mix all the ingredients. Set into 4 balls and flatten into patties.
2. Place the patties into the air fryer basket.
3. Adjust the temperature to 350°F and set the timer for 10 minutes.
4. Flip the patties halfway through the cooking time. Serve warm.

Nutrition Calories: 151 Protein: 14 g. Fiber: 9 g. Fat: 10 g. Carbs: 3 g.

273. Roasted Red Snapper

Preparation time: 20 minutes
Cooking time: 0
Servings: 4
Ingredients

- 4 red snapper fillets; boneless

- 2 garlic cloves; minced
- 1 tbsp. hot chili paste
- 2 tbsp. olive oil
- 2 tbsp. coconut aminos
- 2 tbsp. lime juice
- Pinch salt and black pepper

Directions

1. Take a bowl and mix all the ingredients, except the fish, and whisk well.
2. Rub the fish with this mix, place it in your air fryer's basket and cook at 380°F for 15 minutes.
3. Serve with a side salad.

Nutrition Calories: 220 Fat: 13 g. Fiber: 4 g Carbs: 6 g. Protein: 11 g.

274. Shrimp Scampi

Preparation time: 18 minutes
Cooking time: 0
Servings: 4
Ingredients

- 1 lb. medium shrimp, peeled and deveined
- 1/2 medium lemon
- 1/4 cup heavy whipping cream.
- 1 tbsp. fresh parsley, chopped
- 4 tbsp. salted butter
- 1/4 tsp. xanthan gum
- 1/4 tsp. red pepper flakes
- 1 tsp. roasted garlic, minced

Directions

1. In a saucepan over medium heat, dissolve butter. Zest the lemon, and then squeeze the juice into the pan. Add the garlic.
2. Pour in the cream, xanthan gum, and red pepper flakes. Pour until the mixture begins to thicken, about 2–3 minutes.
3. Place the shrimp into a 4 cup round baking dish. Pour the cream sauce over the shrimp and cover with foil. Place the dish into the air fryer basket.
4. Adjust the temperature to 400°F and set the timer for 8 minutes. Stir twice during cooking. When done, garnish with parsley and serve warm.

Nutrition Calories: 240 Protein: 17 g. Fiber: 4 g. Fat: 10 g. Carbs: 4 g.

275. Tuna Zoodle Casserole

Preparation time: 30 minutes
Cooking time: 0
Servings: 4
Ingredients

- 1 oz. pork rinds, finely ground
- 2 medium zucchinis, spiralized
- 2 cans (5 oz) albacore tuna
- 1/4 cup white onion, diced
- 1/4 cup white mushrooms, chopped
- 2 stalks celery, finely chopped
- 1/2 cup heavy cream
- 1/2 cup vegetable broth
- 2 tbsp. full-fat mayonnaise
- 2 tbsp. butter, salted
- 1/2 tsp. red pepper flakes
- 1/4 tsp. xanthan gum

Directions

1. In a saucepan over medium heat, dissolve the butter. Add the onion, mushrooms, and celery, and sauté until fragrant, about 3–5 minutes.
2. Pour in heavy cream, vegetable broth, mayonnaise, and xanthan gum. Reduce heat and continue cooking an additional 3 minutes until the mixture begins to thicken.
3. Add the red pepper flakes, zucchini, and tuna.
4. Turn off the heat and stir until zucchini noodles are coated.
5. Pour into 4 cups round baking dish. Top with ground pork rinds and cover the top of the dish with foil. Place into the air fryer basket. Adjust the temperature to 370°F and set the timer to 15 minutes.
6. When there are 3 minutes left, remove the foil to brown the top of the casserole.
7. Serve warm.

Nutrition Calories: 339 Protein: 17 g. Fiber: 8 g. Fat: 21 g. Carbs: 1 g.

276. Sea Bass and Rice

Preparation time: 10 minutes
Cooking time: 20 minutes
Servings: 4
Ingredients

- 1 lb. sea bass fillets, boneless, skinless, and cubed

- 1 cup wild rice
- 2 cups chicken stock
- 2 scallions, chopped
- 1 red bell pepper, chopped
- 1 tsp. turmeric powder
- 1 tbsp. chives, chopped
- Salt and black pepper to the taste
- A drizzle olive oil

Directions

1. Grease the air fryer's pan with the oil, add the fish, rice, stock, and the other ingredients, stir gently, cook at 380°F for 20 minutes, stirring halfway.
2. Divide between plates and serve.

Nutrition Calories: 290 Fat: 12 g. Fiber: 2 g.Carbs: 16 g. Protein: 19 g.

277. Sea Bass and Cauliflower

Preparation time: 5 minutes
Cooking time: 20 minutes
Servings: 4
Ingredients

- 1 lb. sea bass fillets, boneless and cubed
- 1 cup cauliflower florets
- 2 tbsp. butter, melted
- 1 tsp. garam masala
- 1/2 cup chicken stock
- 1 tbsp. parsley, chopped
- Salt and black pepper to the taste

Directions

1. In your air fryer, combine the fish with the cauliflower and the other ingredients, stir gently, and cook at 380°F for 20 minutes.
2. Divide everything between plates and serve.

Nutrition Calories: 272 Fat: 4 g. Fiber: 3 g.Carbs: 14 g. Protein: 4 g.

278. Air Fried Catfish

Preparation time: 5 minutes
Cooking time: 20 minutes
Servings: 4
Ingredients

- 4 catfish fillets
- 1 tbsp. olive oil
- 1/4 cup fish seasoning
- 1 tbsp. fresh parsley, chopped
- Cooking spray

Directions

1. Preheat the air fryer to 400°F.
2. Spray the air fryer basket with cooking spray.
3. Season the fish with seasoning and place it into the air fryer basket.
4. Drizzle the fish fillets with oil and cook for 10 minutes.
5. Turn the fish to another side and cook for 10 more minutes.
6. Garnish with parsley and serve.

Nutrition Calories: 120 Fat: 3.41 g.Carbohydrates: 1 g.Protein: 20.99 g.

279. Garlic Parmesan Shrimp

Preparation time: 5 minutes
Cooking time: 20 minutes
Servings: 2
Ingredients

- 1 lb. shrimp, deveined and peeled
- 1/2 cup Parmesan cheese, grated
- 1/4 cup cilantro, diced
- 1 tbsp. olive oil
- 1 tsp. salt
- 1 tsp. fresh cracked pepper
- 1 tbsp. lemon juice
- 6 garlic cloves, diced

Directions

1. Warm the air fryer to 350°F and grease the air fryer basket.
2. Drizzle the shrimp with olive oil and lemon juice; season with garlic, salt, and cracked pepper.
3. Secure the bowl with plastic wrap and refrigerate for a few hours.
4. Stir in the Parmesan cheese and cilantro to the bowl and transfer to the air fryer basket.
5. Cook for 10 minutes and serve immediately.

Nutrition Calories: 282 Fat: 23.41 g.Carbohydrates: 0 g.Protein: 16.59 g.

280. Mango Shrimp Skewers

Preparation time: 5 minutes
Cooking time: 20 minutes
Servings: 2
Ingredients

- 2 tbsp. olive oil
- 1/2 tsp. garlic powder
- 1 tsp. dry mango powder

- 2 tbsp. fresh lime juice
- Salt and black pepper to taste

Directions

1. Mix the garlic powder, mango powder, lime juice, salt, and pepper in a bowl. Add the shrimp and toss to coat. Cover and allow to marinate for minutes.
2. Warm your air fryer to 390°F. Spray the air fryer basket with cooking spray. Transfer the marinated shrimp to the cooking basket and drizzle the olive oil. Cook for 5 minutes, slide out the fryer basket, and shake the shrimp; cook for 5 minutes. Leave to cool and serve.

Nutrition Calories: 220 Fat: 13 g. Fiber: 4 g. Carbs: 6 g. Protein: 11 g.

281. Easy Creamy Shrimp Nachos

Preparation time: 5 minutes
Cooking time: 15 minutes
Servings: 4
Ingredients

- 1 lb. shrimp, cleaned and deveined
- 1 tbsp. olive oil
- 2 tbsp. fresh lemon juice
- 1 tsp. paprika
- 1/4 tsp. cumin powder
- 1/2 tsp. shallot powder
- 1/2 tsp. garlic powder
- Coarse sea salt and black pepper, to flavor
- 1 bag (9 oz.) corn tortilla chips
- 1/4 cup pickled jalapeño, minced
- 1 cup Pepper Jack cheese, grated
- 1/2 cup sour cream

Directions

1. Set the shrimp with olive oil, lemon juice, paprika, cumin powder, shallot powder, garlic powder, salt, and black pepper. Cook in the preheated air fryer at 390°F for 5 minutes.
2. Place the tortilla chips on the aluminum foil-lined cooking basket. Top with the shrimp mixture, jalapeño, and cheese. Cook for another 2 minutes or until cheese has melted.
3. Serve garnished with sour cream, and enjoy!

Nutrition Calories: 225 Fat: 3.41 g.Carbohydrates: 0 g.Protein: 20.9 g.

282. Peppery and Lemony Haddock

Preparation time: 5 minutes
Cooking time: 15 minutes
Servings: 4
Ingredients

- 1 cup breadcrumbs
- 2 tbsp. lemon juice
- 1/2 tsp. black pepper
- 1/4 cup dry air fryer to flakes
- 1 egg, beaten
- 1/4 cup Parmesan cheese
- 3 tbsp. flour
- 1/4 tsp. salt

Directions

1. Combine the flour, black pepper, and salt in a small bowl. In another bowl, combine lemon, breadcrumbs, Parmesan cheese, and potato flakes.
2. Dip the fillets in the flour first, then in the egg, and coat them with the lemony crumbs. Arrange on a lined sheet and place it in the air fryer; cook for 15 minutes at 370°F.

Nutrition Calories: 151 Protein: 14 g. Fiber: 9 g. Fat: 10 g. Carbs: 3 g.

283. Pistachio Crusted Salmon

Preparation time: 5 minutes
Cooking time: 15 minutes
Servings: 1
Ingredients:

- 1 tsp. mustard
- 1 tbsp. pistachios
- Pinch sea salt
- Pinch garlic powder
- Pinch black pepper
- 1 tsp. lemon juice
- 1 tsp. Parmesan cheese, grated
- 1 tsp. olive oil

Directions

1. Warm the air fryer to 350°F, and whisk mustard and lemon juice together.
2. Season the salmon with salt, pepper, and garlic powder.
3. Brush the olive oil on all sides. Brush the mustard mixture onto salmon.

4. Chop the pistachios finely and combine them with the Parmesan cheese; sprinkle on top of the salmon. Set the salmon in the air fryer basket with the skin side down; cook for 15 minutes or to your liking.

Nutrition Calories: 140 Fat: 7 g. Protein: 18 g. Carbs: 3 g. Sugars: 1 g. Fiber: 1 g. Sodium: 141 mg.

284. Fried Crawfish

Preparation time: 5 minutes
Cooking time: 15 minutes
Servings: 4
Ingredients

- 1 lb. crawfish
- 1 tbsp. avocado oil
- 1 tsp. onion powder
- 1 tbsp. rosemary, chopped

Directions

1. Preheat the air fryer to 340°F.
2. Place the crawfish in the air fryer basket and sprinkle with avocado oil and rosemary.
3. Add the onion powder and stir the crawfish gently; cook the meal for 15 minutes.

Nutrition Calories: 38 Protein: 1 g. Fiber: 0 g. Net carbohydrates: 2 g. Fat: 3 g. Sodium: 144 mg.Carbohydrates: 2 g. Sugar: 0 g.

CHAPTER 8:

Meatless Mains

285. Eggplant Surprise

Preparation time: 10–20 minutes
Cooking time: 17 minutes
Servings: 4
Ingredients

- 1 eggplant, roughly chopped
- 3 zucchinis, roughly chopped
- 3 tbsp. extra virgin olive oil
- 3 tomatoes, sliced
- 2 tbsp. lemon juice
- 1 tsp. thyme, dried
- 1 tsp. oregano, dried
- Salt and black pepper to taste

Directions

1. Put eggplant pieces in your instant pot.
2. Add zucchinis and tomatoes.
3. Mix lemon juice with salt, pepper, thyme, oregano, and oil in a bowl and stir well.
4. Pour this over veggie, toss to coat, seal the instant pot lid, and cook at HIGH for 7 minutes.
5. Quickly release the pressure and carefully open the lid; divide among plates and serve.

Nutrition Calories: 160Fat: 7 g.Protein: 1 g.Sugar: 6 g.Carbohydrates: 19 g.Fiber: 8 g.Sodium: 20 mg.

286. Carrots and Turnips

Preparation time: 10–20 minutes
Cooking time: 15 minutes
Servings: 4
Ingredients

- 2 turnips, peeled and sliced
- 1 small onion, chopped
- 1 tsp. lemon juice
- 1 tsp. cumin, ground.
- 3 carrots, sliced
- 1 tbsp. extra-virgin olive oil
- 1 cup water

- Salt and black pepper to taste

Directions

1. Set your instant pot on Sauté mode; add oil and heat it.
2. Add onion, stir and sauté for 2 minutes.
3. Add turnips, carrots, cumin, and lemon juice; stir and cook for 1 minute.
4. Add salt, pepper, and water; then stir well. Close the lid and cook at HIGH for 6 minutes.
5. Quickly release the pressure, open the instant pot lid, and divide turnips and carrots among plates.
6. Serve and enjoy.

Nutrition Calories: 170 Fat: 9 g.Protein: 1 g.Sugar: 5 g.Carbohydrates: 19 g.Fiber: 7 g.Sodium: 475 mg.

287. Shrimp and Asparagus

Preparation time: 10–20 minutes
Cooking time: 8 minutes
Servings: 4
Ingredients

- 1 lb. shrimp, peeled and deveined
- 1 cup water
- 1/2 tbsp. Cajun seasoning
- 1 tsp. extra virgin olive oil
- 1 bunch asparagus, trimmed

Directions

1. Pour the water into your instant pot.
2. Put asparagus in the steamer basket of the pot and add the shrimp on top.
3. Drizzle the olive oil, sprinkle Cajun seasoning, and then stir well. Close the lid and cook on LOW for 2 minutes.
4. Release the pressure naturally, transfer the asparagus and shrimp to plates, and serve.

Nutrition Calories: 20 Fat: 3 g.Protein: 8 g.Sugar: 3 g. Carbohydrates: 0.62 g.

288. Instant Brussels Sprouts With Parmesan

Preparation time: 10–20 minutes
Cooking time: 16 minutes
Servings: 4
Ingredients

- 1 lb. Brussels sprouts, washed
- 1 cup water
- 3 tbsp. Parmesan, grated
- 1 lemon juice
- 2 tbsp. butter
- Salt and black pepper to taste

Directions

1. Put sprouts in your instant pot, add salt, pepper, and water; stir well. Close the lid and cook at HIGH for 3 minutes.
2. Quickly release the pressure, transfer sprouts to a bowl, discard water, and clean your pot.
3. Set your pot on SAUTÉ mode; add butter and melt it.
4. Add the lemon juice and stir well.
5. Add the sprouts, stir and transfer to plates.
6. Add more salt, pepper if needed, and Parmesan cheese on top.

Nutrition Calories: 23 Fat: 10 g. Protein: 8 g. Sugar: 5 g. Carbohydrates: 13.55 g.

289. Braised Fennel

Preparation time: 10–20 minutes
Cooking time: 22 minutes
Servings: 4
Ingredients

- 2 fennel bulbs, trimmed and cut into quarters
- 3 tbsp. extra virgin olive oil
- 1/4 cup white wine
- 1/4 cup Parmesan, grated
- 3/4 cup veggie stock
- 1/2 lemon juice
- 1 garlic clove, chopped
- 1 red pepper, dried
- Salt and black pepper to taste

Directions

1. Set your instant pot on SAUTÉ mode; add oil and heat it.
2. Add the garlic and red pepper, then stir well. Cook for 2 minutes and discard garlic.

3. Add the fennel, stir and brown it for 8 minutes.
4. Add salt, pepper, stock, wine, close the lid and cook at HIGH for 4 minutes.
5. Quickly release the pressure, open the instant pot lid, add lemon juice, more salt and pepper if needed, and the cheese.
6. Mix to coat, divide among plates, and serve.

Nutrition Calories: 230 Fat: 4 g. Protein: 1 g. Sugar: 3 g. Carbohydrates: 13.42 g.

290. Brussels Sprouts and Potatoes Dish

Preparation time: 10–20 minutes
Cooking time: 15 minutes
Servings: 4
Ingredients

- 1 1/2 lb. Brussels sprouts, washed and trimmed
- 1 1/2 tbsp. breadcrumbs
- 1/2 cup beef stock
- 1 cup new potatoes, chopped
- 1 1/2 tbsp. butter
- Salt and black pepper to taste

Directions

1. Put the sprouts and potatoes in your instant pot.
2. Add the stock, salt, and pepper; close the lid and cook at HIGH for 5 minutes.
3. Quickly release the pressure, carefully open the lid, and set on SAUTÉ mode; add the butter and breadcrumbs, toss to coat well, divide among plates, and serve.

Nutrition Calories: 150 Fat: 8 g. Protein: 1 g. Sugar: 2 g. Carbohydrates: 25.34 g.

291. Beet and Orange Salad

Preparation time: 10–20 minutes
Cooking time: 20 minutes
Servings: 4
Ingredients

- 1 1/2 lb. beets
- 3 strips orange peel
- 2 tbsp. cider vinegar
- 1/2 cup orange juice
- 2 tsp. orange zest, grated
- 2 tbsp. brown sugar
- 2 scallions, chopped
- 2 tsp. mustard
- 2 cups arugula and salad greens

Directions

1. Scrub the beets well, cut them in halves, and put them in a bowl.
2. In your instant pot, mix the orange peel strips with vinegar and orange juice, and stir.
3. Add the beets, seal the instant pot lid, cook at HIGH for 7 minutes, and naturally release the pressure.
4. Carefully open the lid, take the beets and transfer them to a bowl.
5. Discard the peel strips from the pot, add mustard and sugar, and stir well.
6. Add the scallions, grated orange zest to beets, and toss them.
7. Add the liquid from the pot over beets, toss to coat and serve on plates over the mixed salad greens.

Nutrition Calories: 164Fat: 5 g.Protein: 2 g.Sugar: 5 g. Carbohydrates: 21.68 g.

292. Endives Dish

Preparation time: 10–20 minutes
Cooking time: 30 minutes
Servings: 4
Ingredients

- 4 endives, trimmed
- 2 tbsp. butter
- 1 tbsp. white flour
- 4 slices ham
- 1/2 tsp. nutmeg
- 14 oz. milk
- Salt and black pepper to taste
- Water

Directions

1. Put the endives in the steamer basket of the instant pot, add some water to the pot, cover, and cook at HIGH for 10 minutes.
2. Meanwhile, heat a pan with the butter over medium heat, stir and melt it.
3. Add flour, stir well, and cook for 3 minutes.
4. Add the milk, salt, pepper, and nutmeg; stir well, reduce heat to low, and cook for 10 minutes.
5. Release the pressure from the pot, uncover it, transfer them to a cutting board, and roll each in a slice of ham.
6. Arrange endives in a pan, add the milk mixture over them, introduce them in

the preheated broiler and broil for 10 minutes.
7. Slice, arrange on plates, and serve.

Nutrition Calories: 175 Fat: 8 g.Protein: 1 g.Sugar: 2 g. Carbohydrates: 7.66 g.

293. Roasted Potatoes

Preparation time: 10–20 minutes
Cooking time: 30 minutes
Servings: 4
Ingredients

- 2 lb. baby potatoes
- 5 tbsp. vegetable oil
- 1/2 cup stock
- 1 rosemary spring
- 5 garlic cloves
- Salt and black pepper to taste

Directions

1. Set your instant pot on SAUTÉ mode; add the oil and heat it.
2. Add the potatoes, rosemary, and garlic, stir and brown them for 10 minutes.
3. Prick each potato with a knife, add the stock, salt, and pepper to the pot.
4. Seal the instant pot lid and cook at HIGH for 7 minutes.
5. Quickly release the pressure, open the instant pot lid, divide potatoes among plates, and serve.

Nutrition Calories: 250Fat: 15 g.Protein: 2 g.Sugar: 1 g. Carbohydrates: 41.93 g.

294. Cabbage Wedges

Preparation time: 10 minutes
Cooking time: 29 minutes
Servings: 6
Ingredients

- 1 small head green cabbage
- 6 strips bacon, thick-cut, pastured
- 1 tsp. onion powder
- 1/2 tsp. ground black pepper
- 1 tsp. garlic powder
- 3/4 tsp. salt
- 1/4 tsp. red chili flakes
- 1/2 tsp. fennel seeds
- 3 tbsp. olive oil

Directions

1. Switch on the air fryer, insert the fryer basket, grease it with olive oil, then shut with its lid, set the fryer to 350°F, and preheat for 5 minutes.

2. Open the fryer, add the bacon strips, close with the lid and cook for 10 minutes until nicely golden and crispy; turning the bacon halfway through the frying.

3. Meanwhile, prepare the cabbage, remove the outer leaves, and cut it into 8 wedges, keeping the core intact.

4. Prepare the spice mix and for this, place the onion powder in a bowl, add black pepper, garlic powder, salt, red chili flakes, and fennel, and stir until mixed.

5. Drizzle cabbage wedges with oil and then sprinkle with spice mix until well coated.

6. When the air fryer beeps, open the lid, transfer the bacon strips to a cutting board and let it rest.

7. Add the seasoned cabbage wedges into the fryer basket, close with the lid, then cook for 8 minutes at 400°F, flip the cabbage, spray with oil and continue air frying for 6 minutes until nicely golden and cooked.

8. When done, transfer cabbage wedges to a plate.

9. Chop the bacon, sprinkle it over cabbage and serve.

Nutrition Calories: 123Carbs: 2 g.Fat: 11 g.Protein: 4 g.Fiber: 0 g.Sugar: 1 g.

295. **Buffalo Cauliflower Wings**
Preparation time: 5 minutes
Cooking time: 30 minutes
Servings: 6
Ingredients

- 1 tbsp. almond flour
- 1 medium head cauliflower
- 1 1/2 tsp. salt
- 4 tbsp. hot sauce
- 1 tbsp. olive oil

Directions

1. Switch on the air fryer, insert the fryer basket, grease it with olive oil, shut with the lid, set the fryer to 400°F, and preheat for 5 minutes.

2. Meanwhile, cut the cauliflower into bite-size florets and set it aside.

3. Place flour in a large bowl, whisk in salt, oil, and hot sauce until combined, add the cauliflower florets and toss until combined.

4. Open the fryer, add the cauliflower florets in a single layer, close with the lid, and cook for 15 minutes until nicely golden and crispy; shaking halfway through the frying.

5. When the air fryer beeps, open the lid, transfer the cauliflower florets onto a serving plate, and keep warm.

6. Cook the remaining cauliflower florets in the same way and serve.

Nutrition Calories: 48Carbs: 1 g. Fat: 4 g. Protein: 1 g. Fiber: 0.5 g.

296. **Sweet Potato Cauliflower Patties**
Preparation time: 20 minutes
Cooking time: 40 minutes
Servings: 7
Ingredients

- 1 green onion, chopped
- 1 large sweet potato, peeled
- 1 tsp. garlic, minced
- 1 cup cilantro leaves
- 2 cup cauliflower florets
- 1/4 tsp. ground black pepper
- 1/4 tsp. salt
- 1/4 cup sunflower seeds
- 1/4 tsp. cumin
- 1/4 cup ground flaxseed
- 1/2 tsp. red chili powder
- 2 tbsp. ranch seasoning mix
- 2 tbsp. arrowroot starch

Directions

1. Cut peeled sweet potato into small pieces, then place them in a food processor and pulse until pieces are broken up.

2. Then add the onion, cauliflower florets, garlic, and pulse until combined; add the remaining ingredients and pulse more until well combined.

3. Tip the mixture into a bowl, shape it into 7 1 1/2-inch thick patties, each about 1/4 cup, then place them on a baking sheet and freeze for 10 minutes.

4. Switch on the air fryer, insert the fryer basket, and grease it with olive oil; close the lid, set the fryer at 400°F, and preheat for 10 minutes.

5. Open the fryer, add patties to it in a single layer, close the lid and cook for 20

minutes until nicely golden and cooked; flipping the patties halfway through the frying.

6. When the air fryer beeps, open the lid, transfer the patties onto a serving plate, and keep them warm.

7. Prepare the continuing patties in the same way and serve.

Nutrition Calories: 85 Carbs: 9 g. Fat: 3 g. Protein: 2.7 g. Fiber: 3.5 g.

297. Okra

Preparation time: 10 minutes
Cooking time: 10 minutes
Servings: 4
Ingredients

- 1 cup almond flour
- 8 oz. fresh okra - 1/2 tsp. sea salt
- 1 cup milk, reduced-fat
- 1 egg, pastured

Directions

1. Break the egg in a container, pour in the milk, and whisk until blended.

2. Cut the stem from each okra, cut it into 1/2-inch pieces, add them into the egg and stir until well coated.

3. Mix the flour and salt and add them into a large plastic bag.

4. Working on one okra piece at a time, drain the okra well by letting excess egg drip off, add it to the flour mixture, seal the bag and shake well until the okra is well coated. Place the coated okra on a grease air fryer basket, coat the remaining okra pieces in the same way and place them into the basket.

5. Switch on the air fryer, insert the fryer basket, spray okra with oil, then shut with the lid, set the fryer to 390°F, and cook for 10 minutes until nicely golden and cooked; stirring okra halfway through the frying.

6. Serve straight away.

Nutrition Calories: 250 Carbs: 38 g. Fat: 9 g. Protein: 3 g. Fiber: 2 g.

298. Creamed Spinach

Preparation time: 10 minutes
Cooking time: 20 minutes
Servings: 2
Ingredients

- 1/2 cup white onion, chopped

- 10 oz. frozen spinach, thawed
- 1 tsp. salt
- 1 tsp. ground black pepper
- 2 tsp. garlic, minced
- 1/2 tsp. ground nutmeg
- 4 oz. cream cheese, reduced-fat, diced
- 1/4 cup shredded Parmesan cheese, reduced-fat
- Olive oil

Directions

1. Switch on the air fryer, insert the fryer basket, grease it with olive oil, then shut with the lid, set the fryer at 350°F, and preheat for 5 minutes.

2. Meanwhile, take a 6-inches baking pan, grease it with oil, and set it aside.

3. Put the spinach in a container, add the remaining ingredients except for Parmesan cheese, stir until well mixed, and add the mixture into a prepared baking pan.

4. Open the fryer, add pan, close with the lid, and cook for 10 minutes until the cheese has melted, stirring halfway through.

5. Then sprinkle Parmesan cheese on top of spinach and continue air frying for 5 minutes at 400°F until the top is nicely golden and cheese has melted.

6. Serve straight away.

Nutrition Calories: 273 Carbs: 8 g. Fat: 23 g. Protein: 8 g. Fiber: 2 g.

299. Eggplant Parmesan

Preparation time: 20 minutes
Cooking time: 15 minutes
Servings: 4
Ingredients

- 1/2 cup and 3 tbsp. almond flour, divided
- 1.25 lb. eggplant, 1/2-inch sliced
- 1 tbsp. parsley, chopped
- 1 tsp. Italian seasoning
- 2 tsp. salt
- 1 cup marinara sauce
- 1 egg, pastured
- 1 tbsp. water
- 3 tbsp. grated Parmesan cheese, reduced-fat

- 1/4 cup grated Mozzarella cheese, reduced-fat

Directions

1. Slice the eggplant into 1/2-inch pieces, place them in a colander, sprinkle with 1 1/2 tsp. of salt on both sides, and let it rest for 15 minutes.
2. Meanwhile, place 1/2 cup flour in a bowl, add the egg and water, and whisk until blended.
3. Place the remaining flour in a shallow dish, add remaining salt, Italian seasoning, and Parmesan cheese, and stir until mixed.
4. Switch on the air fryer, insert the fryer basket, grease it with olive oil, then shut with its lid, set the fryer to 360°F, and preheat for 5 minutes.
5. Meanwhile, drain the eggplant pieces, pat them dry, and then dip each slice into the egg mixture and coat with flour mixture.
6. Open the air fryer, add the coated eggplant slices in a single layer, close the lid, and cook for 8 minutes until nicely golden and cooked; flipping the eggplant slices halfway through the frying.
7. Then top each eggplant slice with a tbsp. of marinara sauce and some Mozzarella cheese, and continue air frying for 1–2 minutes or until cheese has melted.
8. When the air fryer beeps, open the lid, transfer eggplants onto a serving plate, and keep them warm.
9. Cook the remaining eggplant slices in the same way and serve.

Nutrition Calories: 193 Carbs: 27 g. Fat: 5.5 g. Protein: 10 g. Fiber: 6 g.

300. Cauliflower Rice

Preparation time: 10 minutes
Cooking time: 27 minutes
Servings: 3
Ingredients
For the tofu

- 1 cup carrot, diced
- 6 oz. tofu, extra-firm, drained
- 1/2 cup white onion, diced
- 2 tbsp. soy sauce
- 1 tsp. turmeric

For the cauliflower

- 1/2 cup chopped broccoli
- 3 cups cauliflower rice
- 1 tbsp. garlic, minced
- 1/2 cup frozen peas
- 1 tbsp. ginger, minced
- 2 tbsp. soy sauce
- 1 tbsp. apple cider vinegar
- 1 1/2 tsp. toasted sesame oil

Directions

1. Switch on the air fryer, insert the fryer pan, grease it with olive oil, close the lid, set the fryer to 370°F, and preheat for 5 minutes.
2. Meanwhile, place tofu in a bowl, crumble it, then add remaining ingredients and stir until mixed.
3. Open the fryer, add the tofu mixture, and spray with oil; close the lid, and cook for 10 minutes until nicely golden and crispy; stirring halfway through the frying.
4. Meanwhile, place all the ingredients for cauliflower in a bowl and toss until mixed.
5. When the air fryer beeps, open the lid, add cauliflower mixture, shake the pan gently to mix, and continue cooking for 12 minutes, shaking halfway through the frying.
6. Serve straight away.

Nutrition Calories: 258.1 Carbs: 20.8 g. Fat: 13 g. Protein: 18.2 g. Fiber: 7 g.

301. Brussels Sprouts

Preparation time: 5 minutes
Cooking time: 10 minutes
Servings: 2
Ingredients

- 2 cups Brussels sprouts
- 1/4 tsp. sea salt
- 1 tbsp. olive oil
- 1 tbsp. apple cider vinegar

Directions

1. Switch on the air fryer, insert the fryer basket, grease it with olive oil, then close the lid, set the fryer to 400°F, and preheat for 5 minutes.
2. Meanwhile, cut the sprouts lengthwise into 1/4-inch thick pieces, put them in a

bowl, add the remaining ingredients, and toss until well coated.

3. Open the fryer, add the sprouts to it, close the lid and cook for 10 minutes until crispy and cooked; shaking halfway through the frying.

4. When the air fryer beeps, open its lid, transfer the sprouts onto a serving plate and serve.

Nutrition Calories: 88 Carbs: 11 g. Fat: 4.4 g. Protein: 3.9 g. Fiber: 4 g.

302. Green Beans

Preparation time: 5 minutes
Cooking time: 13 minutes
Servings: 4
Ingredients

- 1 lb. green beans
- 3/4 tsp. garlic powder
- 3/4 tsp. ground black pepper
- 1 1/4 tsp. salt
- 1/2 tsp. paprika
- Olive oil

Directions

1. Switch on the air fryer, insert the fryer basket, grease it with olive oil, close the lid, set the fryer to 400°F, and preheat for 5 minutes.

2. Meanwhile, place the beans in a bowl, spray generously with olive oil, sprinkle with garlic powder, black pepper, salt, and paprika, and toss until well coated.

3. Open the fryer, add green beans, close the lid and cook for 8 minutes until nicely golden and crispy, shaking halfway through the frying.

4. When the air fryer beeps, open the lid, transfer green beans onto a serving plate and serve.

Nutrition Calories: 45 Carbs: 7 g. Fat: 1 g. Protein: 2 g. Fiber: 3 g.

303. Asparagus Avocado Soup

Preparation time: 10 minutes
Cooking time: 20 minutes
Servings: 4
Ingredients

- 1 avocado, peeled, pitted, cubed
- 12 oz. asparagus
- 1/2 tsp. ground black pepper
- 1 tsp. garlic powder
- 1 tsp. sea salt

- 2 tbsp. olive oil, divided
- 1/2 lemon, juiced
- 2 cups vegetable stock

Directions

1. Switch on the air fryer, insert the fryer basket, grease it with olive oil, close the lid, set the fryer to 425°F, and preheat for 5 minutes.

2. Meanwhile, place the asparagus in a shallow dish, drizzle with 1 tbsp. of oil, sprinkle with garlic powder, salt, and black pepper, and toss until well mixed.

3. Open the fryer, add the asparagus, close with its lid and cook for 10 minutes until nicely golden and roasted, shaking halfway through the frying.

4. When the air fryer beeps, open the lid and transfer asparagus to a food processor.

5. Add the remaining ingredients into a food processor and pulse until well combined and smooth.

6. Tip the soup in a saucepan, pour in the water if it is too thick, and heat it over medium-low heat for 5 minutes until thoroughly heated.

7. Ladle the soup into bowls and serve.

Nutrition Calories: 208 Carbs: 13 g. Fat: 16 g. Protein: 6 g. Fiber: 5 g.

304. Fried Peppers With Sriracha Mayo

Preparation time: 20 minutes
Cooking time: 10 minutes
Servings: 2
Ingredients

- 4 bell peppers, seeded and sliced (1-inch pieces)
- 1 onion, sliced (1-inch pieces)
- 1 tbsp. olive oil
- 1/2 tsp. rosemary, dried
- 1/2 tsp. basil, dried
- Kosher salt, to taste
- 1/4 tsp. ground black pepper
- 1/3 cup mayonnaise
- 1/3 tsp. Sriracha

Directions

1. Toss the bell peppers and onions with olive oil, rosemary, basil, salt, and black pepper.

2. Place the peppers and onions on an even layer in the cooking basket. Cook at 400°F for 12–14 minutes.

3. Meanwhile, make the sauce by whisking the mayonnaise and sriracha.

4. Serve immediately.

Nutrition Calories: 346 Fat: 34.1 g. Carbs: 9.5 g.Protein: 2.3 g.Sugars: 4.9 g.

305. Spiced Avocado With Jicama Dip

Preparation time: 5 minutes
Cooking time: 0 minutes
Servings: 4
Ingredients

- 1 avocado, cut into cubes
- 1/2 lime juice
- 2 tbsp. red onion, finely chopped
- 2 tbsp. fresh cilantro, chopped
- 1 garlic clove, minced
- 1/4 tsp. sea salt - 1 cup jicama, sliced

Directions

1. Combine the avocado, lime juice, onion, cilantro, garlic, and salt in a small bowl. Mash lightly with a fork.

2. Serve with the jicama for dipping.

Nutrition Calories: 74 Fat: 5.1 g. Protein: 1.1 g. Carbs: 7.9 g. Fiber: 4.9 g. Sugar: 3.0 g. Sodium: 80 mg.

306. Tahini Zucchini With Pepper Dip

Preparation time: 10 minutes
Cooking time: 0 minutes
Servings: 4
Ingredients

- 2 zucchinis, chopped - 3 garlic cloves
- 2 tbsp. extra virgin olive oil
- 2 tbsp. tahini - 1 lemon juice
- 1/2 tsp. sea salt
- 1 red bell pepper, seeded and cut into sticks

Directions

1. Combine the zucchini, garlic, olive oil, tahini, lemon juice, and salt in a blender or food processor. Blend until smooth.

2. Serve with the red bell pepper for dipping.

Nutrition Calories: 120 Fat: 11.1 g. Protein: 2.1 g. Carbs: 6.9 g. Fiber: 2.9 g. Sugar: 4.0 g. Sodium: 155 mg.

307. Simple Acorn Squash With Parmesan

Preparation time: 10 minutes
Cooking time: 20 minutes
Servings: 4
Ingredients

- 1 (1 lb./454 g.) acorn squash
- 1 tbsp. extra virgin olive oil
- 1 tsp. dried sage leaves, crumbled
- 1/4 tsp. nutmeg, freshly grated
- 1/8 Tsp. kosher salt
- 1/8 Tsp. freshly ground black pepper
- 2 tbsp. Parmesan cheese, freshly grated
- 1 cup water

Directions

1. Cut the acorn squash in half lengthwise and remove the seeds. Cut each half in half for a total of 4 wedges. Snap off the stem if it's easy to do.

2. In a small bowl, combine the olive oil, sage, nutmeg, salt, and pepper. Brush the cut sides of the squash with the olive oil mixture.

3. Pour 1 cup of water into the electric pressure cooker and insert a wire rack or trivet.

4. Place the squash on the trivet in a single layer, skin-side down.

5. Close and lock the lid of the pressure cooker. Set the valve to sealing. Cook on high pressure for 20 minutes.

6. When the cooking is complete, hit CANCEL and quickly release the pressure. Once the pin drops, unlock and remove the lid.

7. Carefully, remove the squash from the pot, sprinkle with the Parmesan, and serve.

Nutrition Calories: 86 Fat: 4.1 g. Protein: 2.1 g. Carbs: 11.9 g. Fiber: 2.1 g. Sugar: 0 g. Sodium: 283 mg.

308. Spicy Bread Pot With Mushroom and Kale

Preparation time: 20 minutes
Cooking time: 20 minutes
Servings: 2
Ingredients

- 1 large egg
- 1/2 cup 2% milk
- 1/2 tsp. Dijon mustard

- Pinch freshly grated nutmeg
- Pinch kosher salt
- Pinch freshly ground black pepper
- 1 slice sourdough bread (about 1 oz./28 g.), cut into 1-inch cubes
- 1 tbsp. avocado oil
- 1/4 cup onion, chopped
- 2 oz. (57 g.) mushrooms, sliced (about 3 creminis)
- 1/4 tsp. thyme, dried
- 1 cup chopped lacinato kale, stems and ribs removed (from 2 stems)
- Non-stick cooking spray
- 1/4 cup Gruyère cheese, grated
- 1 tbsp. Parmesan, shredded

Directions

1. In a 2-cup measuring cup with a spout, whisk the egg, milk, mustard, nutmeg, salt, and pepper.
2. Add the bread and submerge it in the liquid.
3. Set the electric pressure cooker to the SAUTÉ setting. When the pot is hot, pour in the avocado oil.
4. Add the onion, mushrooms, and thyme to the pot; sauté for 3–5 minutes or until the onion begins to soften.
5. Stir in the kale and cook for 2 minutes or until it wilted. Hit CANCEL.
6. Spray the ramekins with cooking spray. Divide the mushroom mixture between the ramekins.
7. Top each with 2 tbsp. of Gruyère. Pour half of the egg mixture into each ramekin and stir. Make sure the bread stays submerged. Cover with foil.
8. Pour 1 cup of water into the electric pressure cooker and insert a wire rack or trivet. Place the ramekins on the rack.
9. Close and lock the lid of the pressure cooker. Set the valve to sealing. Cook on high pressure for 8 minutes.
10. When the cooking is complete, hit CANCEL. Allow the pressure to release naturally for 10 minutes, then quickly release any remaining pressure.
11. Using the tongs or the handles of the rack, transfer the ramekins to a cutting board. Carefully lift the foil and sprinkle the Parmesan on top. Replace the foil for

about 5 minutes or until the cheese melts.
12. Remove the foil and serve immediately.

Nutrition Calories: 296 Fat: 17.1 g. Protein: 13.1 g. Carbs: 22.9 g. Fiber: 2.9 g. Sugar: 7.0 g. Sodium: 312 mg.

309. One-Pot Hot Corn

Preparation time: 10 minutes
Cooking time: 20 minutes
Servings: 12
Ingredients

- 6 ears corn
- 1 cup water

Directions

1. Remove the husks and silk from the corn. Cut or break each ear in half.
2. Pour 1 cup of water into the bottom of the electric pressure cooker. Insert a wire rack or trivet.
3. Place the corn upright on the rack, cut-side down. Close and lock the lid of the pressure cooker. Set the valve to sealing.
4. Cook on high pressure for 5 minutes.
5. When the cooking is complete, hit CANCEL and quickly release the pressure.
6. Once the pin drops, unlock and remove the lid.
7. Use the tongs to remove the corn from the pot; season as desired and serve immediately.

Nutrition Calories: 64 Fat: 1.1 g. Protein: 2.1 g. Carbs: 13.9 g. Fiber: 0.9 g. Sugar: 5.0 g. Sodium: 12 mg.

310. Spicy Lemony Broccoli

Preparation time: 10 minutes
Cooking time: 25 minutes
Servings: 8
Ingredients

- 2 large broccoli heads, cut into florets
- 2 tbsp. extra virgin olive oil
- 3 garlic cloves, minced
- 1/4 tsp. salt
- 1/4 tsp. ground black pepper
- 2 tbsp. lemon juice, freshly squeezed

Directions

1. Preheat the oven to 425°F (220°C) and line a large baking sheet with parchment paper.

2. In a large bowl, add the broccoli, olive oil, garlic, salt, and pepper. Toss well until the broccoli is coated completely. Transfer the broccoli to the prepared baking sheet.

3. Roast in the preheated oven for 25 minutes, flipping the broccoli halfway through, or until the broccoli is browned and fork-tender.

4. Remove from the oven to a plate and let cool for 5 minutes.

5. Serve drizzled with lemon juice.

Nutrition Calories: 33 Fat: 2.1 g. Protein: 1.2 g. Carbs: 3.1 g. Fiber: 1.1 g. Sugar: 1.1 g.Sodium: 85 mg.

311. Oven-Baked Lemony Cauliflower

Preparation time: 5 minutes
Cooking time: 25 minutes
Servings: 4
Ingredients

- 1 cauliflower head, broken into small florets
- 2 tbsp. extra virgin olive oil
- 1/2 tsp. salt, or more to taste
- 1/2 tsp. ground chipotle chili powder
- 1 lime juice

Directions

1. Preheat the oven to 450°F (235°C) and line a large baking sheet with parchment paper. Set aside.

2. Mix the cauliflower florets with olive oil in a large bowl; season with salt and chipotle chili powder.

3. Arrange the cauliflower florets on the baking sheet.

4. Roast in the preheated oven for 15 minutes until lightly browned. Flip the cauliflower and continue to roast until crisp and tender, about 10 minutes.

5. Remove from the oven and season as needed with salt.

6. Cool for 6 minutes and drizzle with the lime juice, then serve.

Nutrition Calories: 100 Fat: 7.1 g. Protein: 3.2 g. Carbs: 8.1 g. Fiber: 3.2 g. Sugar: 3.2 g. Sodium: 285 mg.

312. Homemade Veggie Fajitas With Guacamole

Preparation time: 10 minutes
Cooking time: 15 minutes
Servings: 4
Ingredients
For the guacamole

- 2 small avocados, pitted and peeled
- 1 tsp. lime juice, freshly squeezed
- 1/4 tsp. salt
- 9 cherry tomatoes, halved

For the fajitas

- 1 red bell pepper, cut into 1/2-inch slices
- 1 green bell pepper, cut into 1/2-inch slices
- 1 small white onion, cut into 1/2-inch slices
- 1 cup canned low-sodium black beans, drained and rinsed
- 1/4 tsp. garlic powder
- 1/4 tsp. chili powder
- 1/2 tsp. ground cumin
- 4 (6-inch) yellow corn tortillas
- Avocado oil cooking spray

Directions

1. In a bowl, add the avocados and lime juice. Use a fork to mash until a uniform consistency is achieved. Season with salt and fold in the cherry tomatoes. Stir well and set aside.

2. Heat a large skillet over medium heat until hot. Cover the bottom with cooking spray.

3. Add the bell peppers, white onion, black beans, garlic powder, chili powder, and cumin to the skillet. Stir and cook for 15 minutes until the beans are tender.

4. Remove from the heat to a plate. Arrange the corn tortillas on a clean work surface and evenly divide the fajita mixture among the tortillas.

5. Serve topped with guacamole.

Nutrition Calories: 273 Fat: 15.2 g. Protein: 8.1 g. Carbs: 30.1 g. Fiber: 11.2 g. Sugar: 5.2 g. Sodium: 176 mg.

313. Cheesy Spinach Portobello Mushrooms Mix

Preparation time: 5 minutes
Cooking time: 20 minutes
Servings: 4
Ingredients

- 8 large Portobello mushrooms
- 3 tsp. extra virgin olive oil, divided
- 4 cups fresh spinach
- 1 medium red bell pepper, diced
- 1/4 cup feta cheese, crumbled

Directions

1. Preheat the oven to 450°F (235°C).
2. On your cutting board, remove the mushroom stems. Scoop out the gills with a spoon and discard. Grease the mushrooms with 2 tbsp. of olive oil.
3. Arrange the mushrooms, cap-side down, on a baking sheet. Roast in the preheated oven for 20 minutes until browned on top.
4. Meanwhile, in a skillet, heat the remaining olive oil over medium heat until shimmering.
5. Add the spinach and red bell pepper to the skillet and sauté for 8 minutes until the vegetables are tender, stirring occasionally. Remove from the heat to a bowl.
6. Remove the mushrooms from the oven to a plate. Use a spoon to stuff the mushrooms with the vegetables and sprinkle with the feta cheese.
7. Serve warm.

Nutrition Calories: 118 Fat: 6.3 g. Protein: 7.2 g. Carbs: 12.2 g. Fiber: 4.1 g. Sugar: 6.1 g. Sodium: 128 mg.

314. Butter Sautéed Green Beans

Preparation time: 15 minutes
Cooking time: 5 minutes
Servings: 4
Ingredients

- 1 tbsp. butter
- 1 1/2 lbs. (680 g.) green beans, trimmed
- 1 tsp. ground nutmeg
- Sea salt, to taste

Directions

1. Melt the butter in a large skillet over medium heat.
2. Sauté the green beans in the melted butter for 5 minutes until tender but still crisp, stirring frequently.
3. Season with nutmeg and salt and mix well.
4. Remove from the heat and cool for a few minutes before serving.

Nutrition Calories: 83 Fat: 3.2 g. Protein: 3.2 g. Carbs: 12.2 g. Fiber: 6.1 g. Sugar: 3.2 g. Sodium: 90 mg.

315. Garlic Veggie Broth Onion Bowl

Preparation time: 10 minutes
Cooking time: 20 minutes
Servings: 2
Ingredients

- 2 tbsp. extra-virgin olive oil
- 1 onion, chopped
- 1 red bell pepper, seeded and chopped
- 2 garlic cloves, minced
- 1 can (14 oz./397 g.) crushed tomatoes
- 2 cups green beans (fresh or frozen; halved if fresh)
- 3 cups low-sodium vegetable broth
- 1 tbsp. Italian seasoning
- 1/2 cup dried whole-wheat elbow macaroni
- Pinch red pepper flakes or to taste
- 1/2 tsp. sea salt

Directions

1. Heat the olive oil in a large saucepan over medium-high heat until shimmering.
2. Sauté the onion and bell pepper for 3 minutes, stirring frequently, or until they start to soften.
3. Add the garlic and cook for 30 seconds until fragrant, stirring occasionally.
4. Stir in the tomatoes, green beans, vegetable broth, and Italian seasoning, and then bring the mixture to a boil.
5. Add the elbow macaroni, red pepper flakes, and salt. Continue to cook for 8 minutes, stirring occasionally, or until the macaroni is cooked.
6. Remove from the heat to a large bowl and cool for 6 minutes before serving.

Nutrition Calories: 202 Fat: 7.2 g. Protein: 5.2 g. Carbs: 29.2 g. Fiber: 7.2 g. Sugar: 29 g. Sodium: 479 mg.

316. Brown Rice With Tofu Broccoli Stir Fry

Preparation time: 10 minutes
Cooking time: 10 minutes
Servings: 4
Ingredients

- 3 tbsp. extra-virgin olive oil
- 12 oz. (340 g.) firm tofu, cut into 1/2-inch pieces
- 4 cups broccoli, broken into florets
- 4 scallions, sliced
- 1 tsp. fresh ginger, peeled and grated
- 4 garlic cloves, minced
- 2 tbsp. soy sauce (use gluten-free soy sauce if necessary)
- 1/4 cup vegetable broth
- 1 cup cooked brown rice

Directions

1. Heat the olive oil in a large skillet over medium-high heat until simmering.
2. Add the tofu, broccoli, and scallions and stir fry for 6 minutes, or until the vegetables become tender.
3. Add the ginger and garlic and cook for 30 seconds, stirring constantly.
4. Fold in the soy sauce, vegetable broth, and brown rice. Stir to combine and cook for an additional 1–2 minutes until the rice is heated.
5. Let it cool for 5 minutes before serving.

Nutrition Calories: 238 Fat: 13.2 g. Protein: 11.1 g. Carbs: 21.2 g. Fiber: 4.2 g. Sugar: 8.8 g. Sodium: 360 mg.

317. Simple Veggie Eggs Bake

Preparation time: 5 minutes
Cooking time: 25 minutes
Servings: 4
Ingredients

- 2 tbsp. extra-virgin olive oil
- 1 red onion, chopped
- 1 sweet potato, cut into 1/2-inch pieces
- 1 green bell pepper, seeded and chopped
- 1/2 tsp. sea salt
- 1 tsp. chili powder
- 4 large eggs
- 1/2 cup pepper Jack cheese, shredded
- 1 avocado, cut into cubes

Directions

1. Preheat the oven to 350ºF (180ºC).

2. Heat the olive oil in a large skillet over medium-high heat until shimmering.
3. Add the onion, sweet potato, bell pepper, salt, and chili powder. Cook for 10 minutes, stirring constantly, or until the vegetables are lightly browned.
4. Remove from the heat. With the back of a spoon, make 4 wells in the vegetables, then crack an egg into each well. Spread the shredded cheese over the vegetables.
5. Bake in the preheated oven for 10 minutes until the cheese is melted and eggs are set.
6. Remove from the heat and sprinkle the avocado on top before serving.

Nutrition Calories: 286 Fat: 21.3 g. Protein: 12.3 g. Carbs: 16.2 g. Fiber: 5.2 g. Sugar: 9.1 g. Sodium: 266 mg.

318. One Plate Egg Spinach Quiches

Preparation time: 10 minutes
Cooking time: 15 minutes
Servings: 6
Ingredients

- 2 tbsp. olive oil, divided
- 1 onion, finely chopped
- 2 garlic cloves, minced
- 2 cups baby spinach
- 8 large eggs
- 1/4 cup 1% or skim milk
- 1/2 tsp. sea salt
- 1/4 tsp. freshly ground black pepper
- 1 cup Swiss cheese, shredded

Special equipment

- A 6-cup muffin tin

Directions

1. Preheat the oven to 375ºF (190ºC). Grease a 6-cup muffin tin with 1 tbsp. of olive oil.
2. Heat the olive oil in a non-stick skillet over medium-high heat. Add the onion and garlic to the skillet and sauté for 4 minutes until translucent.
3. Add the spinach to the skillet and sauté for 1 minute until tender. Transfer to a plate and set them aside.
4. Whisk together the eggs, milk, salt, and black pepper in a bowl. Dunk the cooked vegetables in the bowl of egg mixture, and then spread the cheese.

5. Divide the mixture among the muffin cups. Bake in the preheated oven for 15 minutes until puffed, and the edges are golden brown.
6. Transfer the quiches to 6 small plates and serve warm.

Nutrition Calories: 220 Fat: 17.2 g. Protein: 14.3 g. Carbs: 4.2 g. Fiber: 0.8 g. Sugar: 27 g. Sodium: 235 mg.

319. Garlic and Soy Sauce Sautéed Cabbage

Preparation time: 10 minutes
Cooking time: 10 minutes
Servings: 8
Ingredients

- 2 tbsp. extra virgin olive oil
- 1 bunch collard greens, stemmed and thinly sliced
- 1/2 small green cabbage, thinly sliced
- 6 garlic cloves, minced
- 1 tbsp. low-sodium soy sauce

Directions

1. Heat the olive oil in a large skillet over medium-high heat.
2. Sauté the collard greens in the oil for 2 minutes, or until the greens start to wilt.
3. Toss in the cabbage and mix well. Reduce the heat to medium-low, cover, and cook for 5–7 minutes, stirring occasionally, or until the greens are softened. Fold in the garlic and soy sauce and stir to combine. Cook for about 30 seconds more until fragrant.
4. Remove from the heat to a plate and serve.

Nutrition Calories: 73 Fat: 4.1 g. Protein: 3.2 g. Carbs: 5.9 g. Fiber: 2.9 g. Sugar: 0 g. Sodium: 128 mg.

320. Oven-Baked Squash With Black Pepper

Preparation time: 10 minutes
Cooking time: 20 minutes
Servings: 4
Ingredients

- 1 (1–1 1/2 lb./454–680 g.) delicate squash, halved, seeded, and cut into 1/2-inch-thick strips
- 1 tbsp. extra virgin olive oil
- 1/2 tsp. thyme, dried
- 1/4 tsp. salt

- 1/4 tsp. freshly ground black pepper

Directions

1. Preheat the oven to 400°F (205°C).
2. Line a baking sheet with parchment paper and set it aside.
3. Add the squash strips, olive oil, thyme, salt, and pepper in a large bowl, and toss until the squash strips are fully coated.
4. Place the squash strips on the prepared baking sheet in a single layer.
5. Roast for about 20 minutes until lightly browned; flipping the strips halfway through.
6. Remove from the oven and serve on plates.

Nutrition Calories: 78 Fat: 4.2 g. Protein: 1.1 g. Carbs: 11.8 g. Fiber: 2.1 g. Sugar: 2.9 g. Sodium: 122 mg.

321. Tender Veggie Spring Peas

Preparation time: 10 minutes
Cooking time: 12 minutes
Servings: 6 (1/2 cup each)
Ingredients

- 1 tbsp. unsalted butter
- 1/2 Vidalia onion, thinly sliced
- 1 cup low-sodium vegetable broth
- 3 cups fresh shelled peas
- 1 tbsp. fresh tarragon, minced

Directions

1. Melt the butter in a skillet over medium heat. Sauté the onion in the melted butter for 3 minutes until translucent; stir occasionally.
2. Pour in the vegetable broth and whisk well. Add the peas and tarragon to the skillet and stir to combine.
3. Reduce the heat to low, cover, and cook for 8 minutes more, or until the peas are tender. Let the peas cool for 5 minutes and serve warm.

Nutrition Calories: 82 Fat: 2.1 g. Protein: 4.2 g. Carbs: 12.0 g. Fiber: 3.8 g. Sugar: 4.9 g. Sodium: 48 mg.

322. Citrusy Butter Yams

Preparation time: 7 minutes
Cooking time: 45 minutes
Servings: 8 (1/2 cup each)
Ingredients

- 2 medium jewel yams cut into 2-inch dices

- 2 tbsp. unsalted butter
- 1 large orange juice
- 11/2 tsp. ground cinnamon
- 1/4 tsp. ground ginger
- 3/4 tsp. ground nutmeg
- 1/8 tsp. ground cloves

Directions

1. Preheat the oven to 350ºF (180ºC).
2. Arrange the yam dices on a rimmed baking sheet in a single layer. Set them aside.
3. Add the butter, orange juice, cinnamon, ginger, nutmeg, and garlic cloves to a medium saucepan over medium-low heat. Cook for 3–5 minutes, stirring continuously, or until the sauce begins to thicken and bubble.
4. Spoon the sauce over the yams and toss to coat well.
5. Bake in the preheated oven for 40 minutes until tender.
6. Let the yams cool for 8 minutes on the baking sheet before removing and serving.

Nutrition Calories: 129 Fat: 2.8 g.Protein: 2.1 g.Carbs: 24.7 g.Fiber: 5.0 g.Sugar: 2.9 g.Sodium: 28 mg.

323. Sundried Tomato With Brussels Sprouts Roast

Preparation time: 15 minutes
Cooking time: 20 minutes
Servings: 4
Ingredients

- 1 lb. (454 g.) Brussels sprouts, trimmed and halved
- 1 tbsp. extra virgin olive oil
- Sea salt and freshly ground black pepper, to taste
- 1/2 cup sun-dried tomatoes, chopped
- 2 tbsp. lemon juice, freshly squeezed
- 1 tsp. lemon zest

Directions

1. Preheat the oven to 400ºF (205ºC).
2. Line a large baking sheet with aluminum foil.
3. Toss the Brussels sprouts with olive oil in a large bowl until well coated. Sprinkle with salt and pepper.

4. Spread out the seasoned Brussels sprouts on the prepared baking sheet in a single layer.
5. Roast in the preheated oven for 20 minutes, shaking the pan halfway through, or until the Brussels sprouts are crispy and browned on the outside.
6. Remove from the oven to a serving bowl.
7. Add the tomatoes, lemon juice, and lemon zest, and stir to incorporate.
8. Serve immediately.

Nutrition Calories: 111 Fat: 5.8 g. Protein: 5.0 g.Carbs: 13.7 g.Fiber: 4.9 g.Sugar: 2.7 g.Sodium: 103 mg.

324. Cardamom Spiced Swiss Chard

Preparation time: 10 minutes
Cooking time: 10 minutes
Servings: 4
Ingredients

- 2 tbsp. extra virgin olive oil
- 1 lb. (454 g.) Swiss chard, coarse stems removed, and leaves chopped
- 1 lb. (454 g.) kale, coarse stems removed, and leaves chopped
- 1/2 tsp. ground cardamom
- 1 tbsp. lemon juice, freshly squeezed
- Sea salt and freshly ground black pepper, to taste

Directions

1. Heat the olive oil in a large skillet over medium-high heat.
2. Add the Swiss chard, kale, cardamom, and lemon juice to the skillet, and stir to combine. Cook for about 10 minutes, stirring continuously, or until the greens are wilted. Sprinkle with salt and pepper and stir well.
3. Serve the greens on a plate while warm.

Nutrition Calories: 139 Fat: 6.8 g.Protein: 5.9 g.Carbs: 15.8 g.Fiber: 3.9 g.Sugar: 1.0 g.Sodium: 350 mg.

325. Aromatic Thyme Spiced Button Mushrooms

Preparation time: 10 minutes
Cooking time: 12 minutes
Servings: 4
Ingredients

- 1 tbsp. butter

- 2 tsp. extra virgin olive oil
- 2 lbs. (907 g.) button mushrooms, halved
- 2 tsp. fresh garlic, minced
- 1 tsp. fresh thyme, chopped
- Sea salt and freshly ground black pepper, to taste

Directions

1. Heat the butter and olive oil in a large skillet over medium-high heat.
2. Add the mushrooms and sauté for 10 minutes, stirring occasionally, or until the mushrooms are lightly browned and cooked.
3. Stir in the garlic and thyme and cook for an additional 2 minutes.
4. Season with salt and pepper and serve on a plate.

Nutrition Calories: 96 Fat: 6.1 g.Protein: 6.9 g.Carbs: 8.2 g.Fiber: 1.7 g.Sugar: 3.9 g.Sodium: 91 mg.

CHAPTER 9:

Legumes, Grains And Beans

326. Enchilada Black Bean Casserole

Preparation time: 15 minutes
Cooking time: 15 minutes
Servings: 6

Ingredients

- 1 tbsp. extra-virgin olive oil
- 1/2 onion, chopped
- 1/2 red bell pepper, seeded and chopped
- 1/2 green bell pepper, seeded and chopped
- 2 small zucchinis, chopped
- 3 garlic cloves, minced
- 1 can (15 oz./425 g.) low-sodium black beans, drained and rinsed
- 1 can (10 oz./283 g.) low-sodium enchilada sauce
- 1 tsp. ground cumin
- 1/4 tsp. salt
- 1/4 tsp. freshly ground black pepper
- 1/2 cup shredded Cheddar cheese, divided
- 2 (6-inch) corn tortillas, cut into strips
- Chopped fresh cilantro, for garnish
- Plain yogurt, for serving

Directions

1. Heat the broiler to high.
2. In a large oven-safe skillet, heat the oil over medium-high heat.
3. Add the onion, red bell pepper, green bell pepper, zucchini, and garlic to the skillet, and cook for 3–5 minutes until the onion softens.
4. Add the black beans, enchilada sauce, cumin, salt, pepper, 1/4 cup of cheese, and tortilla strips; mix well. Top with the remaining 1/4 cup of cheese.
5. Put the skillet under the broiler and broil for 5–8 minutes until the cheese is melted and bubbly.

6. Garnish with cilantro and serve with yogurt on the side.

Nutrition Calories: 172 Fat: 7.1 g.Protein: 8.1 g.Carbs: 20.9 g.Fiber: 6.9 g.Sugar: 3.0 g.Sodium: 566 mg.

327. Crispy Parmesan Bean and Veggie Cups

Preparation time: 10 minutes
Cooking time: 5 minutes
Servings: 4

Ingredients

- 1 cup grated Parmesan cheese, divided
- 1 can (15 oz./425 g.) low-sodium white beans, drained and rinsed
- 1 cucumber, peeled and finely diced
- 1/2 cup red onion, finely diced
- 1/4 cup fresh basil, thinly sliced
- 1 garlic clove, minced
- 1/2 jalapeño pepper, diced
- 1 tbsp. extra virgin olive oil
- 1 tbsp. balsamic vinegar
- 1/4 tsp. salt
- Freshly ground black pepper, to taste

Directions

1. Heat a medium non-stick skillet over medium heat. Sprinkle 2 tbsp. of cheese in a thin circle in the center of the pan, flatten it with a spatula.
2. When the cheese melts, use a spatula to flip the cheese and lightly brown the other side.
3. Remove the cheese "pancake" from the pan and place it into the cup of a muffin tin, bending it gently with your hands to fit in the muffin cup.
4. Repeat with the remaining cheese until you have 8 cups.
5. Combine the beans, cucumber, onion, basil, garlic, jalapeño, olive oil, and vinegar in a mixing bowl, and season with salt and pepper.

6. Fill each cup with the bean mixture just before serving.

Nutrition Calories: 260 Fat: 12.1 g.Protein: 14.9 Carbs: 23.9 g.Fiber: 8.0 g.Sugar: 3.9 g.Sodium: 552 mg.

328. Green Lentils With Summer Vegetables

Preparation time: 15 minutes
Cooking time: 0 minutes
Servings: 4
Ingredients

- 3 tbsp. extra virgin olive oil
- 2 tbsp. balsamic vinegar
- 2 tsp. fresh basil, chopped
- 1 tsp. garlic, minced
- Sea salt and freshly ground black pepper, to taste
- 2 cans (15 oz./425 g.) sodium-free green lentils, rinsed and drained
- 1/2 English cucumber, diced
- 2 tomatoes, diced
- 1/2 cup Kalamata olives, halved
- 1/4 cup fresh chives, chopped
- 2 tbsp. pine nuts

Directions

1. Whisk together the olive oil, vinegar, basil, and garlic in a medium bowl; season with salt and pepper.
2. Stir in the lentils, cucumber, tomatoes, olives, and chives.
3. Top with the pine nuts, and serve.

Nutrition Calories: 400 Fat: 15.1 g.Protein: 19.8 g.Carbs: 48.8 g.Fiber: 18.8 g.Sugar: 7.1 g.Sodium: 439 mg.

329. Herbed Beans and Brown Rice Bowl

Preparation time: 15 minutes
Cooking time: 15 minutes
Servings: 8
Ingredients

- 2 tsp. extra virgin olive oil
- 1/2 sweet onion, chopped
- 1 tsp. jalapeño pepper, minced
- 1 tsp. garlic, minced
- 1 can (15 oz./425 g.) sodium-free red kidney beans, rinsed and drained
- 1 large tomato, chopped
- 1 tsp. fresh thyme, chopped

- Sea salt and freshly ground black pepper, to taste - 2 cups brown rice, cooked

Directions

1. Place a large skillet over medium-high heat and add the olive oil.
2. Sauté the onion, jalapeño, and garlic until softened, about 3 minutes.
3. Stir in the beans, tomato, and thyme.
4. Cook until heated through, about 10 minutes. Season with salt and pepper.
5. Serve over the warm brown rice.

Nutrition Calories: 200 Fat: 2.1 g.Protein: 9.1 g.Carbs: 37.1 g. Fiber: 6.1 g.Sugar: 2.0 g.Sodium: 40 mg.

330. Blueberry Wild Rice

Preparation time: 15 minutes
Cooking time: 45 minutes
Servings: 4
Ingredients

- 1 tbsp. extra virgin olive oil
- 1/2 sweet onion, chopped
- 2 1/2 cups sodium-free chicken broth
- 1 cup wild rice, rinsed and drained
- Pinch sea salt
- 1/2 cup pumpkin seeds, toasted
- 1/2 cup blueberries
- 1 tsp. fresh basil, chopped

Directions

1. Place a medium saucepan over medium-high heat and add the oil.
2. Sauté the onion until softened and translucent, about 3 minutes.
3. Stir in the broth and bring to a boil.
4. Stir in the rice and salt and reduce the heat to low. Cover and simmer until the rice is tender, about 40 minutes.
5. Drain off any excess broth, if necessary. Stir in the pumpkin seeds, blueberries, and basil. Serve warm.

Nutrition Calories: 259 Fat: 9.1 g.Protein: 10.8 g.Carbs: 37.1 g.Fiber: 3.9 g.Sugar: 4.1 g.Sodium: 543 mg.

331. Mushroom Rice With Hazelnut

Preparation time: 20 minutes
Cooking time: 35 minutes
Servings: 8
Ingredients

- 1 tbsp. extra virgin olive oil

- 1 cup button mushrooms, chopped
- 1/2 sweet onion, chopped
- 1 celery stalk, chopped
- 2 tsp. garlic, minced
- 2 cups brown basmati rice
- 4 cups low-sodium chicken broth
- 1 tsp. fresh thyme, chopped
- Sea salt and freshly ground black pepper, to taste
- 1/2 cup hazelnuts, chopped

Directions

1. Place a large saucepan over medium-high heat and add the oil.
2. Sauté the mushrooms, onion, celery, and garlic until lightly browned, about 10 minutes.
3. Add the rice and sauté for 1 more minute. Add the chicken broth and bring to a boil. Reduce the heat to low and cover the pot. Simmer until the liquid is absorbed and the rice is tender, about 20 minutes.
4. Stir in the thyme and season with salt and pepper.
5. Top with the hazelnuts, and serve.

Nutrition Calories: 240 Fat: 6.1 g.Protein: 7.1 g.Carbs: 38.9 g.Fiber: 0.9 g.Sugar: 1.1 g.Sodium: 388 mg.

332. Barley Kale and Squash Risotto

Preparation time: 10 minutes
Cooking time: 15 minutes
Servings: 6
Ingredients

- 1 tsp. extra-virgin olive oil
- 1/2 sweet onion, finely chopped
- 1 tsp. garlic, minced
- 2 cups barley, cooked
- 2 cups kale, chopped
- 2 cups cooked butternut squash, cut into 1/2-inch cubes
- 2 tbsp. pistachios, chopped
- 1 tbsp. fresh thyme, chopped
- Sea salt, to taste

Directions

1. Place a large skillet over medium heat and add the oil. Sauté the onion and garlic until softened and translucent, about 3 minutes.

2. Add the barley and kale, and stir until the grains are heated through and the greens are wilted, about 7 minutes.
3. Stir in the squash, pistachios, and thyme.
4. Cook until the dish is hot, about 4 minutes, and season with salt.

Nutrition Calories: 160 Fat: 1.9 g.Protein: 5.1 g.Carbs: 32.1 g.Fiber: 7.0 g.Sugar: 2.0 g.Sodium: 63 mg.

333. Eggplant and Bulgur Pilaf

Preparation time: 10 minutes
Cooking time: 60 minutes
Servings: 4
Ingredients

- 1 tbsp. extra-virgin olive oil
- 1/2 sweet onion, chopped
- 2 tsp. garlic, minced
- 1 cup eggplant, chopped
- 1 1/2 cups bulgur
- 4 cups low-sodium chicken broth
- 1 cup tomato, diced
- Sea salt and freshly ground black pepper, to taste
- 2 tbsp. fresh basil, chopped

Directions

1. Place a large saucepan over medium-high heat. Add the oil and sauté the onion and garlic until softened and translucent, about 3 minutes.
2. Stir in the eggplant and sauté 4 minutes to soften.
3. Stir in the bulgur, broth, and tomatoes. Bring the mixture to a boil.
4. Reduce the heat to low, cover, and simmer until the water has been absorbed, about 50 minutes.
5. Season the pilaf with salt and pepper.
6. Garnish with the basil, and serve.

Nutrition Calories: 300 Fat: 4.0 g.Protein: 14.0 g.Carbs: 54.0 g.Fiber: 12.0 g.Sugar: 7.0 g.Sodium: 358 mg.

334. Couscous With Balsamic Dressing

Preparation time: 10 minutes
Cooking time: 5 minutes
Servings: 6
Ingredients

For the dressing

- 1/4 cup extra virgin olive oil

- 2 tbsp. balsamic vinegar
- 1 tsp. honey
- Sea salt and freshly ground black pepper, to taste

For the couscous

- 1 1/4 cups whole-wheat couscous
- Pinch sea salt
- 1 tsp. butter
- 2 cups boiling water
- 1 scallion, white and green parts, chopped
- 1/2 cup pecans, chopped
- 2 tbsp. fresh parsley, chopped

Directions

To make the dressing

1. Whisk together the oil, vinegar, and honey.
2. Season with salt and pepper and set it aside.

To make the couscous

3. Put the couscous, salt, and butter in a large heat-proof bowl and pour the boiling water on top. Stir and cover the bowl. Let it sit for 5 minutes. Uncover and fluff the couscous with a fork.
4. Stir in the dressing, scallion, pecans, and parsley.
5. Serve warm.

Nutrition Calories: 250 Fat: 12.9 g.Protein: 5.1 g.Carbs: 30.1 g.Fiber: 2.2 g.Sugar: 1.1 g.Sodium: 77 mg.

335. Quinoa and Lush Vegetable Bowl

Preparation time: 15 minutes
Cooking time: 15 minutes
Servings: 6
Ingredients

- 2 cups vegetable broth
- 1 cup quinoa, well rinsed and drained
- 1 tsp. extra virgin olive oil
- 1/2 sweet onion, chopped
- 2 tsp. garlic, minced
- 1/2 large green zucchini, halved lengthwise and cut into half disks
- 1 red bell pepper, seeded and cut into thin strips
- 1 cup fresh or frozen corn kernels
- 1 tsp. fresh basil, chopped

- Sea salt and freshly ground black pepper, to taste

Directions

1. Place a medium saucepan over medium heat and add the vegetable broth. Bring the broth to a boil and add the quinoa. Cover and reduce the heat to low.
2. Cook until the quinoa has absorbed all the broth, about 15 minutes. Remove from the heat and let it cool slightly.
3. While the quinoa is cooking, place a large skillet over medium-high heat and add the oil.
4. Sauté the onion and garlic until softened and translucent, about 3 minutes.
5. Add the zucchini, bell pepper, corn, and sauté until the vegetables are tender-crisp, about 5 minutes.
6. Remove the skillet from the heat. Add the cooked quinoa and the basil to the skillet, stirring to combine.
7. Season with salt and pepper, and serve.

Nutrition Calories: 159 Fat: 3.0 g.Protein: 7.1 g.Carbs: 26.1 g.Fiber: 2.9 g. Sugar: 3.0 g.Sodium: 300 mg.

336. Easy Coconut Quinoa

Preparation time: 15 minutes
Cooking time: 25 minutes
Servings: 4
Ingredients

- 2 tsp. extra-virgin olive oil
- 1 sweet onion, chopped
- 1 tbsp. fresh ginger, grated
- 2 tsp. garlic, minced
- 1 cup low-sodium chicken broth
- 1 cup coconut milk
- 1 cup quinoa, well rinsed and drained
- Sea salt, to taste
- 1/4 cup unsweetened coconut, shredded

Directions

1. Place a large saucepan over medium-high heat and add the oil.
2. Sauté the onion, ginger, and garlic until softened, about 3 minutes.
3. Add the chicken broth, coconut milk, and quinoa.
4. Bring the mixture to a boil, then reduce the heat to low and cover. Simmer the quinoa, occasionally stirring, until the

DIABETIC COOKBOOK FOR BEGINNERS

quinoa is tender and most of the liquid has been absorbed, about 20 minutes.

5. Season the quinoa with salt, and serve topped with coconut.

Nutrition Calories: 355 Fat: 21.1 g.Protein: 9.1 g.Carbs: 35.1 g.Fiber: 6.1 g.Sugar: 4.0 g.Sodium: 33 mg.

337. Linguine With Kale Pesto

Preparation time: 10 minutes
Cooking time: 20 minutes
Servings: 6
Ingredients

- 1/2 cup kale, shredded
- 1/2 cup fresh basil
- 1/2 cup sun-dried tomatoes
- 1/4 cup almonds, chopped
- 2 tbsp. extra virgin olive oil
- 8 oz. (227 g.) dry whole-wheat linguine
- 1/2 cup Parmesan cheese, grated

Directions

1. Place the kale, basil, sun-dried tomatoes, almonds, and olive oil in a food processor or blender, and pulse until chunky paste forms, about 2 minutes. Scoop the pesto into a bowl and set it aside.
2. Place a large pot filled with water on high heat and bring to a boil.
3. Cook the pasta al dente, according to the package directions.
4. Drain the pasta and toss it with the pesto and the Parmesan cheese.
5. Serve immediately.

Nutrition Calories: 218 Fat: 10.1 g. P Protein: 9.1 g.Carbs: 25.1 g. Fiber: 1.1 g.Sugar: 2.9 g.Sodium: 195 mg.

338. Lemon Wax Beans

Preparation time: 5 minutes
Cooking time: 15 minutes
Servings: 4
Ingredients

- 2 lbs. (907 g.) wax beans
- 2 tbsp. extra virgin olive oil
- Sea salt and freshly ground black pepper, to taste
- 1/2 lemon juice

Directions

1. Preheat the oven to 400°F (205°C).
2. Line a baking sheet with aluminum foil.

3. In a large bowl, toss the beans and olive oil. Season lightly with salt and pepper.
4. Transfer the beans to the baking sheet and spread them out.
5. Roast the beans until caramelized and tender, about 10–12 minutes.
6. Transfer the beans to a serving platter and sprinkle with lemon juice.

Nutrition Calories: 99 Fat: 7.1 g.Protein: 2.1 g.Carbs: 8.1 g.Fiber: 4.2 g.Sugar: 3.9 g.Sodium: 814 mg.

339. Navy Bean Pico de Gallo

Preparation time: 20 minutes
Cooking time: 0 minutes
Servings: 4
Ingredients

- 2 1/2 cups cooked navy beans
- 1 tomato, diced
- 1/2 red bell pepper, seeded and chopped
- 1/4 jalapeño pepper, chopped
- 1 scallion, white and green parts, chopped
- 1 tsp. garlic, minced
- 1 tsp. ground cumin
- 1/2 tsp. ground coriander
- 1/2 cup low-sodium feta cheese

Directions

1. Put the beans, tomato, bell pepper, jalapeño, scallion, garlic, cumin, and coriander in a medium bowl and stir until well mixed.
2. Top with the feta cheese and serve.

Nutrition Calories: 225 Fat: 4.1 g. Protein: 14.1 g.Carbs: 34.1 g.Fiber: 13.1 g.Sugar: 3.9 g.Sodium: 165 mg.

340. Tomato and Navy Bean Bake

Preparation time: 10 minutes
Cooking time: 25 minutes
Servings: 8
Ingredients

- 1 tsp. extra-virgin olive oil
- 1/2 sweet onion, chopped
- 2 tsp. garlic, minced
- 2 sweet potatoes, peeled and diced
- 1 can (28 oz./794 g.) low-sodium diced tomatoes
- 1/4 cup sodium-free tomato paste
- 2 tbsp. granulated sweetener

- 2 tbsp. hot sauce
- 1 tbsp. Dijon mustard
- 3 cans (15 oz./425 g.) sodium-free navy or white beans, drained
- 1 tbsp. fresh oregano, chopped

Directions

1. Place a large saucepan over medium-high heat and add the oil.
2. Sauté the onion and garlic until translucent, about 3 minutes.
3. Stir in the sweet potatoes, diced tomatoes, tomato paste, sweetener, hot sauce, and mustard, and bring to a boil.
4. Reduce the heat and simmer the tomato sauce for 10 minutes.
5. Stir in the beans and simmer for 10 minutes more.
6. Stir in the oregano and serve.

Nutrition Calories: 256 Fat: 2.1 g. Protein: 15.1 g. Carbs: 48.1 g.Fiber: 11.9 g. Sugar: 8.1 g. Sodium: 150 mg.

341. Triple Bean Chili

Preparation time: 20 minutes
Cooking time: 60 minutes
Servings: 8
Ingredients

- 1 tsp. extra-virgin olive oil
- 1 sweet onion, chopped
- 1 red bell pepper, seeded and diced
- 1 green bell pepper, seeded and diced
- 2 tsp. garlic, minced
- 1 can (28 oz./794 g.) can low-sodium diced tomatoes
- 1 can (15 oz./425 g.) can sodium-free black beans, rinsed and drained
- 1 can (15 oz./425 g.) can sodium-free red kidney beans, rinsed and drained
- 1 can (15 oz./425 g.) can sodium-free navy beans, rinsed and drained
- 2 tbsp. chili powder
- 2 tsp. ground cumin
- 1 tsp. ground coriander
- 1/4 tsp. red pepper flakes

Directions

1. Place a large saucepan over medium-high heat and add the oil.
2. Sauté the onion, red and green bell peppers, and garlic until the vegetables have softened, about 5 minutes.

3. Add the tomatoes, black beans, red kidney beans, navy beans, chili powder, cumin, coriander, and red pepper flakes to the pan.
4. Bring the chili to a boil, then reduce the heat to low.
5. Simmer the chili, occasionally stirring, for at least 1 hour.
6. Serve hot.

Nutrition Calories: 480 Fat: 28.1 g.Protein: 15.1 g.Carbs: 45.1 g.Fiber: 16.9 g.Sugar: 4.0 g.Sodium: 16 mg.

342. Farro and Avocado Bowl

Preparation time: 5 minutes
Cooking time: 25 minutes
Servings: 4
Ingredients

- 3 cups water
- 1 cup uncooked farro
- 1 tbsp. extra-virgin olive oil
- 1 tsp. ground cumin
- 1/2 tsp. salt
- 1/2 tsp. freshly ground black pepper
- 4 hardboiled eggs, sliced
- 1 avocado, sliced
- 1/3 cup plain low-fat Greek yogurt
- 4 lemon wedges

Directions

1. In a medium saucepan, bring the water to a boil over high heat.
2. Pour the farro into the boiling water, and stir to submerge the grains. Reduce the heat to medium and cook for 20 minutes. Drain and set aside.
3. Heat a medium skillet over medium-low heat. When hot, pour in the oil, add the cooked farro, cumin, salt, and pepper. Cook for 3–5 minutes, stirring occasionally.
4. Divide the farro into 4 equal portions, and top each with one-quarter of the eggs, avocado, and yogurt. Add a squeeze of lemon over the top of each portion.

Nutrition Calories: 333 Fat: 16.1 g. Protein: 15.1 g. Carbs: 31.9 g. Fiber: 7.9 g.Sugar: 2.0 g.Sodium: 360 mg.

343. Black-Eyed Peas Curry

Preparation time: 15 minutes
Cooking time: 40 minutes
Servings: 12
Ingredients

- 1 lb. (454 g.) dried black-eyed peas, rinsed and drained
- 4 cups vegetable broth
- 1 cup coconut water
- 1 cup onion, chopped
- 4 large carrots, coarsely chopped
- 11/2 tbsp. curry powder
- 1 tbsp. garlic, minced
- 1 tsp. fresh ginger, peeled and minced
- 1 tbsp. extra-virgin olive oil
- Kosher salt (optional)
- Lime wedges, for serving

Directions

1. Combine the black-eyed peas, broth, coconut water, onion, carrots, curry powder, garlic, and ginger in the electric pressure cooker. Drizzle the olive oil over the top.
2. Close and lock the lid of the pressure cooker. Set the valve to sealing.
3. Cook on high pressure for 25 minutes.
4. When the cooking is complete, hit CANCEL, allow the pressure to release naturally for 10 minutes, and quickly release any remaining pressure.
5. Once the pin drops, unlock and remove the lid.
6. Season with salt (if using) and squeeze some fresh lime juice on each serving.

Nutrition Calories: 113 Fat: 3.1 g.Protein: 10.1 g.Carbs: 30.9 g.Fiber: 6.1 Sugar: 6.0 g.Sodium: 672 mg.

344. Classic Texas Caviar

Preparation time: 10 minutes
Cooking time: 20 minutes
Servings: 6
Ingredients
For the salad

- 1 ear fresh corn, kernels removed
- 1 cup cooked lima beans
- 1 cup cooked black-eyed peas
- 1 red bell pepper, chopped
- 2 celery stalks, chopped
- 1/2 red onion, chopped

For the dressing

- 3 tbsp. apple cider vinegar
- 1 tsp. paprika
- 2 tbsp. extra-virgin olive oil

Directions

1. Combine the corn, beans, peas, bell pepper, celery, and onion in a large bowl. Stir to mix well.
2. Combine the vinegar, paprika, and olive oil in a small bowl. Stir to combine well.
3. Pour the dressing into the salad and toss to mix well. Let sit for 20 minutes to infuse before serving.

Nutrition Calories: 170 Fat: 5.0 g.Protein: 10.0 g.Carbs: 29.0 g.Fiber: 10.0 g.Sugar: 4.0 g.Sodium: 20 mg.

345. Crispy Cowboy Black Bean Fritters

Preparation time: 10 minutes
Cooking time: 25 minutes
Servings: 20 Fritters
Ingredients

- 13/4 cups all-purpose flour
- 1/2 tsp. cumin
- 2 tsp. baking powder
- 2 tsp. salt
- 1/2 tsp. black pepper
- 4 egg whites, lightly beaten
- 1 cup salsa
- 2 cans (16 oz./454 g.) no-salt-added black beans, rinsed and drained
- 1 tbsp. canola oil, plus extra if needed

Directions

1. Combine the flour, cumin, baking powder, salt, and pepper in a large bowl, then mix the egg whites and salsa. Add the black beans and stir to mix well.
2. Heat the canola oil in a non-stick skillet over medium-high heat.
3. Spoon 1 tsp. of the mixture into the skillet to make a fritter. Make more fritters to coat the bottom of the skillet. Keep a little space between every 2 fritters. You may need to work in batches to avoid overcrowding.
4. Cook for 3 minutes or until the fritters are golden brown on both sides. Flip them and flatten them with a spatula halfway through the cooking time.

Repeat with the remaining mixture. Add more oil as needed.

5. Serve immediately.

Nutrition Calories: 115 Fat: 1.0 g.Protein: 6.0 g.Carbs: 20.0 g.Fiber: 5.0 g.Sugar: 2.0 g.Sodium: 350 mg.

346. Cauliflower Puree

Preparation time: 10 minutes
Cooking time: 15 minutes
Servings: 6
Ingredients

- 2 1/2 lbs. cauliflower florets
- 1/2 leek, white and pale green part, halved
- 4 tbsp. butter
- 2 tsp. fresh parsley, diced
- 2 tbsp. low sodium chicken broth
- 2 tsp. extra virgin olive oil
- 4 garlic cloves, diced fine
- 1/4 tsp. salt
- 1/4 tsp. pepper

Directions

1. Place the cauliflower in a steamer basket over boiling water. Cover and steam for 10–15 minutes or until fork-tender.
2. Rinse the leek under water and pat dry. Chop into thin slices.
3. Heat the oil in a large skillet over medium-low heat. Add the leek and cook 2–3 minutes, or until soft. Add the garlic and cook 1 minute more.
4. Add all the ingredients to a food processor and pulse until almost smooth. Serve warm, or refrigerate for later use.

Nutrition Calories: 146 Total carbs: 14 g.Net carbs: 8 g.Protein: 5 g.Fat: 9 g.Sugar: 6 g.Fiber: 6 g.

347. Cauliflower "Rice"

Preparation time: 5 minutes
Cooking time: 10 minutes
Servings: 4
Ingredients

- 1 small head cauliflower, separated into small florets
- 1 tbsp. olive oil
- 1 garlic clove, diced fine
- 1/2 tsp. salt

Directions

1. Use a cheese grater to rice the cauliflower, using the big holes. Or, use a food processor and short pulses until it resembles rice.
2. In a non-stick skillet, over medium-high heat, heat oil until hot. Add the garlic and salt cook for 1 minute, stirring frequently. Add cauliflower and cook, stirring, for 7–9 minutes, or until it is tender and starts to brown.
3. Serve it as is, or use it in your favorite recipes.

Nutrition Calories: 48 Total carbs: 4 g.Net carbs: 2 g Protein: 1 g.Fat: 4 g.Sugar: 2 g.Fiber: 2 g.

348. Cauliflower Pizza Crust

Preparation time: 15 minutes
Cooking time: 30 minutes
Servings: 8
Ingredients

- 1 1/2 lb. cauliflower, separated in florets
- 1 egg
- 1 1/2 cup reduced-fat Parmesan cheese
- 1/2 tbsp. Italian seasoning
- 1/2 tsp. garlic powder

Directions

1. Heat oven to 400°F.
2. Line a pizza pan or stone with parchment paper.
3. Place the cauliflower in a food processor and pulse until it resembles rice.
4. Cook the cauliflower in a skillet over medium heat, frequently stirring, until soft, about 10 minutes.
5. In a large bowl, whisk the egg, cheese, and seasonings. Place the cauliflower in a clean kitchen towel and squeeze out any excess moisture. Stir into cheese mixture to form a soft dough, press with a spatula if needed. Spread the dough on the prepared pan about 1/4-inch thick. Bake for 20 minutes, or until the top is dry and firm and edges are golden brown. Let it cool for 5–10 minutes; the crust will firm up as it cools. Add desired toppings and bake for 5–10 minutes more. Slice and serve.

Nutrition Calories: 158 Total carbs: 10 g.Net carbs: 6 g.Protein: 12 g.Fat: 9 g.Sugar: 4 g.Fiber: 4 g.

349. Cheese Biscuits

Preparation time: 20 minutes
Cooking time: 20 minutes
Servings: 16
Ingredients

- 8 oz. low-fat cream cheese
- 3 cup Mozzarella cheese, grated
- 4 eggs
- 2 tbsp. margarine, melted
- 1 1/3 cup almond flour
- 4 tbsp. baking powder
- Non-stick cooking spray

Directions

1. Heat the oven to 400°F.
2. Spray a 12-inch cast-iron skillet with cooking spray
3. In a saucepan over low heat, melt the cream cheese and mozzarella together. Stir until smooth. Remove from heat.
4. In a large bowl, combine the melted cheese, eggs, baking powder, and flour. Mix until smooth. Let rest for 10–20 minutes.
5. Use a large cookie spoon to scoop out the dough and place it in a prepared skillet. Refrigerate for 10 minutes.
6. Bake for 20–25 minutes, until golden brown. Brush biscuits with melted margarine.

Nutrition Calories: 106 Total carbs: 5 g. Net carbs: 4 g. Protein: 7 g. Fat: 8 g. Sugar: 0 g. Fiber: 1 g.

350. Cheesy Cauliflower Puree

Preparation time: 5 minutes
Cooking time: 15 minutes
Servings: 6
Ingredients

- 2 1/2 lbs. cauliflower florets, steamed
- 4 oz. reduced-fat sharp cheddar cheese, grated
- 2 tbsp. half-n-half
- 1 tbsp. butter
- 1/2 tsp. salt
- 1/2 tsp. pepper

Directions

1. Steam the cauliflower until it is fork-tender, drain.
2. Add the cauliflower and the remaining ingredients to a food processor. Pulse until almost smooth.

3. Serve warm.
4. You can make it ahead of time and just reheat it as needed also.

Nutrition Calories: 145 Total carbs: 10 g. Net carbs: 5 g. Protein: 9 g. Fat: 9 g. Sugar: 5 g. Fiber: 5 g.

351. Chickpea Tortillas

Preparation time: 5 minutes
Cooking time: 10 minutes
Servings: 4
Ingredients

- 1 cup chickpea flour
- 1 cup water
- 1/4 tsp. salt
- Non-stick cooking spray

Directions

1. In a large bowl, whisk all the ingredients together until no lumps remain.
2. Spray a skillet with cooking spray and place over medium-high heat.
3. Pour the batter in 1/4 cup at a time, and tilt the pan to spread it well.
4. Cook until golden brown on each side for 2 minutes per side.
5. Use it for taco shells, enchiladas, quesadillas, or whatever you desire.

Nutrition Calories: 89 Total carbs: 13 g. Net carbs: 10 g. Protein: 5 g. Fat: 2 g. Sugar: 3 g. Fiber: 3 g.

352. "Cornbread" Stuffing

Preparation time: 15 minutes
Cooking time: 40 minutes
Servings: 6
Ingredients

- 1 strip bacon, diced
- 1 egg
- 1 cup onion, diced
- 1 cup celery, diced
- 2 tbsp. margarine, divided
- 1 cup almond flour
- 1/4 cup low-sodium chicken broth
- 3 cloves garlic, diced fine
- 2 tbsp. stone-ground cornmeal
- 1 tsp. thyme
- 1 tsp. sage
- 3/4 tsp. salt
- Fresh ground black pepper, to taste

Directions

1. Heat the oven to 375°F.

2. Melt 1 tbsp. of margarine in a skillet over low heat. Add the onions and celery and cook, stirring, until soft, about 10 minutes. Add the garlic and seasonings and cook for 1–2 minutes more. Remove from heat and let it cool.

3. Place the almond flour, cornmeal, and bacon in a food processor, and pulse until combined. Add the broth and egg, and pulse to combine. Add the onion mixture and pulse just until mixed.

4. Place the remaining tbsp. of margarine in a cast-iron skillet or baking dish, and melt in the oven until hot. Swirl the pan to coat with melted margarine.

5. Spread the dressing in the pan and bake for 30 minutes or until the top is nicely browned and the center is cooked.

6. Serve.

Nutrition Calories: 177 Total carbs: 9 g.Net carbs: 6 g.Protein: 6 g.Fat: 14 g.Sugar: 2 g.Fiber: 3 g.

353. "Flour" Tortillas

Preparation time: 10 minutes
Cooking time: 15 minutes
Servings: 4
Ingredients

- 3/4 cup egg whites
- 1/3 cup water
- 1/4 cup coconut flour
- 1 tsp. sunflower oil
- 1/2 tsp. salt
- 1/2 tsp. cumin
- 1/2 tsp. chili powder

Directions

1. Add all the ingredients, except oil, to a food processor and pulse until combined. Let rest for 7–8 minutes.

2. Heat the oil in a large skillet over med-low heat. Pour 1/4 cup batter into the center and tilt to spread to 7–8-inch circle.

3. When the top is no longer shiny, flip the tortilla and cook for 1–2 minutes. Repeat with the remaining batter.

4. Place each tortilla on parchment paper and lightly wipe off excess oil.

Nutrition Calories: 27 Total carbs: 1 g.Protein: 5 g.Fat: 0 g.Sugar: 0 g.Fiber: 0 g.

354. Flourless "Burger Buns"

Preparation time: 10 minutes
Cooking time: 35 minutes
Servings: 4
Ingredients

- 4 egg yolks, room temp
- 4 egg whites, room temp
- 1/4 cup low-fat ricotta cheese
- 1/4 cup reduced-fat Parmesan cheese
- 1/4 tsp. cream tartar

Directions

1. Heat oven to 300°F.

2. Line a baking sheet with parchment paper.

3. In a large bowl, whisk the egg yolks, ricotta, and parmesan cheese until smooth. In a separate bowl, beat the egg whites until foamy, then add in cream of tartar and beat until stiff peaks form.

4. Add some beaten egg white to the egg yolk mixture and mix lightly. Slowly and lightly fold in the remaining egg white to the egg yolk mixture until just blended.

5. Spoon the batter onto the prepared pan to make 8 buns; bake for 35 minutes. Use it like bread for sandwiches or eat it alone.

Nutrition Calories: 50 Total carbs: 1 g.Protein: 4 g.Fat: 3 g.Sugar: 1 g.Fiber: 0 g.

355. Fried Rice

Preparation time: 5 minutes
Cooking time: 15 minutes
Servings: 8
Ingredients

- 2 cups sugar snap peas
- 2 egg whites - 1 egg
- 1 cup instant brown rice, cooked according to directions
- 2 tbsp. lite soy sauce

Directions

1. Add the peas to the cooked rice and mix to combine.

2. In a small skillet, scramble the egg and egg whites. Add the rice and peas to the skillet and stir in soy sauce.

3. Cook, frequently stirring, about 2–3 minutes, or until heated. Serve.

Nutrition Calories: 107 Total carbs: 20 g.Net carbs: 19 g.Protein: 4 g.Fat: 1 g.Sugar: 1 g.Fiber: 1 g.

356. Garlic Basil Breadsticks

Preparation time: 10 minutes
Cooking time: 10 minutes
Servings: 4
Ingredients

- 2 eggs, beaten
- 2 cup mozzarella cheese, grated
- 2 tbsp. cream cheese
- 2 tbsp. fresh basil, diced
- 4 tbsp. coconut flour
- 4 cloves garlic, crushed
- Non-stick cooking spray

Directions

1. Heat oven to 400°F.
2. Spray a baking sheet with cooking spray.
3. Add mozzarella, cream cheese, crushed garlic, and basil to a microwaveable bowl. Mix and then cook for 1 minute. Stir well to make sure the cheeses are melted, and then add in the flour and egg.
4. Mix well; use your hands if needed to form into a dough.
5. Break off the pieces of the dough and roll into a long finger shape. Place on prepared pan.
6. Bake for 8–10 minutes or until the dough begins to brown. Remove from heat and let it cool slightly before serving.

Nutrition Calories: 153 Total carbs: 10 g.Net carbs: 5 g.Protein: 9 g.Fat: 8 g.Sugar: 1 g.Fiber: 5 g.

357. Healthy Loaf of Bread

Preparation time: 10 minutes
Cooking time: 30 minutes
Servings: 20
Ingredients

- 6 eggs, separated
- 4 tbsp. butter, melted
- 1 1/2 cup almond flour, sifted
- 3 tsp. baking powder
- 1/4 tsp. cream of tartar
- 1/8 tsp. salt
- Butter flavored cooking spray

Directions

1. Heat oven to 375°F. Spray an 8-inch loaf pan with cooking spray.
2. In a large bowl, beat the egg whites and cream of tartar until soft peaks form.

3. Add the yolks, 1/3 of egg whites, butter, flour, baking powder, and salt to a food processor and pulse until combined.
4. Add the remaining egg whites and pulse until thoroughly combined, being careful not to over mix the dough.
5. Pour into prepared pan and bake 30 minutes, or until bread passes the toothpick test.
6. Cool 10 minutes in the pan, then invert and cool completely before slicing.

Nutrition Calories: 81 Total carbs: 2 g.Net carbs: 1 g.Protein: 3 g.Fat: 7 g.Sugar: 0 g.Fiber: 1 g.

358. Homemade Pasta

Preparation time: 20 minutes
Cooking time: 5 minutes
Servings: 8
Ingredients

- 1 egg
- 2 egg yolks
- 1 3/4 cup soy flour
- 1/4 cup ground wheat germ
- 3–4 tbsp. cold water
- 1 tsp. light olive oil
- 1/2 tsp. salt

Directions

1. In a large bowl, whisk egg, the egg yolks, oil, and 3 tbsp. of water until smooth.
2. In a separate bowl, combine flour, wheat germ, and salt. Stir into egg mixture until smooth. Use the last tbsp. of water if needed to make a smooth dough.
3. Turn out onto a lightly floured surface and knead for 5–8 minutes or until smooth. Cover and let it rest for 10 minutes.
4. Divide the dough into 4 equal pieces and roll out, one at a time, as thin as possible, or run it through a pasta machine until it reaches the thinnest setting.
5. Let the dough dry out for 30 minutes. Cut into the desired size with a pasta machine or pizza cutter. If not used right away, let it dry overnight on a pasta or cooling rack. Fresh pasta should be used within 3 days.
6. After drying for just 1 hour, it will be stored in the freezer in an airtight bag for 6–8 months. Pasta dried overnight can

be stored in an airtight container for up to 1 week.

7. To cook it when fresh, add to a pot of boiling water for 4–5 minutes or until tender. Drying the pasta will take a couple of minutes longer.

NutritionCalories: 152 Total carbs: 12 g.Net carbs: 9 g.Protein: 16 g.Fat: 5 g.Sugar: 6 g.Fiber: 3 g.

359. Light Beer Bread

Preparation time: 5 minutes
Cooking time: 55 minutes
Servings: 14
Ingredients

- 1/4 cup butter, soft
- 12 oz. light beer
- 3 cup low-carb baking mix
- 1/3 cup Splenda®

Directions

1. Heat oven to 375°F. Use 1 tbsp. of butter to grease the bottom of a 9x5-inch loaf pan.
2. In a large bowl, whisk together beer, baking mix, and Splenda®. Pour into the prepared pan.
3. Bake for 45–55 minutes or until golden brown. Cool in pan 10 minutes, remove from pan, and cool on wire rack.
4. Melt the remaining butter in a microwave and brush over a warm loaf in a small glass bowl; cool for 15 minutes before slicing.

Nutrition Calories: 162 Total carbs: 16 g.Net carbs: 12 g.Protein: 9 g.Fat: 5 g.Sugar: 5 g.Fiber: 4 g.

360. Mexican "Rice"

Preparation time: 5 minutes
Cooking time: 10 minutes
Servings: 6
Ingredients

- 2 cups cauliflower rice, cooked
- 1 small jalapeño, seeded and diced fine
- 1/2 white onion, diced
- 1/2 cup water
- 1/2 cup tomato paste
- 3 garlic cloves, diced fine
- 2 tsp. salt
- 2 tsp. olive oil

Directions

1. Heat oil in a skillet over medium heat.
2. Add onion, garlic, jalapeño, and salt and cook 3–4 minutes, stirring frequently.
3. In a small bowl, whisk water and tomato paste together. Add to the skillet.
4. Cook, frequently stirring, for 3–5 minutes.
5. Stir in the cauliflower, and cook just until heated through and most of the liquid is absorbed.
6. Serve.

Nutrition Calories: 46 Total carbs: 7 g.Net carbs: 5 g.Protein: 2 g.Fat: 2 g.Sugar: 4 g.Fiber: 2 g.

361. No Corn "Cornbread"

Preparation time: 10 minutes
Cooking time: 25 minutes
Servings: 16
Ingredients

- 4 eggs, room temperature
- 1/3 cup butter, melted
- 1 1/2 cup almond flour, sifted
- 1/3 cup Splenda®
- 1 tsp. baking powder

Directions

1. Heat oven to 350°F.
2. Line an 8-inch baking dish with parchment paper.
3. In a large bowl, whisk together eggs, butter, and Splenda®. Stir in the flour and baking powder until no lumps remain.
4. Pour batter into prepared dish and smooth the top. Bake 25–30 minutes or until edges are golden brown and it passes the toothpick test.
5. Let cool 5 minutes before slicing and serving.

Nutrition Calories: 121 Total carbs: 6 g.Net carbs: 5 g.Protein: 3 g.Fat: 9 g.Sugar: 4 g.Fiber: 1 g.

362. Quick Coconut Flour Buns

Preparation time: 5 minutes
Cooking time: 20 minutes
Servings: 4
Ingredients

- 3 eggs, room temperature
- 2 tbsp. coconut milk, room temperature
- 1/4 cup coconut flour
- 2 tbsp. coconut oil, soft

- 1 tbsp. honey
- 1/2 tsp. baking powder
- 1/2 tsp. salt

Directions

1. Heat oven to 375°F.
2. Line a cookie sheet with parchment paper.
3. In a small bowl, sift together flour, baking powder, and salt.
4. In a medium bowl, combine eggs, coconut oil, milk, and honey, mix well. Slowly add the dry ingredients to the egg mixture; the batter will be thick but make sure there are no lumps.
5. Form into 4 balls and place on prepared pan. Press down into rounds 1/2-inch thick. Bake for 15–20 minutes or until the buns pass the toothpick test.

Nutrition Calories: 143 Total carbs: 6 g Protein: 4 g.Fat: 12 g.Sugar: 5 g.Fiber: 0 g.

363. Pizza Crust

Preparation time: 20 minutes
Cooking time: 40 minutes
Servings: 4
Ingredients

- 1 1/2 cup Mozzarella cheese, grated
- 2 oz. cream cheese
- 1 egg, beaten
- 3/4 cup almond flour
- 1/2 tsp. Italian seasoning
- 1/2 tsp. salt
- 1/2 tsp. garlic powder
- 1/2 tsp. onion powder

Directions

1. Heat oven to 400°F.
2. Line a large baking sheet with parchment paper.
3. In a large bowl, microwave cream cheese and Mozzarella for 60 seconds. Remove from the microwave and stir. Return to microwave and cook another 30 seconds. Stir until well combined.
4. Add the flour, salt, onion powder, garlic powder, and egg. Stir until almond flour is well incorporated into the cheese. If the mixture becomes too sticky, microwave for another 10–15 seconds to warm up.

5. Place the dough on parchment paper and roll out thin. Poke holes in the crust with a fork. Bake for 10 minutes.
6. Remove from the oven and turn over. Bake for another 10 minutes.
7. Remove from the oven and top with your desired pizza toppings.
8. Return to oven and bake another 10 minutes, until toppings are hot and cheese is melted.

Nutrition Calories: 198 Total carbs: 5 g.Net carbs: 3 g.Protein: 9 g.Fat: 17 g.Sugar: 1 g.Fiber: 2 g.

364. Kidney Bean Stew

Preparation time: 10 minutes
Cooking time: 15 minutes
Servings: 2
Ingredients

- 1 lb. cooked kidney beans
- 1 cup tomato passata
- 1 cup low-sodium beef broth
- 3 tbsp. Italian herbs

Directions

1. Mix all the ingredients in your instant pot.
2. Cook on STEW for 15 minutes.
3. Release the pressure naturally.

Nutrition Calories: 270Carbs: 16 g.Sugar: 3 g.Fat: 10 g.Protein: 23 g.

365. Chickpea Soup

Preparation time: 15 minutes
Cooking time: 35 minutes
Servings: 2
Ingredients

- 1 lb. cooked chickpeas
- 1 lb. vegetables, chopped
- 1 cup low-sodium vegetable broth
- 2 tbsp. mixed herbs

Directions

1. Mix all the ingredients in your instant pot.
2. Cook on STEW for 35 minutes.
3. Release the pressure naturally.

Nutrition Calories: 310Carbs: 20 g. Sugar: 3 g. Fat: 5 g.Protein: 27 g.

CHAPTER 10:

Salad And Vegetables

366. Classic Fried Pickles

Preparation time: 20 minutes
Cooking time: 10 minutes
Servings: 2
Ingredients

- 1 egg, whisked - 2 tbsp. buttermilk
- 1/2 cup fresh breadcrumbs
- 1/4 cup Romano cheese, grated
- 1/2 tsp. onion powder
- 1/2 tsp. garlic powder
- 1 1/2 cups dill pickle chips, pressed dry with kitchen towels

For mayo sauce

- 1/4 cup mayonnaise
- 1/2 tbsp. mustard
- 1/2 tsp. molasses - 1 tbsp. ketchup
- 1/4 tsp. ground black pepper

Directions

1. In a small bowl, whisk the egg with buttermilk. In another bowl, mix the breadcrumbs, cheese, onion powder, and garlic powder. Dredge the pickle chips in the egg mixture, then in the breadcrumb/cheese mixture. Cook in the preheated air fryer at 400°F for 5 minutes; shake the basket and cook for 5 minutes more.
2. Meanwhile, mix all the sauce ingredients until well combined.
3. Serve the fried pickles with the mayo sauce for dipping.

Nutrition Calories: 342 Fat: 28.5 gCarbs: 12.5 g.Protein: 9.1 g. Sugars: 4.9 g.

367. Fried Green Beans With Pecorino Romano

Preparation time: 15 minutes
Cooking time: 10 minutes
Servings: 3
Ingredients

- 2 tbsp. buttermilk

- 1 egg
- 4 tbsp. cornmeal
- 4 tbsp. tortilla chips, crushed
- 4 tbsp. Pecorino Romano cheese, finely grated
- Coarse salt and crushed black pepper, to taste
- 1 tsp. smoked paprika
- 12 oz. green beans, trimmed

Directions

1. In a small bowl, whisk together the buttermilk and egg.
2. Combine the cornmeal, tortilla chips, Pecorino Romano cheese, salt, black pepper, and paprika in a separate bowl.
3. Incline the green beans in the egg mixture, then in the cornmeal/cheese mixture. Place the green beans in the lightly greased cooking basket.
4. Cook in the preheated air fryer at 390°F for 4 minutes. Shake the basket and cook for a further 3 minutes.
5. Taste, adjust the seasonings, and serve with the dipping sauce if desired. Bon appétit!

Nutrition Calories: 340 Fat: 9.7 g. Carbs: 50.9 g. Protein: 12.8 g. Sugars: 4.7 g.

368. Spicy Glazed Carrots

Preparation time: 20 minutes
Cooking time: 10 minutes
Servings: 3
Ingredients

- 1 lb. carrots, cut into matchsticks
- 2 tbsp. peanut oil
- 1 tbsp. agave syrup
- 1 jalapeño, seeded and minced
- 1/4 tsp. dill
- 1/2 tsp. basil
- Salt and white pepper to taste

Directions

1. Preheat the air fryer to 380°F.

Toss all the ingredients together and place them in the air fryer basket.
3. Prepare for 15 minutes, pulsating the basket halfway through the cooking time.
4. Transfer to a serving platter and enjoy!

Nutrition Calories: 162 Fat: 9.3 g. Carbs: 20.1 g. Protein: 1.4 g. Sugars: 12.8 g.

369. Rainbow Vegetable Fritters

Preparation time: 20 minutes
Cooking time: 10 minutes
Servings: 2
Ingredients

- 1 zucchini, grated and squeezed
- 1 cup corn kernels
- 1/2 cup canned green peas
- 4 tbsp. all-purpose flour
- 2 tbsp. fresh shallots, minced
- 1 tsp. fresh garlic, minced
- 1 tbsp. peanut oil
- Sea salt and pepper, to taste
- 1 tsp. cayenne pepper

Directions

1. In a mixing bowl, thoroughly combine all the ingredients until everything is well incorporated.
2. Shape the mixture into patties. Spritz the air fryer carrier with cooking spray.
3. Cook in the preheated air fryer at 365°F for 6 minutes. Fit them over and cook for a further 6 minutes
4. Serve immediately and enjoy!

Nutrition Calories: 215 Fat: 8.4 g. Carbs: 31.6 g. Protein: 6 g. Sugars: 4.1 g.

370. Mediterranean Vegetable Skewers

Preparation time: 30 minutes
Cooking time: 10 minutes
Servings: 4
Ingredients

- 2 medium zucchinis, cut into 1-inch pieces
- 2 red bell peppers, cut into 1-inch pieces
- 1 green bell pepper, cut into 1-inch pieces
- 1 red onion, cut into 1-inch pieces
- 2 tbsp. olive oil
- Sea salt, to taste

- 1/2 tsp. black pepper, preferably freshly cracked
- 1/2 tsp. red pepper flakes

Directions

1. Soak the wooden skewers in water for 15 minutes.
2. Thread the vegetables on skewers; drizzle olive oil all over the vegetable skewers; sprinkle with spices.
3. Cook in the preheated air fryer at 400°F for 13 minutes.
4. Serve warm and enjoy!

Nutrition Calories: 138 Fat: 10.2 g. Carbs: 10.2 g. Protein: 2.2 g. Sugars: 6.6 g.

371. Roasted Veggies With Yogurt-Tahini Sauce

Preparation time: 20 minutes
Cooking time: 10 minutes
Servings: 4
Ingredients

- 1 lb. Brussels sprouts
- 1 lb. button mushrooms
- 2 tbsp. olive oil
- 1/2 tsp. white pepper
- 1/2 tsp. dill weed, dried
- 1/2 tsp. cayenne pepper
- 1/2 tsp. celery seeds
- 1/2 tsp. mustard seeds
- Salt, to taste

For the yogurt tahini sauce

- 1 cup plain yogurt
- 2 tbsp. tahini paste
- 1 tbsp. lemon juice
- 1 tbsp. extra-virgin olive oil
- 1/2 tsp. Aleppo pepper, minced

Directions

1. Toss the Brussels sprouts and mushrooms with olive oil and spices. Preheat your air fryer to 380°F.
2. Add the Brussels sprouts to the cooking basket and cook for 10 minutes.
3. Add the mushrooms, turn the temperature to 390°F and cook for 6 minutes more.
4. While the vegetables are cooking, make the sauce by whisking all ingredients. Serve the warm vegetables with the sauce on the side. Bon appétit!

Nutrition Calories: 254 Fat: 17.2 g. Carbs: 19.6 g. Protein: 11.1 g. Sugars: 8.1 g.

372. Swiss Cheese and Vegetable Casserole

Preparation time: 50 minutes
Cooking time: 48 minutes
Servings: 4
Ingredients

- 1 lb. (1/4-inch thick) potatoes, peeled and sliced
- 2 tbsp. olive oil
- 1/2 tsp. red pepper flakes, crushed
- 1/2 tsp. freshly ground black pepper
- Salt to taste
- 3 bell peppers, thinly sliced
- 1 Serrano pepper, thinly sliced
- 2 medium tomatoes, sliced
- 1 leek, thinly sliced
- 2 garlic cloves, minced
- 1 cup Swiss cheese, shredded
- Cooking oil

Directions

1. Preheat the air fryer to 350°F. Spray a casserole dish with cooking oil.
2. Place the potatoes in the casserole dish in an even layer; drizzle 1 tbsp. of olive oil over the top. Then swell the red pepper, black pepper, and salt.
3. Add 2 bell peppers and 1/2 of the leeks. Add the tomatoes and the remaining 1 tbsp. of olive oil.
4. Add the remaining peppers, leeks, and minced garlic. Top with the cheese.
5. Cover the casserole with foil and bake for 32 minutes. Remove the foil and increase the temperature to 400°F; bake an additional 16 minutes. Bon appétit!

Nutrition Calories: 328 Fat: 16.5 g. Carbs: 33.1 g. Protein: 13.1 g. Sugars: 7.6 g.

373. American-Style Brussels Sprout Salad

Preparation time: 35 minutes
Cooking time: 10 minutes
Servings: 4
Ingredients

- 1 lb. Brussels sprouts
- 1 apple, cored and diced
- 1/2 cup mozzarella cheese, crumbled
- 1/2 cup pomegranate seeds
- 1 small red onion, chopped
- 4 eggs, hardboiled and sliced
- Cooking spray

For the dressing

- 1/4 cup olive oil
- 2 tbsp. champagne vinegar
- 1 tsp. Dijon mustard
- 1 tsp. honey
- Sea salt and ground black pepper, to taste

Directions

1. Preheat the air fryer to 380°F.
2. Add the Brussels sprouts to the cooking basket. Grease with cooking spray and cook for 15 minutes. Let it cool to room temperature for 15 minutes.
3. Toss the Brussels sprouts with apple, cheese, pomegranate seeds, and red onion.
4. Mix all the ingredients for the dressing and toss to combine well. Serve topped with hard-boiled eggs. Bon appétit!

Nutrition Calories: 319 Fat: 18.5 g. Carbs: 27 g. Protein: 14.7 g. Sugars: 14.6 g.

374. The Best Cauliflower Tater Tots

Preparation time: 25 minutes
Cooking time: 10 minutes
Servings: 4
Ingredients

- 1 lb. cauliflower florets
- 2 eggs
- 1 tbsp. olive oil
- 2 tbsp. scallions, chopped
- 1 garlic clove, minced
- 1 cup Colby cheese, shredded
- 1/2 cup breadcrumbs
- Sea salt and ground black pepper, to taste
- 1/4 tsp. dill weed, dried
- 1 tsp. paprika

Directions

1. Blanch the cauliflower in salted boiling water for about 3–4 minutes until al dente. Drain well and pulse in a food processor.
2. Add the remaining ingredients; mix to combine well. Shape the cauliflower mixture into bite-sized tots.
3. Grease the air fryer basket with cooking spray.

4. Cook in the preheated air fryer at 375°F for 16 minutes, shaking halfway through the cooking time. Serve with your favorite sauce for dipping. Bon appétit!

Nutrition Calories: 267 Fat: 19.2 g. Carbs: 9.6 g. Protein: 14.9 g. Sugars: 2.9 g.

375. 3-Cheese Stuffed Mushrooms

Preparation time: 15 minutes
Cooking time: 10 minutes
Servings: 3
Ingredients

- 9 large button mushrooms, stems removed
- 1 tbsp. olive oil
- Salt and ground black pepper, to taste
- 1/2 tsp. rosemary, dried
- 6 tbsp. Swiss cheese, shredded
- 6 tbsp. Romano cheese, shredded
- 6 tbsp. cream cheese
- 1 tsp. soy sauce
- 1 tsp. garlic, minced
- 3 tbsp. green onion, minced

Directions

1. Brush the mushroom caps with olive oil; sprinkle with salt, pepper, and rosemary.
2. In a mixing bowl, thoroughly combine the remaining ingredients, mix them well, and divide the filling mixture among the mushroom caps.
3. Cook in the preheated air fryer at 390°F for 7 minutes.
4. Let the mushrooms cool slightly before serving. Bon appétit!

Nutrition Calories: 345 Fat: 28 g. Carbs: 11.2 g. Protein: 14.4 g. Sugars: 8.1 g.

376. Sweet Corn Fritters With Avocado

Preparation time: 20 minutes
Cooking time: 10 minutes
Servings: 3
Ingredients

- 2 cups sweet corn kernels
- 1 small onion, chopped
- 1 garlic clove, minced
- 2 eggs, whisked
- 1 tsp. baking powder
- 2 tbsp. fresh cilantro, chopped
- Sea salt and ground black pepper, to taste
- 1 avocado, peeled, pitted, and diced
- 2 tbsp. sweet chili sauce

Directions

1. Thoroughly combine the corn, onion, garlic, eggs, baking powder, cilantro, salt, and black pepper in a mixing bowl.
2. Shape the corn mixture into 6 patties and transfer them to the lightly greased air fryer basket.
3. Cook in the preheated air fryer at 370°F for 8 minutes; turn them over and cook for 7 minutes longer.
4. Serve the cakes with avocado and chili sauce.

Nutrition Calories: 383 Fat: 21.3 g. Carbs: 42.8 g. Protein: 12.7 g. Sugars: 9.2 g.

377. Greek-Style Vegetable Bake

Preparation time: 35 minutes
Cooking time: 10 minutes
Servings: 4
Ingredients

- 1 eggplant, peeled and sliced
- 2 bell peppers, seeded and sliced
- 1 red onion, sliced
- 1 tsp. fresh garlic, minced
- 4 tbsp. olive oil
- 1 tsp. mustard
- 1 tsp. oregano, dried
- 1 tsp. smoked paprika
- Salt and ground black pepper, to taste
- 1 tomato, sliced
- 6 oz. halloumi cheese, sliced lengthways

Directions

1. Start by preheating your air fryer to 370°F. Spritz a baking pan with non-stick cooking spray.
2. Place the eggplant, peppers, onion, and garlic on the baking pan's bottom. Add the olive oil, mustard, and spices. Transfer to the cooking basket and cook for 14 minutes.
3. Top with the tomatoes and cheese; increase the temperature to 390°F and cook for 5 minutes more until bubbling. Let it sit on a cooling rack for 10 minutes before serving. Bon appétit!

Nutrition Calories: 296 Fat: 22.9 g.Carbs: 16.1 g. Protein: 9.3 g. Sugars: 9.9 g.

378. Japanese Tempura Bowl

Preparation time: 20 minutes
Cooking time: 10 minutes
Servings: 3
Ingredients

- 1 cup all-purpose flour
- Kosher salt and ground black pepper, to taste
- 1/2 tsp. paprika
- 2 eggs
- 3 tbsp. soda water
- 1 cup panko crumbs
- 2 tbsp. olive oil
- 1 cup green beans
- 1 onion, cut into rings
- 1 zucchini, cut into slices
- 2 tbsp. soy sauce
- 1 tbsp. mirin
- 1 tsp. dashi granules

Directions

1. In a shallow bowl, mix the flour, salt, black pepper, and paprika.
2. In a separate bowl, whisk the eggs and soda water.
3. In a third shallow bowl, combine the panko crumbs with olive oil.
4. Dip the vegetables in the flour mixture, then in the egg mixture; lastly, roll over the panko mixture to coat evenly.
5. Cook in the preheated air fryer at 400°F for 10 minutes, shaking the basket halfway through the cooking time. Work in batches until the vegetables are crispy and golden brown.
6. Then, make the sauce by whisking the soy sauce, mirin, and dashi granules. Bon appétit!

Nutrition Calories: 446 Fat: 14.7 g.Carbs: 63.5 g. Protein: 14.6 g. Sugars: 3.8 g.

379. Balsamic Root Vegetables

Preparation time: 25 minutes
Cooking time: 17 minutes
Servings: 3
Ingredients

- 2 potatoes, cut into 1 1/2-inch piece
- 2 carrots, cut into 1 1/2-inch piece
- 2 parsnips, cut into 1 1/2-inch piece
- 1 onion, cut into 1 1/2-inch piece
- Pink Himalayan salt and ground black pepper, to taste
- 1/4 tsp. smoked paprika
- 1 tsp. garlic powder
- 1/2 tsp. thyme, dried
- 1/2 tsp. marjoram, dried
- 2 tbsp. olive oil
- 2 tbsp. balsamic vinegar

Directions

1. Toss all the ingredients in a large mixing dish.
2. Roast in the preheated air fryer at 400°F for 10 minutes. Shake the basket and cook for 7 minutes more.
3. Serve with some extra fresh herbs if desired. Bon appétit!

Nutrition Calories: 405 Fat: 9.7 g. Carbs: 74.7 g. Protein: 7.7 g. Sugars: 15.2 g.

380. Winter Vegetable Braise

Preparation time: 25 minutes
Cooking time: 10 minutes
Servings: 2
Ingredients

- 4 potatoes, peeled and cut into 1-inch pieces
- 1 celery root, peeled and cut into 1-inch pieces
- 1 cup winter squash
- 2 tbsp. unsalted butter, melted
- 1/2 cup chicken broth
- 1/4 cup tomato sauce
- 1 tsp. parsley
- 1 tsp. rosemary
- 1 tsp. thyme

Directions

1. Start by preheating the air fryer to 370°F. Add all the ingredients to a lightly greased casserole dish. Stir to combine well.
2. Bake in the preheated air fryer for 10 minutes.
3. Gently stir the vegetables with a large spoon and increase the temperature to 400°F; cook for 10 minutes more.
4. Serve in individual bowls with a few drizzles of lemon juice. Bon appétit!

Nutrition Calories: 358 Fat: 12.3 g. Carbs: 55.7 g. Protein: 7.7 g. Sugars: 7.4 g.

381. Family Vegetable Gratin

Preparation time: 35 minutes
Cooking time: 10 minutes
Servings: 4
Ingredients

- 1 lb. Chinese cabbage, roughly chopped
- 2 bell peppers, seeded and sliced
- 1 jalapeño pepper, seeded and sliced
- 1 onion, thickly sliced
- 2 garlic cloves, sliced
- 1/2 stick butter
- 4 tbsp. all-purpose flour
- 1 cup milk
- 1 cup cream cheese
- Sea salt and freshly ground black pepper, to taste
- 1/2 tsp. cayenne pepper
- 1 cup Monterey Jack cheese, shredded

Directions

1. Heat a pan of salted water and bring to a boil. Boil the Chinese cabbage for 2–3 minutes. Transfer it to cold water to stop the cooking process.
2. Place the cabbage in a lightly greased casserole dish. Add the peppers, onion, and garlic.
3. Next, melt the butter in a saucepan over moderate heat. Gradually add the flour and cook for 2 minutes to form a paste.
4. Slowly pour in the milk, stirring continuously, until a thick sauce forms. Add the cream cheese.
5. Season with salt, black pepper, and cayenne pepper. Add the mixture to the casserole dish.
6. Top with the shredded Monterey Jack cheese and bake in the preheated air fryer at 390°F for 25 minutes.
7. Serve hot.

Nutrition Calories: 373 Fat: 26.1 g. Carbs: 17.7 g. Protein: 18.7 g. Sugars: 7.7 g.

382. Sweet-and-Sour Mixed Veggies

Preparation time: 25 minutes
Cooking time: 10 minutes
Servings: 4
Ingredients

- 1/2 lb. sterling asparagus, cut into 1 1/2-inch piece
- 1/2 lb. broccoli, cut into 1 1/2-inch piece
- 1/2 lb. carrots, cut into 1 1/2-inch piece
- 2 tbsp. peanut oil
- Salt and white pepper, to taste
- 1/2 cup water
- 4 tbsp. raisins
- 2 tbsp. honey
- 2 tbsp. apple cider vinegar

Directions

1. Place the vegetables in a single layer in a lightly greased cooking basket. Drizzle the peanut oil over the vegetables.
2. Sprinkle with salt and white pepper.
3. Cook at 380°F for 15 minutes, shaking the basket halfway through the cooking time.
4. Add 1/2 cup of water to a saucepan; bring a rapid boil and add the raisins, honey, and vinegar. Prepare for 5–7 minutes or until the sauce has been reduced by half.
5. Spoon the sauce over the warm vegetables and serve immediately. Bon appétit!

Nutrition Calories: 153 Fat: 7.1 g. Carbs: 21.6 g. Protein: 3.6 g. Sugars: 14.2 g.

383. Carrot and Oat Balls

Preparation time: 25 minutes
Cooking time: 10 minutes
Servings: 3
Ingredients

- 4 carrots, grated
- 1 cup rolled oats, ground
- 1 tbsp. butter, room temperature
- 1 tbsp. chia seeds
- 1/2 cup scallions, chopped
- 2 cloves garlic, minced
- 2 tbsp. tomato ketchup
- 1 tsp. cayenne pepper
- 1/2 tsp. sea salt
- 1/4 tsp. ground black pepper
- 1/2 tsp. ancho chili powder
- 1/4 cup fresh breadcrumbs

Directions

1. Preheat your air fryer to 380°F.
2. In a bowl, mix all the ingredients until everything is well incorporated. Shape the batter into bite-sized balls.

3. Cook the balls for 15 minutes, shaking the basket halfway through the cooking time. Bon appétit!

Nutrition Calories: 215 Fat: 4.7 g. Carbs: 37.2 g. Protein: 7.5 g. Sugars: 5.6 g

384. Broccoli and Bacon Salad

Preparation time: 10 minutes
Cooking time: 0 minutes
Servings: 4
Ingredients

- 2 cups broccoli, separated into florets
- 4 slices bacon, chopped and cooked crisp
- 1/2 cup cheddar cheese, cubed
- 1/4 cup low-fat Greek yogurt
- 1/8 cup red onion, diced fine
- 1/8 cup almonds, sliced
- 1/4 cup reduced-fat mayonnaise
- 1 tbsp. lemon juice
- 1 tbsp. apple cider vinegar
- 1 tbsp. granulated sugar substitute
- 1/4 tsp. salt
- 1/4 tsp. pepper

Directions

1. In a large bowl, combine the broccoli, onion, cheese, bacon, and almonds.
2. In a small bowl, whisk the remaining ingredients together until combined.
3. Pour the dressing over the broccoli mixture and stir.
4. Cover and chill at least 1 hour before serving.

Nutrition Calories: 217 Total carbs: 12 g.Net carbs: 10 g.Protein: 11 g.Fat: 14 g.Sugar: 6 g.Fiber: 2 g.

385. Broccoli and Mushroom Salad

Preparation time: 10 minutes
Cooking time: 0 minutes
Servings: 4
Ingredients

- 4 sun-dried tomatoes, cut in half
- 3 cup torn leaf lettuce
- 1 1/2 cup broccoli florets
- 1 cup mushrooms, sliced
- 1/3 cup radishes, sliced
- 2 tbsp. water
- 1 tbsp. balsamic vinegar

- 1 tsp. vegetable oil
- 1/4 tsp. chicken bouillon granules
- 1/4 tsp. parsley
- 1/4 tsp. dry mustard
- 1/8 tsp. cayenne pepper

Directions

1. Place tomatoes in a small bowl and pour boiling water over, just enough to cover. Let stand 5 minutes, drain.
2. Chop tomatoes and place them in a large bowl. Add the lettuce, broccoli, mushrooms, and radishes.
3. In a jar with a tight-fitting lid, add the remaining ingredients and shake well. Pour over salad and toss to coat.
4. Serve.

Nutrition Calories: 54 Total carbs: 9 g.Net carbs: 7 g.Protein: 3 g.Fat: 2 g.Sugar: 2 g.Fiber: 2 g.

386. Cantaloupe and Prosciutto Salad

Preparation time: 15 minutes
Cooking time: 0 minutes
Servings: 4
Ingredients

- 6 mozzarella balls, quartered
- 1 medium cantaloupe, peeled and cut into small cubes
- 4 oz. prosciutto, chopped
- 1 tbsp. fresh lime juice
- 1 tbsp. fresh mint, chopped
- 2 tbsp. extra virgin olive oil
- 1 tsp. honey

Directions

1. Whisk together the oil, lime juice, honey, and mint; season with salt and pepper to taste.
2. Add the cantaloupe and mozzarella and toss to combine.
3. Arrange the mixture on a serving plate and add prosciutto. Serve.

Nutrition Calories: 240 Total carbs: 6 g.Protein: 18 g.Fat: 16 g.Sugar: 4 g.Fiber: 0 g.

387. Caprese Salad

Preparation time: 10 minutes
Cooking time: 0 minutes
Servings: 4
Ingredients

- 3 medium tomatoes, cut into 8 slices

- 2 (1 oz.) slices mozzarella cheese, cut into strips
- 1/4 cup fresh basil, sliced thin
- 2 tsp. extra-virgin olive oil
- 1/8 tsp. salt
- Pinch black pepper

Directions

1. Place the tomatoes and cheese on serving plates. Sprinkle with salt and pepper. Drizzle oil over and top with basil. Serve.

Nutrition Calories: 77 Total carbs: 4 g.Protein: 5 g.Fat: 5 g.Sugar: 2 g.Fiber: 1 g.

388. Celery Apple Salad

Preparation time: 5 minutes
Cooking time: 1 minutes
Servings: 4
Ingredients

- 2 green onions, diced
- 2 Medjool dates, pitted and diced fine
- 1 honey crisp apple, sliced thin
- 2 cup celery, sliced
- 1/2 cup celery leaves, diced
- 1/4 cup walnuts, chopped
- ½ cup Maple Shallot Vinaigrette

Directions

1. Heat the oven to 375°F.
2. Place the walnuts on a cookie sheet and bake for 10 minutes, stirring to toast.
3. In a large bowl, combine all the ingredients and toss to mix.
4. Drizzle the vinaigrette over and toss to coat.
5. Serve immediately.

Nutrition Calories: 171 Total carbs: 25 g.Net carbs: 21 g Protein: 3 g.Fat: 8 g Sugar: 15 g.Fiber: 4 g.

389. Chicken Guacamole Salad

Preparation time: 10 minutes
Cooking time: 20 minutes
Servings: 6
Ingredients

- 1 lb. chicken breast, boneless & skinless
- 2 avocados
- 1–2 jalapeño peppers, seeded & diced
- 1/3 cup onion, diced
- 3 tbsp. cilantro, diced
- 2 tbsp. fresh lime juice
- 2 garlic cloves, diced

- 1 tbsp. olive oil
- Salt and pepper, to taste

Directions

1. Heat oven to 400°F.
2. Line a baking sheet with foil.
3. Season the chicken with salt and pepper and place it on a prepared pan; bake for 20 minutes, or until chicken is cooked through. Let cool completely.
4. Once the chicken has cooled, shred or dice and add to a large bowl. Add the remaining ingredients and mix well, mashing the avocado as you mix it in; taste and season with salt and pepper as desired.
5. Serve immediately.

Nutrition Calories: 324 Total carbs: 12 g.Net carbs: 5 g.Protein: 23 g.Fat: 22 g.Sugar: 1 g.Fiber: 7 g.

390. Chopped Veggie Salad

Preparation time: 15 minutes
Cooking time: 0 minutes
Servings: 4
Ingredients

- 1 cucumber, chopped
- 1 pint cherry tomatoes, cut in half
- 3 radishes, chopped
- 1 yellow bell pepper chopped
- 1/2 cup fresh parsley, chopped
- 3 tbsp. lemon juice
- 1 tbsp. olive oil
- Salt to taste

Directions

1. Place all the ingredients in a large bowl and toss to combine.
2. Serve immediately, or cover and chill until ready to serve.

Nutrition Calories: 70 Total carbs: 9 g.Net carbs: 7 g.Protein: 2 g.Fat: 4 g.Sugar: 5 g.Fiber: 2 g.

391. Creamy Crab Slaw

Preparation time: 10 minutes, chill time: 1 hour
Cooking time: 0 minutes
Servings: 4
Ingredients

- 1/2 lb. cabbage, shredded
- 1/2 lb. red cabbage, shredded
- 2 eggs, hard-boiled and chopped
- 1/2 lemon juice

- 2 cans (6 oz.) crabmeat, drained
- 1/2 cup lite mayonnaise
- 1 tsp. celery seeds
- Salt and pepper, to taste

Directions

1. In a large bowl, combine both kinds of cabbage.
2. In a small bowl, combine mayonnaise, lemon juice, and celery seeds. Add to the cabbage and toss to coat.
3. Add the crab and eggs and toss to mix, season with salt and pepper.
4. Cover and refrigerate 1 hour before serving.

Nutrition Calories: 380 Total carbs: 25 g.Net carbs: 17 g.Protein: 18 g.Fat: 24 g.Sugar: 13 g.Fiber: 8 g.

392. Festive Holiday Salad

Preparation time: 10 minutes, chill time: 1 hour
Cooking time: 0 minutes
Servings: 8
Ingredients

- 1 head broccoli, separated into florets
- 1 head cauliflower, separated into florets
- 1 red onion, sliced thin
- 2 cup cherry tomatoes, halved
- 1/2 cup fat-free sour cream
- 1 cup lite mayonnaise
- 1 tbsp. Splenda®

Directions

1. In a large bowl, combine vegetables.
2. In a small bowl, whisk together mayonnaise, sour cream, and Splenda®. Pour over the vegetables and toss to mix.
3. Cover and refrigerate at least 1 hour before serving.

Nutrition Calories: 152 Total carbs: 12 g.Net carbs: 10 g.Protein: 2 g.Fat: 10 g.Sugar: 5 g.Fiber: 2 g.

393. Grilled Vegetable and Noodle Salad

Preparation time: 15 minutes
Cooking time: 10 minutes
Servings: 4
Ingredients

- 2 ears corn on the cob, husked
- 1 red onion, cut in 1/2-inch thick slices
- 1 tomato, diced fine
- 1/3 cup fresh basil, diced

- 1/3 cup feta cheese, crumbled
- 1 recipe Homemade Noodles, cook and drain
- 4 tbsp. Herb Vinaigrette,
- Non-stick cooking spray

Directions

1. Heat the grill to medium heat and spray the rack with cooking spray.
2. Place the corn and onions on the grill and cook, turning when needed, until lightly charred and tender, about 10 minutes.
3. Cut the corn off the cob and place it in a medium bowl. Chop the onion and add to the corn.
4. Stir in noodles, tomatoes, basil, and vinaigrette, toss to mix. Sprinkle cheese over the top and serve.

Nutrition Calories: 330 Total carbs: 19 g.Net carbs: 16 g.Protein: 10 g.Fat: 9 g.Sugar: 5 g.Fiber: 3 g.

394. Harvest Salad

Preparation time: 15 minutes
Cooking time: 25 minutes
Servings: 6
Ingredients

- 10 oz. kale, deboned and chopped
- 1 1/2 cup blackberries
- 1/2 butternut squash, cubed
- 1/4 cup goat cheese, crumbled

Maple Mustard Salad Dressing:

- 1 cup raw pecans
- 1/3 cup raw pumpkin seeds
- 1/4 cup cranberries, dried
- 3 1/2 tbsp. olive oil
- 1 1/2 tbsp. sugar-free maple syrup
- 3/8 tsp. salt, divided
- Pepper, to taste
- Non-stick cooking spray

Directions

1. Heat oven to 400°F.
2. Spray a baking sheet with cooking spray.
3. Spread the squash on the prepared pan, add 1 1/2 tbsp. of oil, 1/8 tsp. of salt, and pepper to squash and stir to coat the squash evenly. Bake for 20–25 minutes.
4. Place the kale in a large bowl. Add 2 tbsp. of oil and 1/2 tsp. of salt and massage it into the kale with your hands for 3–4 minutes.

5. Spray a clean baking sheet with cooking spray.

6. In a medium bowl, stir together pecans, pumpkin seeds, and maple syrup until the nuts are coated. Pour onto a prepared pan and bake 8–10 minutes; these can be baked simultaneously as the squash.

To assemble the salad: Place all of the ingredients in a large bowl. Pour dressing over and toss to coat. Serve.

Nutrition Calories: 436 Total carbs: 24 g.Net carbs: 17 g.Protein: 9 g.Fat: 37 g.Sugar: 5 g.Fiber: 7 g.

395. Healthy Taco Salad

Preparation time: 15 minutes
Cooking time: 10 minutes
Servings: 4
Ingredients

- 2 whole Romaine hearts, chopped
- 1 lb. lean ground beef
- 1 whole avocado, cubed
- 3 oz. grape tomatoes, halved
- 1/2 cup cheddar cheese, cubed
- 2 tbsp. red onion, sliced
- 1/2 batch Tangy Mexican Salad Dressing (chapter 16)
- 1 tsp. ground cumin
- Salt and pepper to taste

Directions

1. Cook ground beef in a skillet over medium heat. Cut the meat into little pieces as it cooks. Add seasonings and stir to combine. Drain the grease and let it cool for 5 minutes.

2. To assemble the salad, place all the ingredients into a large bowl. Toss to mix, add the dressing, and toss. Top with reduced-fat sour cream and/or salsa if desired.

Nutrition Calories: 449 Total carbs: 9 g.Net carbs: 4 g.Protein: 40 g.Fat: 22 g.Sugar: 3 g.Fiber: 5 g.

396. Holiday Apple and Cranberry Salad

Preparation time: 15 minutes
Cooking time: 0 minutes
Servings: 10
Ingredients

- 12 oz. salad greens

- 3 Honeycrisp apples, sliced thin
- 1/2 lemon
- 1/2 cup blue cheese, crumbled
- Apple Cider Vinaigrette
- 1 cup pecan halves, toasted
- 3/4 cup dried cranberries

Directions

1. Put the apple slices in a large plastic bag and squeeze the half lemon over them. Close the bag and shake to coat.

2. In a large bowl, layer the greens, apples, pecans, cranberries, and blue cheese. Just before serving, drizzle with enough vinaigrette to dress the salad. Toss to coat all the ingredients evenly.

Nutrition Calories: 291 Total carbs: 19 g.Net carbs: 15 g.Protein: 5 g.Fat: 23 g.Sugar: 13 g.Fiber: 4 g.

397. Layered Salad

Preparation time: 10 minutes
Cooking time: 0 minutes
Servings: 10
Ingredients

- 6 slices bacon, chopped and cooked crisp - 2 tomatoes, diced
- 2 stalks celery, sliced
- 1 head romaine lettuce, diced
- 1 red bell pepper, diced
- 1 cup frozen peas, thawed
- 1 cup sharp cheddar cheese, grated
- 1/4 cup red onion, diced fine
- 1 cup fat-free ranch dressing

Direction:

1. Use a 9x13-inch glass baking dish and layer half the lettuce, pepper, celery, tomatoes, peas, onion, cheese, bacon, and dressing. Repeat.

2. Serve or cover and chill until ready to serve.

Nutrition Calories: 130 Total arbs: 14 g.Net carbs: 12 g.Protein: 6 g.Fat: 6 g.Sugar: 5 g.Fiber: 2 g.

398. Lobster Roll Salad With Bacon Vinaigrette

Preparation time: 10 minutes
Cooking time: 35 minutes
Servings: 6
Ingredients

- 6 slices bacon

- 2 whole grain ciabatta rolls, halved horizontally
- 3 medium tomatoes, cut into wedges
- 2 (8 oz.) spiny lobster tails, fresh or frozen (thawed)
- 2 cups fresh baby spinach
- 2 cups romaine lettuce, torn
- 1 cup seeded cucumber, diced
- 1 cup red sweet peppers, diced
- 2 tbsp. shallot, diced fine
- 2 tbsp. fresh chives, diced fine
- 2 garlic cloves, diced fine
- 3 tbsp. white wine vinegar
- 3 tbsp. olive oil, divided

Direction

1. Heat a grill to medium heat or medium heat charcoals.
2. Rinse the lobster and pat dry; butterfly lobster tails. Place on the grill, cover, and cook for 25–30 minutes, or until meat is opaque.
3. Remove the lobster and let cool.
4. In a small bowl, whisk together 2 tbsp. of olive oil and garlic. Brush the cut sides of the rolls with the oil mixture. Place on the grill, cut side down, and cook until crisp, about 2 minutes; transfer to a cutting board.
5. While the lobster is cooking, chop bacon and cook in a medium skillet until crisp. Transfer to paper towels. Reserve 1 tbsp. of bacon grease.

To make the vinaigrette:

6. Combine the reserved bacon grease, vinegar, shallot, remaining 1 tbsp. of oil, and chives in a glass jar with an air-tight lid. Screw on the lid and shake to combine.
7. Remove the lobster from the shells and cut it into 1 1/2-inch piece. Cut rolls into 1-inch cubes.

To assemble salad:

8. Combine the spinach, romaine lettuce, tomatoes, cucumber, peppers, lobster, and bread cubes in a large bowl. Toss to combine; transfer to serving platter and drizzle with vinaigrette. Sprinkle bacon over the top and serve.

Nutrition Calories: 255 Total carbs: 18 g.Net carbs: 16 g.Protein: 20 g.Fat: 11 g.Sugar: 3 g.Fiber: 2 g.

399. Mustard "Potato" Salad

Preparation time: 15 minutes
Cooking time: 5 minutes
Servings: 8
Ingredients

- 2 lbs. cauliflower, separated into small florets
- 1 boiled egg, peeled and diced
- 1/2 cup celery, diced
- 1/4 cup red onion, diced
- 1/4 cup light mayonnaise
- 1 tbsp. pickle relish
- 1 tbsp. Dijon mustard
- 1/4 tsp. celery seed
- 1/4 tsp. black pepper

Directions

1. Place the cauliflower in a vegetable steamer and cook for 5 minutes, or until almost tender. Drain and let it cool.
2. In a small bowl, whisk together mayonnaise, relish, mustard, celery seed, and pepper.
3. Once cauliflower is cooled off, pat dry, and place it in a large bowl. Add the egg, celery, and onion.
4. Pour dressing over vegetables and mix gently to combine; cover and chill at least 2 hours before serving.

Nutrition Calories: 71 Total carbs: 9 g.Net carbs: 6 g.Protein: 3 g.Fat: 3 g.Sugar: 4 g.Fiber: 3 g.

400. Pecan Pear Salad

Preparation time: 15 minutes
Cooking time: 0 minutes
Servings: 8
Ingredients

- 10 oz. mixed greens
- 3 pears, chopped
- 1/2 cup blue cheese, crumbled
- 2 cup pecan halves
- 1 cup cranberries, dried
- 1/2 cup olive oil
- 6 tbsp. champagne vinegar
- 2 tbsp. Dijon mustard
- 1/4 tsp. salt

Directions

1. In a large bowl, combine greens, pears, cranberries, and pecans.

2. Whisk the remaining ingredients, except blue cheese, together in a small bowl.
3. Pour over the salad and toss to coat.
4. Serve topped with blue cheese crumbles.

Nutrition Calories: 325 Total carbs: 20 g.Net carbs: 14 g.Protein: 5 g.Fat: 26 g.Sugar: 10 g.Fiber: 6 g.

401. Pickled Cucumber and Onion Salad

Preparation time: 10 minutes
Cooking time: 0 minutes
Servings: 2
Ingredients

- 1/2 cucumber, peeled and sliced
- 1/4 cup red onion, sliced thin
- 1 tbsp. olive oil
- 1 tbsp. white vinegar
- 1 tsp. dill

Directions

1. Place all the ingredients in a medium bowl and toss to combine.
2. Serve.

Nutrition Calories: 79 Total carbs: 4 g.Net carbs: 3 g.Protein: 1 g.Fat: 7 g.Sugar: 2 g.Fiber: 1 g.

402. Pomegranate and Brussels Sprouts Salad

Preparation time: 10 minutes
Cooking time: 0 minutes
Servings: 6
Ingredients

- 3 slices bacon, cooked crisp and crumbled
- 3 cup Brussels sprouts, shredded
- 3 cup kale, shredded
- 1 1/2 cup pomegranate seeds
- 1/2 cup almonds, toasted and chopped
- 1/4 cup reduced-fat parmesan cheese, grated
- ½ cup Citrus Vinaigrette

Directions

1. Combine all the ingredients in a large bowl. Drizzle the vinaigrette over salad, and toss to coat well.
2. Serve garnished with more cheese if desired.

Nutrition Calories: 256 Total carbs: 15 g.Net carbs: 10 g.Protein: 9 g.Fat: 18 g.Sugar: 5 g.Fiber: 5 g.

403. Shrimp and Avocado Salad

Preparation time: 20 minutes
Cooking time: 5 minutes
Servings: 4
Ingredients

- 1/2 lb. raw shrimp, peeled and deveined
- 3 cups romaine lettuce, chopped
- 1 cup napa cabbage, chopped
- 1 avocado, pit removed and sliced
- 1/4 cup red cabbage, chopped
- 1/4 cucumber, julienned
- 2 tbsp. green onions, diced fine
- 2 tbsp. fresh cilantro, diced
- 1 tsp. fresh ginger, diced fine
- 2 tbsp. coconut oil
- 1 tbsp. sesame seeds
- 1 tsp. Chinese 5-spice
- 3 tbsp. Fat-free Ranch dressing

Directions

1. Toast the sesame seeds in a medium skillet over medium heat. Shake the skillet to prevent them from burning. Cook until they start to brown, about 2 minutes. Set aside.
2. Add the coconut oil to the skillet. Pat the shrimp dry and sprinkle with the 5-spice seasoning. Add to hot oil. Cook 2 minutes per side, or until they turn pink. Set aside.
3. Arrange the lettuce and cabbage on a serving platter. Top with green onions, cucumber, and cilantro. Add shrimp and avocado.
4. Drizzle with the desired amount of dressing and sprinkle sesame seeds over the top. Serve.

Nutrition Calories: 306 Total carbs: 20 g. Net carbs: 15 g.Protein: 15 Fat: 19 g.Sugar: 4 g.Fiber: 5 g.

404. Southwest Chicken Salad

Preparation time: 10 minutes
Cooking time: 0 minutes
Servings: 6
Ingredients

- 2 cups chicken, cooked and shredded
- 1 small red bell pepper, diced fine
- 1/4 cup red onion, diced fine
- 1/4 cup reduced-fat mayonnaise
- 1 1/2 tsp. ground cumin

- 1 tsp. garlic powder
- 1/2 tsp. coriander
- Salt and pepper to taste

Directions

1. Combine all the ingredients in a large bowl and mix to combine thoroughly. Taste and adjust seasonings as desired. Cover and chill until ready to serve.

Nutrition Calories: 117 Total carbs: 4 g.Net carbs: 0 g.Protein: 14 g.Fat: 5 g.Sugar: 2 g.Fiber: 0 g.

CHAPTER 11:

Sauces Dips And Dressing

405. Alfredo Sauce

Preparation time: 10 minutes
Cooking time: 10 minutes
Servings: 6
Ingredients

- 1/4 cup butter, grass-fed
- 1 cup cream cheese
- 1 1/2 cups heavy (whipping) cream
- 2 tsp. garlic, minced
- 1/4 tsp. salt
- 1/4 tsp. freshly ground black pepper
- 1 cup Parmesan cheese, grated

Directions

1. In a medium saucepan over medium heat, stir together the butter, cream cheese, and cream. Cook, whisking until the sauce is smooth and the butter and cheese are melted.
2. Add the garlic, salt, and pepper and whisk until well blended. Whisk in the Parmesan. Bring the sauce to a simmer and cook until it is slightly thickened about 5 minutes.
3. Cool the sauce completely and store it in a sealed container in the refrigerator for up to 3 days.

Nutrition Calories: 478 Fats: 48 g.Protein: 10 g.Carbs: 4 g.Net carbs: 4 g.Fiber: 0 g.

406. Classic Meat Sauce

Preparation time: 15 minutes
Cooking time: 40 minutes
Servings: 4
Ingredients

- 2 tbsp. olive oil
- 1 lb. (454 g.) grass-fed ground beef
- 1 onion, chopped
- 2 celery stalks, chopped
- 2 tbsp. garlic, minced - 1 can (28 oz./794 g.) sodium-free diced tomatoes
- 1/4 cup red wine

- 1/4 cup tomato paste
- 2 tsp. oregano, dried
- 2 tsp. basil, dried
- 1 tsp. parsley, dried - 1/2 tsp. sea salt
- 1/4 tsp. red pepper flakes

Directions

1. In a large pot over medium-high heat, warm the olive oil; brown the ground beef, stirring it occasionally until it's cooked through, about 6 minutes.
2. Stir in the onion, celery, and garlic and sauté them until they've softened about 3 minutes.
3. Add the rest of the ingredients.
4. Bring the sauce to a boil, then reduce the heat to low and simmer it for 25–30 minutes, stirring occasionally.
5. Cool the sauce completely and store it in a sealed container in the refrigerator for up to 4 days or freeze for 1 month.

Nutrition Calories: 457 Fats: 35 g.Protein: 21 g.Carbs: 13 g.Net carbs: 8 g.Fiber: 5 g.

407. Sriracha Peanut Sauce

Preparation time: 5 minutes
Cooking time: 0 minutes
Servings: 4
Ingredients

- 1/2 cup creamy peanut butter
- 2 tbsp. soy sauce (or coconut aminos)
- 1 tsp. Sriracha sauce
- 1 tsp. toasted sesame oil
- 1 tsp. garlic powder

Directions

1. In a food processor (or blender), blend the peanut butter, soy sauce, Sriracha sauce, sesame oil, and garlic powder until thoroughly mixed.
2. Pour into an airtight glass container and keep in the refrigerator for up to 1 week.

Nutrition Calories: 185 Fats: 15 g.Protein: 7 g.Carbs: 8 g.Net carbs: 6 g.Fiber: 2 g.

408. Tzatziki

Preparation time: 10 minutes
Cooking time: 0 minutes
Servings: 4
Ingredients

- 1/2 large English cucumber, unpeeled
- 1 1/2 cups Greek yogurt
- 2 tbsp. olive oil
- Pinch pink Himalayan salt
- Pinch freshly ground black pepper
- 1/2 lemon juice
- 2 garlic cloves, finely minced
- 1 tbsp. fresh dill

Directions

1. Halve the cucumber lengthwise, and use a spoon to scoop out and discard the seeds.
2. Grate the cucumber with a zester or grater onto a large plate lined with a few layers of paper towels. Close the paper towels around the grated cucumber, and squeeze as much water out of it as you can. (This can take a while and can require multiple paper towels. You can also allow it to drain overnight in a strainer or wrapped in a few layers of cheesecloth in the fridge if you have the time.) In a food processor (or blender), blend the yogurt, olive oil, pink Himalayan salt, pepper, lemon juice, and garlic until fully combined. Transfer the mixture to a medium bowl, and mix in the fresh dill and grated cucumber.
3. I like to chill this sauce for at least 30 minutes before serving. Keep in a sealed glass container in the refrigerator for up to 1 week.

Nutrition Calories: 149 Fats: 11 g.Protein: 8 g.Carbs: 5 g.Net carbs: 4 g.Fiber: 1 g.

409. Cheesy Hot Crab Sauce

Preparation time: 10 minutes
Cooking time: 5–6 hours
Servings: 4
Ingredients

- 8 oz. (227 g.) cream cheese
- 8 oz. (227 g.) goat cheese
- 1 cup sour cream
- 1/2 cup Asiago cheese, grated
- 1 sweet onion, finely chopped
- 1 tbsp. granulated erythritol
- 2 tsp. garlic, minced
- 12 oz. (340 g.) crab meat, flaked - 1 scallion, white and green parts, chopped

Directions

1. Stir together the cream cheese, goat cheese, sour cream, Asiago cheese, onion, erythritol, garlic, crab meat, and scallion in a large bowl until well mixed.
2. Transfer the mixture to an 8x4-inch loaf pan and place it in the pan in the insert of the slow cooker.
3. Cover and cook on LOW for 5–6 hours.
4. Serve warm.

Nutrition Calories: 361 Fats: 28 g.Protein: 17 g.Carbs: 10 g.Net carbs: 8 g.Fiber: 2 g.

410. Enchilada Sauce

Preparation time: 10 minutes
Cooking time: 7–8 hours
Servings: 4
Ingredients

- 1/4 cup extra-virgin olive oil, divided
- 2 cups tomatoes, puréed
- 1 cup water - 1 sweet onion, chopped
- 2 jalapeño peppers, chopped
- 2 tsp. garlic, minced
- 2 tbsp. chili powder
- 1 tsp. ground coriander

Directions

1. Lightly grease the container of the slow cooker with 1 tbsp. of olive oil.
2. Place in the container the remaining 3 tbsp. of the olive oil, tomatoes, water, onion, jalapeño peppers, garlic, chili powder, and coriander.
3. Cover and cook on LOW for 7–8 hours.
4. Serve over poultry or meat. After cooling, store the sauce in a sealed container in the refrigerator for up to 1 week.

Nutrition Calories: 92 Fats: 8 g.Protein: 2 g.Carbs: 4 g.Net carbs: 2 g.Fiber: 2 g.

411. Salsa de Queso

Preparation time: 10 minutes
Cooking time: 3–4 hours
Servings: 4
Ingredients

- 1 tbsp. extra-virgin olive oil
- 12 oz. (340 g.) cream cheese
- 1 cup sour cream - 2 cups salsa verde

- 1 cup Monterey Jack cheese, shredded

Directions

1. Lightly grease the container of the slow cooker with olive oil. Stir together the cream cheese, sour cream, salsa verde, and Monterey Jack cheese in a large bowl until blended.
2. Transfer the mixture to the container.
3. Cover and cook on LOW for 3–4 hours.
4. Serve warm.

Nutrition Calories: 278 Fats: 25 g.Protein: 9 g.Carbs: 4 g.Net carbs: 4 g.Fiber: 0 g.

412.   Bolognese Sauce

Preparation time: 15 minutes
Cooking time: 7–8 hours
Servings: 10
Ingredients

- 3 tbsp. extra-virgin olive oil, divided
- 1 lb. (454 g.) ground pork
- 1/2 lb. (227 g.) ground beef
- 1/2 lb. (227 g.) bacon, chopped
- 1 sweet onion, chopped
- 1 tbsp. garlic, minced
- 2 celery stalks, chopped
- 1 carrot, chopped
- 2 cans (28 oz./794 g.) diced tomatoes
- 1/2 cup coconut milk
- 1/4 cup apple cider vinegar

Directions

1. Lightly grease the container of the slow cooker with 1 tbsp. of olive oil.
2. In a large skillet over medium-high heat, heat the remaining 2 tbsp. of the olive oil. Add the pork, beef, and bacon, and sauté until cooked through, about 7 minutes. Stir in the onion and garlic and sauté for an additional 2 minutes. Transfer the meat mixture to the insert and add the celery, carrot, tomatoes, coconut milk, and apple cider vinegar.
3. Cover and cook on LOW for 7–8 hours.
4. Serve, or cool completely, and store in the refrigerator in a sealed container for up to 4 days, or in the freezer for 1 month.

Nutrition Calories: 333 Fats: 23 g.Protein: 25 g Carbs: 9 g.Net carbs: 6 g.Fiber: 3 g.

413.   Carolina BBQ Sauce

Preparation time: 10 minutes
Cooking time: 3 hours
Servings: 2
Ingredients

- 3 tbsp. extra virgin olive oil, divided
- 2 cans (6 oz./170 g.) tomato paste
- 1/2 cup apple cider vinegar
- 1/2 cup water
- 1/4 cup granulated erythritol
- 1 tbsp. smoked paprika
- 1 tsp. garlic powder
- 1 tsp. onion powder
- 1/2 tsp. chili powder
- 1/4 tsp. salt

Directions

1. Grease the container of the slow cooker with 1 tbsp. of olive oil.
2. In a large bowl, whisk the tomato paste, remaining olive oil, vinegar, water, erythritol, paprika, garlic powder, onion powder, chili powder, and salt until blended.
3. Pour the mixture into the slow cooker container.
4. Cover and cook on LOW for 3 hours.
5. After cooling, store the sauce in a container in the refrigerator for up to 2 weeks.

Nutrition Calories: 21 Fats: 1 g.Protein: 0 g.Carbs: 2 g.Net carbs: 1 g.Fiber: 1 g.

414.   Aioli

Preparation time: 10 minutes
Cooking time: 0 minutes
Servings: 8
Ingredients

- 1 large egg
- 2 tsp. Dijon mustard
- 1 1/2 tsp. garlic, minced
- 1 cup olive oil
- 1 tbsp. lemon juice, freshly squeezed
- Sea salt to taste, for seasoning

Directions

1. In a medium bowl, whisk together the egg, mustard, and garlic until they're well blended, about 2 minutes.

2. Slowly add the olive oil in a thin, continuous stream, constantly whisking until the aioli is thick. Whisk in the lemon juice and season the aioli with salt.

3. Store the aioli in an airtight container in the refrigerator for up to 4 days.

Nutrition Calories: 124 Fats: 14 g.Protein: 0 g.Carbs: 0 g.Net carbs: 0 g.Fiber: 0 g.

415. Basil and Spinach Pesto

Preparation time: 10 minutes
Cooking time: 0 minutes
Servings: 2 cups
Ingredients

- 2 cups fresh spinach
- 1 cup fresh basil leaves
- 3 garlic cloves, smashed
- 1/4 cup pecans
- 1/4 cup Parmesan cheese, grated
- 1/2 cup olive oil
- Sea salt to taste, for seasoning
- Freshly ground black pepper to taste, for seasoning

Directions

1. Put the spinach, basil, garlic, pecans, and Parmesan in a blender and pulse until the mixture is finely chopped, scraping down the sides of the blender once.

2. While the blender is running, pour the olive oil in a thin stream and blend until the pesto is smooth. Season it with salt and pepper.

3. Store in a sealed container in the refrigerator for up to 1 week.

Nutrition Calories: 60 Fats: 6 g.Protein: 1 g.Carbs: 1 g.Net carbs: 1 g.Fiber: 0 g.

416. Arugula Walnut Pesto

Preparation time: 5 minutes
Cooking time: 0 minutes
Servings: 8–10
Ingredients

- 6 cups arugula, packed
- 1 cup walnuts, chopped
- 1/2 cup Parmesan cheese, shredded
- 2 garlic cloves, peeled
- 1/2 tsp. salt
- 1 cup extra virgin olive oil

Directions

1. Combine the arugula, walnuts, cheese, and garlic in a food processor and process until very finely chopped. Add the salt. With the processor running, stream in the olive oil until well blended.

2. If the mixture seems too thick, add warm water, 1 tbsp. at a time, until smooth and creamy.

3. Store in a sealed container in the refrigerator.

Nutrition Calories: 296 Fats: 31 g.Protein: 4 g.Carbs: 3 g.Net carbs: 2 g.Fiber: 1 g.

417. 5-Minute Sriracha Mayonnaise

Preparation time: 5 minutes
Cooking time: 0 minutes
Servings: 4
Ingredients

- 1/2 cup mayonnaise
- 2 tbsp. Sriracha sauce
- 1/2 tsp. garlic powder
- 1/2 tsp. onion powder
- 1/4 tsp. paprika

Directions

1. In a small bowl, whisk all the ingredients until well mixed.

2. Pour into an airtight glass container, and keep in the refrigerator for up to 1 week.

Nutrition Calories: 201 Fats: 22 g.Protein: 1 g.Carbs: 2 g.Net carbs: 1 g.Fiber: 1 g.

418. Avocado Cilantro Lime Crema

Preparation time: 5 minutes
Cooking time: 0 minutes
Servings: 4
Ingredients

- 1/2 cup sour cream
- 1/2 avocado
- 1 garlic clove, finely minced
- 1/4 cup fresh cilantro leaves
- 1/2 lime juice
- Pinch pink Himalayan salt
- Pinch freshly ground black pepper

Directions

1. In a food processor (or blender), mix all the ingredients until smooth and fully combined.

2. Spoon the sauce into an airtight glass jar and keep it in the refrigerator for up to 3 days.

Nutrition Calories: 87 Fats: 8 g.Protein: 1 g.Carbs: 4 g.Net carbs: 2 g.Fiber: 2 g.

419. Ketchup

Preparation time: 10 minutes
Cooking time: 6–7 hours
Servings: 2 cups
Ingredients

- 1 tbsp. extra-virgin olive oil
- 1 can (28 oz./794 g.) crushed tomatoes
- 1/2 cup apple cider vinegar
- 1/4 cup granulated erythritol
- 1 sweet onion, finely chopped
- 2 tsp. garlic, minced
- 1/4 tsp. allspice
- 1/8 tsp. ground cloves
- 1/8 tsp. celery salt
- 2 bay leaves

Directions

1. Lightly grease the container of the slow cooker with olive oil.
2. Add the rest of the ingredients to the container.
3. Cook uncovered for 6–7 hours on low, until thick.
4. Remove the bay leaves. Use an immersion blender or a regular blender to purée the mixture.
5. Cool and transfer the ketchup to jars, seal, and refrigerate.
6. Store the ketchup in the refrigerator for up to 1 week or in the freezer for 2 months.

Nutrition Calories: 17 Fats: 1 g.Protein: 0 g.Carbs: 2 g.Net carbs: 1 g.Fiber: 1 g.

420. Artichoke Dip

Preparation time: 15 minutes
Cooking time: 0 minutes
Servings: 3
Ingredients

- 1 can (14 oz./397 g.) artichoke hearts, drained
- 1 lb. (454 g.) goat cheese
- 2 tbsp. extra virgin olive oil
- 2 tsp. lemon juice
- 1 garlic clove, minced
- 1 tbsp. parsley, chopped

- 1 tbsp. chives, chopped
- 1/2 tbsp. basil, chopped
- 1/2 tsp. sea salt
- 1/2 tsp. freshly ground black pepper
- Dash cayenne pepper to taste (optional)
- 1/2 cup Pecorino Romano, freshly grated

Directions

1. In a food processor, combine all the ingredients, except the Pecorino Romano, and process until well incorporated and creamy.
2. Top with the freshly grated Pecorino Romano.
3. Store in an airtight container in the refrigerator for up to 3 days.

Nutrition Calories: 455 Fats: 36 g.Protein: 22 g.Carbs: 13 g.Net carbs: 10 g.Fiber: 3 g.

421. Roasted Cauliflower Dill Dip

Preparation time: 10 minutes
Cooking time: 25 minutes
Servings: 8

Ingredients

- 1 small cauliflower
- 2 garlic cloves
- 2 tbsp. extra virgin olive oil, plus additional as needed
- 1/2 shallot
- 1/4 cup tahini
- 1/4 cup extra virgin olive oil
- 2 oz. (57 g.) cream cheese
- 1/4 cup fresh dill, stemmed
- Pinch salt

Directions

1. Preheat the oven to 425°F (220°C).
2. Remove the leaves and large stem, then chop the cauliflower.
3. Place the cauliflower and garlic cloves on a baking sheet and toss with the olive oil. Roast for 20–25 minutes, tossing halfway through. Remove from the oven and let cool.
4. Place the vegetables in a food processor or high-speed blender. Add the remaining ingredients and pulse until it forms a dip consistency. Add additional olive oil 1 tbsp. at a time if a thinner consistency is desired.

5. Store in an airtight container in the refrigerator for 3–4 days.

Nutrition Calories: 169 Fats: 17 g. Protein: 2 g.Carbs: 4 g.Net carbs: 3 g.Fiber: 1 g.

422. Whipped Feta Dip

Preparation time: 5 minutes
Cooking time: 0 minutes
Servings: 8
Ingredients

- 8 oz. (227 g.) feta cheese
- 1/4 cup full-fat organic Greek yogurt
- 1 tsp. garlic, minced
- 1/2 tsp. sea salt
- 1/4 cup extra-virgin olive oil

Directions

1. Crumble the feta into a food processor or a high-speed blender.
2. Add the Greek yogurt, garlic, and salt. Pulse several times until the feta is fully broken up, scraping down the sides as needed.
3. Turn the blender on medium speed and slowly add in the olive oil. Turn off, scrape the sides, and blend again.
4. When the dip reaches the desired consistency, transfer it to a bowl. Top with a bit more olive oil, if desired.
5. Store in an airtight container in the refrigerator for up to a week.

Nutrition Calories: 121 Fats: 11 g.Protein: 6 g.Carbs: 0 g.Net carbs: 0 g.Fiber: 0 g.

423. Dijon Vinaigrette

Preparation time: 5 minutes
Cooking time: 0 minutes
Servings: 4
Ingredients

- 2 tbsp. Dijon mustard
- 1/2 lemon juice
- 1 garlic clove, finely minced
- 11/2 tbsp. red wine vinegar
- Pink Himalayan salt, to taste
- Freshly ground black pepper, to taste
- 3 tbsp. olive oil

Directions

1. Whisk the mustard, lemon juice, garlic, and red wine vinegar until well combined in a small bowl. Season with pink Himalayan salt and pepper, and whisk again.

2. Slowly add the olive oil, a little bit at a time, whisking constantly.
3. Keep in a sealed glass container in the refrigerator for up to 1 week.

Nutrition Calories: 99 Fats: 11 g.Protein: 1 g.Carbs: 2 g.Net carbs: 1 g.Fiber: 1 g.

424. Creole Seasoning

Preparation time: 10 minutes
Cooking time: 40 minutes
Servings: 3/4 cup
Ingredients

- 2 tbsp. garlic powder
- 2 tbsp. basil, dried
- 1 tbsp. sweet paprika
- 1 tbsp. smoked paprika
- 1 tbsp. freshly ground black pepper
- 1 tbsp. onion powder
- 1 tbsp. cayenne pepper
- 1 tbsp. thyme, dried
- 1 tbsp. oregano, dried
- 1 tsp. ground red sweet pepper

Directions

1. Combine the garlic powder, basil, sweet paprika, smoked paprika, black pepper, onion powder, cayenne, thyme, oregano, and sweet pepper in an airtight container.

Nutrition Calories: 15 Fat: 0 g. Protein: 1.1 g. Carbs: 2.9 g.Fiber: 1.1 g. Sugar: 1.0 g.Sodium: 4 mg.

425. BBQ Sauce

Preparation time: 5 minutes
Cooking time: 15 minutes
Servings: 3 cups
Ingredients

- 1 1/4 cup tomato purée
- 1 1/2 cup white vinegar
- 1 tbsp. yellow mustard
- 1 tsp. mustard seeds
- 1 tsp. ground turmeric
- 1 tsp. sweet paprika
- 1 tsp. garlic powder
- 1 tsp. celery seeds
- 1/2 tsp. cayenne pepper
- 1/2 tsp. onion powder
- 1/2 tsp. freshly ground black pepper

Directions

1. In a medium pot, combine the tomato purée, vinegar, mustard, mustard seeds, turmeric, paprika, garlic powder, celery seeds, cayenne, onion powder, and black pepper. Simmer over low heat for 15 minutes or until the flavors come together.
2. Remove the sauce from the heat, and let cool for 5 minutes. Transfer to a blender, and purée until smooth.

Nutrition Calories: 10 Fat: 0 g.Protein: 0.3 g.Carbs: 1.5 g.Fiber: 0.3 g.Sugar: 1.0 g.Sodium: 14 mg.

426. Chicken Gravy

Preparation time: 5 minutes
Cooking time: 15 minutes
Servings: 1 1/2 cup
Ingredients

- 2 cups low-sodium chicken broth, divided
- 4 tbsp. whole-wheat flour, divided
- 1 medium yellow onion, chopped
- 1/2 bunch fresh thyme, roughly chopped - 2 garlic cloves, minced
- 1 bay leaf
- 1/2 tsp. celery seeds
- Freshly ground black pepper, to taste
- 1 tsp. Worcestershire sauce

Directions

1. In a shallow stockpot, combine 1/2 cup of broth and 1 tbsp. of whole-wheat flour and cook over medium-low heat; whisking until the flour is dissolved. Continue to add about 1/2 cup of broth and the remaining 3 tbsp. of flour in increments for 2 minutes or until a thick sauce is formed.
2. Add the onion, thyme, garlic, bay leaf, and 1/2 cup of broth, stirring well.
3. Add the celery seeds, pepper, Worcestershire sauce, and the remaining 1/2 cup of broth. Stir and cook for 2–3 minutes, or until the gravy is thickened. Discard the bay leaf.
4. Serve spooned over a baked chicken stuffed with collard greens or your protein of choice.

Nutrition Calories: 17 Fat: 0 g.Protein: 1.1 g.Carbs: 3.0 g.Fiber: 0 g.Sugar: 1.0 g.Sodium: 17 mg.

427. Ranch Dressing

Preparation time: 10 minutes
Cooking time: 0 minutes
Servings: 8–10
Ingredients

- 8 oz. (227 g.) fat-free plain Greek yogurt
- 1/4 cup low-fat buttermilk
- 1 tbsp. garlic powder
- 1 tbsp. dill, dried
- 1 tbsp. chives, dried
- 1 tbsp. onion powder
- 1 tbsp. parsley, dried
- Pinch freshly ground black pepper

Directions

1. In a shallow, medium bowl, combine the Greek yogurt and buttermilk.
2. Stir in the garlic powder, dill, chives, onion powder, parsley, and pepper and mix well.
3. Serve with animal protein or vegetable of your choice, or place in an airtight container.

Nutrition Calories: 30 Fat: 0 g.Protein: 3.0 g.Carbs: 3.0 g.Fiber: 0 g.Sugar: 2.0 g.Sodium: 24 mg.

428. Greek or Italian Vinaigrette

Preparation time: 5 minutes
Cooking time: 0 minutes
Servings: 4
Ingredients
For the Greek vinaigrette

- 1/4 cup extra virgin olive oil
- 3 garlic cloves, minced
- 1 tbsp. freshly squeezed lemon juice
- 1 tbsp. red wine vinegar
- 1 tsp. marjoram, dried
- 1 tsp. oregano, dried
- 1/2 tsp. lemon zest
- 1/4 tsp. sea salt

For the Italian vinaigrette

- 1/4 cup extra-virgin olive oil
- 2 tbsp. red wine vinegar
- 1 tsp. Dijon mustard
- 2 tsp. Italian seasoning
- 1 garlic clove, finely minced
- 1 tbsp. shallot, minced
- 1/4 tsp. sea salt
- 1/8 tsp. freshly ground black pepper

Directions

1. Stir together all ingredients in a medium bowl until completely mixed and emulsified.

Nutrition Calories: 129 Fat: 14.3 g.Protein: 0 g.Carbs: 1.1 g.Fiber: 0.8 g.Sugar: 0.2 g.Sodium: 76 mg.

429. Quick Peanut Sauce

Preparation time: 5 minutes
Cooking time: 0 minutes
Servings: 4
Ingredients

- 1/4 cup peanut butter - 1 lime juice
- 1 tbsp. honey - 1 garlic clove, minced
- 1 tbsp. reduced-sodium soy sauce
- 1 tbsp. fresh ginger, grated and peeled
- Pinch red pepper flakes

Directions

1. Put all ingredients in a medium bowl and whisk until well blended.

Nutrition Calories: 120 Fat: 8.3 g.Protein: 4.2 g.Carbs: 9.2 g.Fiber: 1.1 g.Sugar: 7.3 Sodium: 138 mg.

430. Creamy Lemon Sauce

Preparation time: 5 minutes
Cooking time: 3 to 5 minutes
Servings: 2 cups
Ingredients

- 1 cup half-and-half
- 1 tbsp. unsalted butter
- 2 tbsp. Parmesan cheese, shredded
- 1 tsp. freshly squeezed lemon juice
- 1/4 tsp. garlic powder

Directions

1. Add all the ingredients to a saucepan and cook over medium-low heat for about 3–5 minutes, stirring frequently, or until the sauce is through heated.
2. Remove from the heat to a bowl. Let it cool for a few minutes before serving.

Nutrition Calories: 55 Fat: 5.2 g.Protein: 3 g.Carbs: 1 g.Fiber: 0 g.Sugar: 0 g.Sodium: 40 mg.

431. Lemony Dill and Yogurt Dressing

Preparation time: 5 minutes
Cooking time: 0 minutes
Servings: 2/3 cup
Ingredients

- 2 tbsp. mayonnaise

- 1 tsp. freshly squeezed lemon juice
- 1 tsp. fresh dill, chopped
- 1/2 cup plain Greek yogurt
- 1/4 tsp. garlic powder
- 1/4 tsp. salt

Directions

1. Combine all the ingredients in a bowl. Stir to mix well.

Nutrition Calories: 36 Fat: 1.0 g.Protein: 3.2 g.Carbs: 3.1 g.Fiber: 0 g.Sugars: 1.9 g.Sodium: 176 mg.

432. Fresh Cucumber Dip

Preparation time: 10 minutes
Cooking time: 0 minutes
Servings: 1 1/2 cups
Ingredients

- 1 medium cucumber, peeled and grated
- 1/4 tsp. salt
- 1 cup plain Greek yogurt
- 2 garlic cloves, minced
- 1 tbsp. freshly squeezed lemon juice
- 1 tbsp. extra virgin olive oil
- 1/4 tsp. freshly ground black pepper

Directions

1. Put the cucumber in a colander, then sprinkle with salt. Set it aside.
2. Combine the remaining ingredients in a bowl. Stir to mix well.
3. Wrap the cucumber in a muslin cloth and squeeze the liquid out as much as possible.
4. Put the cucumber in the bowl of mixture, then stir to mix well.
5. Wrap the bowl in plastic and refrigerate to marinate for 2 hours.

Nutrition Calories: 50 Fat: 3.0 g. Protein: 4.0 g.Carbs: 3.0 g.Fiber: 0 g.Sugars: 2.0 g.Sodium: 102 mg.

433. Avocado Cilantro Dressing

Preparation time: 5 minutes
Cooking time: 0 minutes
Servings: 1 cup
Ingredients

- 1 large avocado, peeled and pitted
- 1/2 cup plain Greek yogurt
- 3/4 cup fresh cilantro - 1 tbsp. water
- 2 tsp. lime juice, freshly squeezed
- 1/8 tsp. garlic powder
- Pinch salt

Directions

1. Process the avocado, yogurt, cilantro, water, lime juice, garlic powder, and salt in a blender until creamy and emulsified.
2. Chill for at least 30 minutes in the refrigerator to let the flavors blend.

Nutrition Calories: 92 Fat: 6.8 g.Protein: 4.1 g.Carbs: 4.9 g.Fiber: 2.3 g.Sugar: 1.0 g.Sodium: 52 mg.

434. Lemon Tahini Dressing With Honey

Preparation time: 5 minutes
Cooking time: 0 minutes
Servings: 1 cup
Ingredients

- 1/2 cup water
- 3/4 cup unsalted tahini
- 1/3 cup lemon juice, freshly squeezed
- 3 tbsp. honey
- 1/2 tsp. salt

Directions

1. Mix the water, tahini, lemon juice, honey, and salt in a medium bowl, and stir vigorously until well incorporated.
2. Store the leftover dressing in an airtight container in the fridge for up to 2 weeks and shake before using.

Nutrition Calories: 168 Fat: 13.1 g.Protein: 4.7 g.Carbs: 10.3 g.Fiber: 2.8 g.Sugar: 8.0 g.Sodium: 148 mg.

435. Red Pepper and Chickpea Spread

Preparation time: 5 minutes
Cooking time: 0 minutes
Servings: 1 1/4 cups
Ingredients

- 1 jar (16 oz./454 g.) roasted red bell peppers
- 1 cup canned low-sodium chickpeas, drained and rinsed
- 1/2 small jalapeño pepper, deseeded and stemmed
- 2 tbsp. water
- 2 tbsp. extra virgin olive oil
- 1–2 tsp. lime juice, freshly squeezed
- 1/4 tsp. garlic powder
- 1/2 tsp. salt
- 1/4 tsp. ground cumin
- 1/8 tsp. freshly ground black pepper

Directions

1. In a food processor, add the bell peppers, chickpeas, jalapeño pepper, water, oil, lime juice, garlic powder, salt, cumin, and black pepper, and pulse until the mixture has a spreadable consistency.
2. Transfer to an airtight container and store it in the fridge for up to 1 week.

Nutrition Calories: 52 Fat: 2.8 g.Protein: 1.1 g.Carbs: 4.7 g.Fiber: 2.2 g.Sugar: 2.0 g. Sodium: 138 mg.

436. Spicy Asian Dipping Sauce

Preparation time: 5 minutes
Cooking time: 0 minutes
Servings: 1/2 cup
Ingredients

- 1/3 cup low-fat mayonnaise
- 1–2 tsp. hot sauce, to your liking
- 2 tsp. rice vinegar
- 1 tsp. sesame oil

Directions

1. Stir together the mayo, hot sauce, rice vinegar, and oil in a small bowl until thoroughly smooth.
2. Chill for at least 30 minutes to blend the flavors.

Nutrition Calories: 54 Fat: 4.7 g.Protein: 0 g.Carbs: 1.7 g.Fiber: 0 g.Sugar: 1.0 g.Sodium: 190 mg.

437. Easy Thai Peanut Sauce

Preparation time: 10 minutes
Cooking time: 0 minutes
Servings: 2/3 cup
Ingredients

- 1/2 cup natural peanut butter
- 2 tbsp. rice vinegar
- 4 tsp. sesame oil
- 2–4 tsp. freshly squeezed lime juice, to your liking
- 2–2 1/2 tsp. hot sauce (optional)
- 1 tsp. low-sodium soy sauce
- 1 tsp. fresh ginger, chopped and peeled
- 1 tsp. honey

Directions

1. Mix the peanut butter, rice vinegar, sesame oil, lime juice, hot sauce (if desired), soy sauce, ginger, and honey in a small bowl, and whisk to combine well.

2. You can store it in an airtight container in the fridge for up to 2 weeks.

Nutrition Calories: 206 Fat: 16.7 g.Protein: 7.9 g.Carbs: 8.2 g.Fiber: 3.1 g.Sugar: 3.0 g.Sodium: 113 mg.

438. Maple Mustard Salad Dressing

Preparation time: 5 minutes
Cooking time: 0 minutes
Servings: 6
Ingredients

- 2 tbsp. balsamic vinegar
- 2 tbsp. olive oil
- 1 tbsp. sugar-free maple syrup
- 1 tsp. Dijon mustard
- 1/8 tsp. sea salt

Directions

1. Place all the ingredients in a jar with a tight-fitting lid. Screw on the lid and shake to combine. Store in refrigerator until ready to use.

Nutrition Calories: 48 Total carbs: 2 g.Protein: 0 g.Fat: 5 g. Sugar: 0 g.Fiber: 0 g.

439. Maple Shallot Vinaigrette

Preparation time: 3 minutes
Cooking time: 5 minutes
Servings: 4
Ingredients

- 1 tbsp. shallot, diced fine
- 2 tbsp. apple cider vinegar
- 1 tbsp. spicy brown mustard
- 1 tbsp. olive oil
- 2 tsp. sugar-free maple syrup

Directions

1. Place all the ingredients in a small jar with an airtight lid. Shake well to mix. Refrigerate until ready to use.
2. The serving size is 1 tbsp.

Nutrition Calories: 45 Total carbs: 5 g.Protein: 0 g. Fat: 2 g.Sugar 0 g.Fiber: 0 g.

440. Marinara Sauce

Preparation time: 10 minutes
Cooking time: 30 minutes
Servings: 6
Ingredients

- 1 can (28 oz.) diced tomatoes, undrained
- 4–6 garlic cloves, diced fine
- 4 tbsp. extra virgin olive oil

- 2 tbsp. tomato paste
- 1 tbsp. basil,
- 1 tsp. Splenda®
- 1 tsp. salt

Directions

1. Heat oil in a saucepan over medium heat. Add the garlic and cook for 1 minute.
2. Stir in the tomato paste and cook 1 minute more. Add the tomatoes and basil and simmer for 10–15 minutes, breaking up the tomatoes as they cook.
3. Stir in Splenda® and salt. Use an immersion blender and process to desired consistency.
4. Let cool and store in a jar with an airtight lid in the refrigerator for up to 7 days. Or use right away.

Nutrition Calories: 179 Total carbs: 13 g.Net carbs: 10 g.Protein: 2 g.Fat: 14 g.Sugar: 8 g. Fiber: 3 g.

441. Orange Marmalade

Preparation time: 30 minutes
Cooking time: 30 minutes
Servings: 48
Ingredients

- 4 navel oranges
- 1 lemon
- 2 1/2 cup water
- 1/4 cup warm water
- 4 tbsp. Splenda®
- 1 oz. gelatin

Directions

1. Quarter the oranges and remove all the pulp. Scrap the white part off the rind and cut it into thin 2-inch strips. Remove as much of the membrane between orange segments as you can and place the seeds in a small piece of cheesecloth, pull up the sides to make a "bag," and tie closed.
2. Repeat with the lemon but discard the seeds. Cut the lemon rind into smaller strips than the orange rind.
3. Chop the orange and lemon pulp and add it to a medium saucepan along with 2 1/2 cups water. Bring to a rapid boil over medium-high heat.
4. Reduce heat to medium-low and add the bag of seeds. Boil gently for 30 minutes

or until the citrus fruit is soft. Remove and discard the seed bag.

5. Dissolve the gelatin in warm water. Add it to the orange mixture with 1/2 the Splenda®. Be careful not to burn yourself, taste the marmalade and adjust sweetener as desired.

6. Spoon the marmalade into 3 1/2-pint jars with air-tight lids; seal and chill.

Nutrition Calories: 15 Total carbs: 3 g. Protein: 1 g. Fat: 0 g. Sugar: 3 g.Fiber: 0 g.

442. Peach Pepper Relish

Preparation time: 10 minutes, chill time: 2 hours

Cooking time: 0 minutes

Servings: 16

Ingredients

- 2 peaches, peeled and diced
- 1 green onion, diced fine
- 1/3 cup bell pepper, diced
- 1/3 cup red pepper, diced
- 2 tbsp. fresh mint, diced
- 1 tbsp. lemon juice
- 1 tbsp. sugar-free peach preserves

Directions

1. In a medium bowl, stir together the peaches, onion, peppers, and mint.

2. In a small bowl, combine the lemon juice and preserves. Pour over peach mixture and toss to coat.

3. Place in an airtight container and refrigerate for up to 2 hours or overnight.

4. The serving size is 2 tbsp.

Nutrition Calories:10 Total carbs: 3 g.Protein: 0 g.Fat: 0 g.Sugar: 2 g.Fiber: 0 g.

443. Pear and Poppy Jam

Preparation time: 2 hours

Cooking time: 30 minutes

Servings: 32

Ingredients

- 3 pears, peeled, seeded and chopped
- 1/2 lemon
- 3/4 cup Splenda®
- 1 tbsp. poppy seeds

Directions

1. Place the pears in a large bowl, sprinkle with Splenda,® and toss to coat.

2. Squeeze the lemon over the pears and toss again. Let sit for 2 hours so the fruit will release its juice.

3. Place poppy seeds in a medium saucepan over medium heat. Cook, stirring, 1–2 minutes to lightly toast the. Transfer them to a bowl.

4. Add the pears with the juice to the saucepan and bring to a boil, stirring frequently. Reduce the heat and let boil 10 minutes or until thickened.

5. Spoon 1/2 the pears into a blender and process until smooth. Add the puree back to the saucepan along with the poppy seeds. Continue cooking for 5–10 minutes, or the jam is thick.

6. Spoon into 2-pint sized jars with air-tight lids. Let cool completely, screw on the lids, and store in the refrigerator.

7. The serving size is 1 tbsp.

Nutrition Calories: 36 Total carbs: 8 g.Net carbs: 7 g.Protein: 0 g.Fat: 0 g.Sugar: 6 g.Fiber: 1 g.

444. Pineapple Mango Hot Sauce

Preparation time: 10 minutes

Cooking time: 20 minutes

Servings: 16

Ingredients

- 2 cherry peppers, diced
- 1 ghost pepper, diced
- 1 cup pineapple, diced
- 1/2 cup mango, diced
- 2 tbsp. cilantro, diced
- 1 cup water
- 1/2 cup vinegar
- 1 tsp. olive oil
- 1 tsp. Splenda®
- 1 tsp. paprika
- Salt, to taste

Directions

1. Heat the oil in a large saucepan over medium heat.

2. Add the peppers and fruit and cook 8 minutes to soften.

3. Add the remaining ingredients and bring to a boil.
4. Reduce the heat and simmer for 20 minutes. Remove from heat and let cool.
5. Add the mixture to a food processor and pulse until smooth. Pour into sterilized bottles, secure lids and refrigerate until ready to use.

Nutrition Calories: 16 Total carbs: 3 g.Protein: 0 g.Fat: 0 g.Sugar: 2 g.Fiber: 0 g.

CHAPTER 12:

Dessert And Smoothie

445. Pineapple and Strawberry Smoothie

Preparation time: 7 minutes
Cooking time: 0 minute
Servings: 2
Ingredients

- 1 cup strawberries
- 1 cup pineapple, chopped
- 3/4 cup almond milk
- 1 tbsp. almond butter

Directions

1. Add all the ingredients to a blender.
2. Blend until smooth.
3. Add more almond milk until it reaches your desired consistency.
4. Chill before serving.

Nutrition Calories: 255 Carbohydrates: 39 g.Protein: 5.6 g.Fat: 5.88 g.

446. Cantaloupe Smoothie

Preparation time: 11 minutes
Cooking time: 0-minute
Servings: 2
Ingredients

- 3/4 cup carrot juice
- 4 cups cantaloupe, sliced into cubes
- Pinch salt
- 2 Frozen melon balls
- 1 tsp. chopped fresh basil

Directions

1. Add the carrot juice and cantaloupe cubes to a blender. Sprinkle with salt.
2. Process until smooth.
3. Transfer to a bowl.
4. Chill in the refrigerator for at least 30 minutes.
5. Top with the frozen melon balls and basil before serving.

Nutrition Calories: 135 Carbohydrates: 31 g.Protein: 3.4 g.Fat: 0.81 g.

447. Berry Smoothie With Mint

Preparation time: 7 minutes
Cooking time: 0 minute
Servings: 2
Ingredients

- 1/4 cup orange juice
- 1/2 cup blueberries
- 1/2 cup blackberries
- 1 cup reduced-fat plain kefir
- 1 tbsp. honey
- 1 tbsp. fresh mint leaves

Directions

1. Add all the ingredients to a blender.
2. Blend until smooth.

Nutrition Calories: 137 Carbohydrates: 27 g.Protein: 6 g.Fat: 49.3 g.

448. Green Smoothie

Preparation time: 12 minutes
Cooking time: 0 minute
Servings: 2
Ingredients

- 1 cup vanilla almond milk (unsweetened)
- 1/4 ripe avocado, chopped
- 1 cup kale, chopped
- 2 bananas - 1 tsp. honey
- 1 tbsp. chia seeds
- 1 cup ice cubes

Directions

1. Combine all the ingredients in a blender.
2. Process until creamy.

Nutrition Calories: 343 Carbohydrates: 14.7 g.Protein: 5.9 g.Fat: 13.39 g.

449. Banana, Cauliflower, and Berry Smoothie

Preparation time: 9 minutes
Cooking time: 0 minute
Servings: 2
Ingredients

- 1 1/2 cups almond milk(unsweetened)

- 1 cup banana, sliced
- 1/2 cup blueberries
- 1/2 cup blackberries
- 1 cup cauliflower rice
- 2 tsp. maple syrup

Directions
1. Pour almond milk into a blender.
2. Stir in the rest of the ingredients.
3. Process until smooth.
4. Chill before serving.

Nutrition Calories: 149 Carbohydrates: 29 g.Protein: 3 g. Fat: 15.76 g.

450. Berry and Spinach Smoothie

Preparation time: 11 minutes
Cooking time: 0 minute
Servings: 2
Ingredients

- 2 cups strawberries
- 1 cup raspberries
- 1 cup blueberries
- 1 cup fresh baby spinach leaves
- 1 cup pomegranate juice
- 3 tbsp. milk powder, unsweetened

Directions
1. Mix all the ingredients in a blender.
2. Blend until smooth.
3. Chill before serving.

Nutrition Calories: 118 Carbohydrates: 25.7 g.Protein: 4.6 g.Fat: 1.45 g.

451. Peanut Butter Smoothie With Blueberries

Preparation time: 12 minutes
Cooking time: 0 minute
Servings: 2
Ingredients

- 2 tbsp. creamy peanut butter
- 1 cup vanilla almond milk (unsweetened)
- 6 oz. soft silken tofu
- 1/2 cup grape juice
- 1 cup blueberries Crushed ice

Directions
1. Mix all the ingredients in a blender.
2. Process until smooth.

Nutrition Calories: 247 Carbohydrates: 30 g.Protein: 10.7 g.Fat: 13.56 g.

452. Peach and Apricot Smoothie

Preparation time: 11 minutes
Cooking time: 0 minute
Servings: 2
Ingredients

- 1 cup almond milk, unsweetened
- 1 tsp. honey - 1/2 cup apricots, sliced
- 1/2 cup peaches, sliced
- 1/2 cup carrot, chopped
- 1 tsp. vanilla extract

Directions
1. Mix the milk and honey.
2. Pour into a blender.
3. Add the apricots, peaches, and carrots.
4. Stir in the vanilla.
5. Blend until smooth.

Nutrition Calories: 153 Carbohydrates: 30 g.Protein: 32.6 g.Fat: 1.8 g.

453. Tropical Smoothie

Preparation time: 8 minutes
Cooking time: 0 minute
Servings: 2
Ingredients

- 1 banana, sliced
- 1 cup mango, sliced
- 1 cup pineapple, sliced
- 1 cup peaches, sliced
- 6 oz. non-fat coconut yogurt
- 1/2 cup pineapple wedges

Directions
1. Freeze the fruit slices for 1 hour.
2. Transfer to a blender.
3. Stir in the rest of the ingredients except pineapple wedges.
4. Process until smooth.
5. Garnish with pineapple wedges.

Nutrition Calories: 102 Carbohydrates: 22.6 g.Protein: 2.5 g.Fat: 0.76 g.

454. Banana and Strawberry Smoothie

Preparation time: 7 minutes
Cooking time: 0 minute
Servings: 2
Ingredients

- 1 banana, sliced
- 4 cups fresh strawberries, sliced
- 1 cup ice cubes
- 6 oz. yogurt - 1 kiwi fruit, sliced

Directions

1. Add the banana, strawberries, ice cubes, and yogurt in a blender.
2. Blend until smooth.
3. Garnish with kiwi fruit slices and serve.

Nutrition Calories: 54 Carbohydrates: 11.8 g.Protein: 1.7 g.Fat: 9.58 g.

455. Cantaloupe and Papaya Smoothie

Preparation time: 9 minutes
Cooking time: 0 minute
Servings: 2

Ingredients

- 3/4 cup low-fat milk
- 1/2 cup papaya, chopped
- 1/2 cup cantaloupe, chopped
- 1/2 cup mango, cubed
- 4 ice cubes - 2 lime zest

Directions

1. Pour the milk into a blender.
2. Add the chopped fruits and ice cubes.
3. Blend until smooth.
4. Garnish with lime zest and serve.

Nutrition Calories: 207 Carbohydrates: 18.4 g.Protein: 7.7 g.Fat: 11.11 g.

456. Watermelon and Cantaloupe Smoothie

Preparation time: 10 minutes
Cooking time: 0 minute
Servings: 2

Ingredients

- 1 1/2 cups watermelon, sliced
- 1 cup cantaloupe, sliced
- 1/2 cup nonfat yogurt
- 1/4 cup orange juice

Directions

1. Add all the ingredients to a blender.
2. Blend until creamy and smooth.
3. Chill before serving.

Nutrition Calories: 114 Carbohydrates: 13 g.Protein: 4.8 g.Fat: 0.38 g.

457. Raspberry and Peanut Butter Smoothie

Preparation time: 10 minutes
Cooking time: 0 minute
Servings: 2

Ingredients

- 2 tbsp. peanut butter, smooth and natural

- 2 tbsp. skim milk
- 1 1/2 cups raspberries, fresh
- 1 cup ice cubes
- 1 tsp. stevia

Directions

1. Place all the ingredients in your blender. Set the mixer to puree.
2. Serve.

Nutrition

- Calories: 170
- Fat: 8.6 g.
- Carbohydrates: 20 g.
- Protein: 12.57 g.

458. Strawberry, Kale, and Ginger Smoothie

Preparation time: 13 minutes
Cooking time: 0 minute
Servings: 2

Ingredients

- 6 pcs. curly kale leaves, fresh and large with stems removed
- 2 tsp. grated ginger, raw and peeled
- 1/2 cup water, cold
- 3 tbsp. lime juice
- 2 tsp. honey
- 1 or 1 1/2 cups strawberries, fresh and trimmed
- 1 cup ice cubes

Directions

1. Place all the ingredients in your blender. Set to puree.
2. Serve.

Nutrition Calories: 205 Fat: 2.9 g.Carbohydrates: 42.4 g.Protein: 2.73 g.

459. Green Detox Smoothie

Preparation time: 10 minutes
Cooking time: 0 minutes
Servings: 4

Ingredients

- 1 1/2 cups baby spinach
- 2 cups baby kale
- 2 ribs celery, chopped
- 1 medium green apple, chopped
- 1 cup frozen sliced banana
- 1 cup almond milk
- 1 tbsp. grated fresh ginger
- 1 tbsp. chia seeds
- 1 tbsp. honey

Directions

1. Combine all the ingredients in a blender and blend until smooth. Serve.

Nutrition Calories: 136 Fat: 1 g.Protein: 1 g.Carbohydrates: 13.76 g.

460. Classic Apple Detox Smoothie

Preparation time: 5 minutes
Cooking time: 0 minute
Servings: 2
Ingredients

- 1 1/2 oz. baby spinach
- 2 oz. celery, chopped
- 1 lemon, juiced - 1 cup water
- 1 apple, chopped
- 1 mini cucumber, chopped
- 1/2 inch ginger, peeled and chopped
- 1 cup ice

Directions

1. Blend everything in a blender and enjoy.

Nutrition Calories: 66 Fat: 0.1 g.Protein: 1 g.Carbohydrates: 22.27 g.

461. Energy-Booting Green Smoothie

Preparation time: 15 minutes
Cooking time: 0 minutes
Servings: 4
Ingredients

- 1 handful greens
- 1/2 cucumber, seeded
- 1 apple - 1 burro banana
- 1/2 tsp. Bromide Plus Powder
- 1 tbsp. walnuts
- 1/2 lb. soft-jelly coconut milk

Directions

1. To prepare your green smoothie, first, mix all the ingredients in a food processor.
2. Pour into a glass and enjoy.

Nutrition Fat: 16.5 g. Protein: 2.9 g.Calories: 222 Carbohydrates: 10.98 g.

462. Zucchini Relaxing Smoothie

Preparation time: 15 minutes
Cooking time: 10 minutes
Servings: 4
Ingredients

- 1 zucchini, chopped

- 0.2 lb. herbal tea
- 1/2 lb. soft jelly coconut water

Directions

1. First, brew the tea according to the instructions and let it cool to make your smoothie relaxed.
2. Combine all the ingredients in a blender. Blend well.
3. Pour into serving glasses and enjoy!

Nutrition Fat: 0.4 g. Protein: 1.1 g. Calories: 52 Carbohydrates: 2.19 g.

463. Magnesium-Boosting Smoothie

Preparation time: 10 minutes
Cooking time: 0 minutes
Servings: 2
Ingredients

- 1/2 lb. fresh spring water
- 0.7 lb. Brazil nuts
- 1/2 burro banana
- 2 strawberries
- 1/2 lb. figs

Directions

1. Mix all the ingredients using a high-speed mixer.
2. Enjoy.

Nutrition Calories: 182 Fat: 3 g.Protein: 2.8 g.Carbohydrates: 91.99 g.

464. Detox Smoothie

Preparation time: 20 minutes
Cooking time: 0 minutes
Servings: 4
Ingredients

- 1/2 avocado
- 1/2 lb. homemade soft-jelly coconut milk
- 1 handful "approved" greens, such as callaloo, watercress, or dandelion greens
- 1 squeeze key lime
- 1 tsp. Dr. Sebi's® Bromide Plus Powder

Directions

1. Mix all the ingredients in a high-speed mixer.
2. Fill in more water if the mixture is too concentrated.
3. Enjoy.

Nutrition Calories: 202 Fat: 19.4 g.Protein: 2.4 g.Carbohydrates: 6.21 g.

465. Immunity-Boosting Smoothie

Preparation time: 35 minutes
Cooking time: 20 minutes
Servings: 2
Ingredients

- 1 mango
- 1 Seville orange
- 1/2 lb. brewed Dr. Sebi's® Immune Support Herbal Tea
- 1 tbsp. coconut oil
- 1 tbsp. date sugar or agave syrup
- 1 lime, juiced

Directions

1. Boil distilled water and pour 1 half tsp. of Dr. Sebi's® Immune Support Herbal Tea. Cook for about 15 minutes. Let cool, strain. Add the Seville orange peel and mango cut into pieces.
2. Mix all the ingredients in a high-speed mixer. Add to serving glasses and enjoy!

Nutrition Calories: 97 Fat: 3.7 g.Protein: 9 g.Carbohydrates: 10.53 g.

466. Crestless Berry Cheesecake

Preparation time: 10 minutes
Cooking time: 40 minutes
Servings: 12
Ingredients

- 16 oz. cream cheese, softened
- 1 cup powdered erythritol
- 1/4 cup sour cream
- 2 tsp. vanilla extract
- 2 eggs
- 2 cups water
- 1/4 cup blackberries and strawberries, as the topping

Directions

1. Beat the erythritol and cream cheese until smooth.
2. Add the eggs, vanilla, and sour cream and combine.
3. Pour batter into a springform pan.
4. Cover top with tinfoil.
5. Pour water into the instant pot and place the steam rack in the pot.
6. Place the pan on top of the rack.
7. Close and press CAKE.
8. Cook 40 minutes and do a natural release when done.
9. Remove and cool.
10. Top with berries and serve.

Nutrition Calories: 153 Fat: 12.7 g.Carb: 1.9 g. Protein: 3.4 g.

467. Almond Butter Fat Bomb

Preparation time: 3 minutes
Cooking time: 3 minutes
Servings: 6
Ingredients

- 1/4 cup Coconut oil
- 1/4 cup no-sugar-added almond butter
- 2 tbsp. cacao powder
- 1/4 cup powdered erythritol

Directions

1. Melt the coconut oil on SAUTÉ in the instant pot.
2. Press CANCEL and stir in remaining ingredients.
3. Pour the mixture into 6 silicone molds.
4. Freeze and serve.

Nutrition Calories: 142 Fat: 14.1 g.Carb: 1.4 g.Protein: 2 g.

468. Chocolate Chip Fat Bomb

Preparation time: 2 minutes
Cooking time: 2 minutes
Servings: 12
Ingredients

- 1/2 cup coconut oil
- 1/2 cup no-sugar-added peanut butter
- 2 oz. cream cheese, warmed
- 1/4 cup powdered erythritol
- 1/4 cup low-carb chocolate chips

Direction

1. Melt coconut oil in the instant pot on SAUTÉ.
2. Add erythritol, cream cheese, and peanut butter. Mix well.
3. Pour mixture into silicone baking cups.
4. Sprinkle the cups with chocolate chips.
5. Freeze in the freezer and serve.

Nutrition Calories: 181 Fat: 16.8 g.Carb: 3.6 g.Protein: 3 g.

469. Chocolate Mousse

Preparation time: 5 minutes
Cooking time: 5 minutes
Servings: 4
Ingredients

- 1 cup heavy whipping cream
- 1/2 tsp. gelatin
- 1 tbsp. erythritol

- 1 tsp. vanilla extract
- 1 cup chocolate pudding, no sugar added

Directions

1. Place the gelatin and heavy cream in a bowl.
2. Add into the instant pot on SAUTÉ.
3. Whisk until the gelatin is dissolved.
4. Press CANCEL and add the vanilla and erythritol.
5. Whisk until soft peaks form.
6. Gently fold in chocolate pudding.
7. Serve chilled.

Nutrition Calories: 289 Fat: 23.2 g.Carb: 8 g.Protein: 2.7 g.

470. Blackberry Crunch

Preparation time: 5 minutes
Cooking time: 5 minutes
Servings: 1
Ingredients

- 10 blackberries
- 1/2 tsp. vanilla extract
- 2 tbsp. powdered erythritol
- 1/8 tsp. xanthan gum
- 1 tbsp. butter
- 1/4 cup pecans, chopped
- 3 tsp. almond flour
- 1/2 tsp. cinnamon
- 2 tsp. powdered erythritol
- 1 cup water

Directions

1. Place the xanthan gum, erythritol, vanilla, and blackberries in a 4-inch ramekin.
2. Stir to coat the blackberries.
3. Mix the remaining ingredients in another bowl.
4. Sprinkle over blackberries and cover with foil. Press MANUAL and cook for 4 minutes.
5. Do a quick release and serve.

Nutrition Calories: 346 Fat: 30.7 g.Carb: 5.5 g.Protein: 3.4 g.

471. Peanut Butter Cheesecake Bites

Preparation time: 10 minutes
Cooking time: 15 minutes
Servings: 8
Ingredients

- 16 oz. cream cheese, softened

- 1 cup powdered erythritol
- 1/2 cup peanut flour
- 1/4 cup sour cream
- 2 tsps. vanilla extract
- 2 eggs
- 2 cups water
- 1/4 cup low-carb chocolate chips
- 1 tbsp. coconut oil

Directions

1. Beat the erythritol and cream cheese until smooth in a bowl.
2. Gently fold in sour cream, flour, and vanilla. Fold in eggs until mixed.
3. Pour batter into silicone cupcake molds or 4-inch springform pans.
4. Cover with foil and pour water into the instant pot.
5. Place steam rack in the pot and add foil-covered pan on top.
6. Close the lid and press CAKE.
7. Cook for 15 minutes.
8. Do a natural release. Remove and cool.
9. Add coconut oil and chocolate chips to a bowl.
10. Melt in the microwave for 30 seconds and whisk until smooth.
11. Drizzle over cheesecakes.
12. Chill and serve.

Nutrition Calories: 290 Fat: 22.8 g.Carbs: 6.5 g.Protein: 7 g.

472. Pecan Clusters

Preparation time: 5 minutes
Cooking time: 5 minutes
Servings: 8
Ingredients

- 3 tbsp. butter
- 1/4 cup heavy cream
- 1 tsp. vanilla extract
- 1 cup pecans, chopped
- 1/4 cup low-carb chocolate chips

Directions

1. Melt the butter on SAUTÉ in the instant pot.
2. Once the butter is brown, add heavy cream and press CANCEL.
3. Add the chopped pecans and vanilla.
4. Cool and occasionally stir for 10 minutes.
5. Line a baking sheet with parchment and spoon mixture on it to form 8 clusters.

6. Scatter chocolate chips over the clusters.
7. Cool and serve.

Nutrition Calories: 194 Fat: 18.2 g.Carbs: 4 g.Protein: 1.5 g.

473. Classic Fudge

Preparation time: 5 minutes
Cooking time: 3 minutes
Servings: 10
Ingredients

- 1 cup low-carb chocolate chips
- 8 oz. cream cheese
- 1/4 cup erythritol
- 1/4 tsp. cinnamon
- 1 tsp. vanilla extract
- 1 cup water

Directions

1. Place the vanilla, cinnamon, erythritol, cream cheese, and chocolate chips in a bowl. Cover with foil.
2. Pour water into the instant pot and place it on the steam rack.
3. Place the bowl on the rack and cover the lid.
4. Press the MANUAL bottom and cook for 3 minutes.
5. Do a natural release.
6. Remove the bowl carefully and stir until smooth.
7. Line a pan with parchment paper and pour the mixture on it.
8. Chill, slice, and serve.

Nutrition Calories: 190 Fat: 13.9 g.Carbs: 9 g.Protein: 1.4 g.

474. Lemon Poppy Seed Cake

Preparation time: 10 minutes
Cooking time: 25 minutes
Servings: 6
Ingredients

- 1 cup almond flour
- 2 eggs
- 1/2 cup erythritol
- 2 tsp. vanilla extract
- 1 tsp. lemon extract
- 1 tbsp. poppy seeds
- 4 tbsp. butter, melted
- 1/4 cup heavy cream
- 1/8 cup sour cream
- 1/2 tsp. baking powder
- 1 cup water

- 1/4 cup powdered erythritol, for garnish

Directions

1. Mix the poppy seeds, lemon, vanilla, erythritol, eggs, and almond flour in a bowl.
2. Add the baking powder, sour cream, heavy cream, and butter.
3. Pour into a 7-inch round cake pan and cover with foil.
4. Pour the water into the instant pot and place it on a steam rack.
5. Place the cake pan on top of the rack.
6. Close the lid and press CAKE.
7. Cook for 25 minutes.
8. Do a natural release.
9. Cool and sprinkle with powdered erythritol.
10. Serve.

Nutrition Calories: 240 Fat: 20.8 g.Carb: 3 g.Protein: 2.7 g.

475. Brownies

Preparation time: 15 minutes
Cooking time: 25 minutes
Servings: 6
Ingredients

- 1 cup low-carb chocolate chips
- 1 tbsp. coconut oil
- 1 oz. cream cheese, warmed
- 1/4 cup heavy cream
- 1 cup almond flour
- 2 eggs
- 1/2 tsp. baking soda
- 4 tbsp. melted butter
- 3/4 cup powdered erythritol
- 1 tsp. gelatin
- 1/2 cup cocoa powder
- 1 cup water

Directions

1. Melt coconut oil and chocolate chips in the microwave. Whisk until smooth. Set aside.
2. Mix cocoa powder, gelatin, erythritol, butter, baking soda, eggs, almond flour, heavy cream, and cream cheese in another bowl. Fold in melted chocolate.
3. Pour mixture into 7-inch round cake pan and cover with foil.
4. Pour water into the Instant Pot and place the steam rack.

5. Place the pan on the steam rack and close the lid.
6. Press manual adds cook for 25 minutes.
7. Do a natural release and serve.

Nutrition Calories: 460 Fat: 35.9 g.Carb: 11 g.Protein: 5.1 g.

476. Peanut Butter Fudge

Preparation time: 5 minutes
Cooking time: 2 hours
Servings: 12
Ingredients

- 1 cup low-carb chocolate chips
- 8 oz. cream cheese
- 1/4 cup erythritol
- 1/4 cup peanut butter, no-sugar-added
- 1 tsp. vanilla extract

Directions

1. Add all the ingredients and cover with a slow cooker lid.
2. Cook on LOW for 1 hour and stir.
3. Smooth mixture and cook for 30 minutes more.
4. Line a pan with parchment and pour the mixture on it.
5. Chill and serve.

Nutrition Calories: 159 Fat: 11.5 g.Carb: 9.5 g.Protein: 1.9 g.

477. Chocolate Pudding

Preparation time: 5 minutes
Cooking time: 15 minutes
Servings: 4
Ingredients

- 2 cups vanilla almond milk, unsweetened, and divided
- 1/2 cup heavy cream
- 2 egg yolks
- 1 tsp. vanilla extract
- 1/8 tsp. cinnamon
- 2 tbsps. cocoa powder
- 3/4 tsp. guar gum
- 1/4 cup low-carb chocolate chips

Directions

1. Press SAUTÉ and add half of the almond milk and heavy cream into the instant pot; bring to a gentle boil.
2. Add the guar gum, cocoa powder, cinnamon, vanilla, and yolks and whisk to mix in a bowl.

3. Slowly whisk this mixture into the instant pot mixture. Mix until smooth.
4. Press CANCEL and add chocolate chips.
5. Whisk until melted.
6. Pour the mixture into a large bowl and refrigerate for 2 hours.
7. Serve.

Nutrition Calories: 224 Fat: 18.7 g.Carb: 8 g.Protein: 3 g.

478. Chocolate Mug Cake

Preparation time: 5 minutes
Cooking time: 20 minutes
Servings: 1
Ingredients

- 1 cup water
- 1/4 cup almond flour
- 2 tbsps. coconut flour
- 1 egg
- 2 tbsps. erythritol
- 1/2 tsp. vanilla extract
- 1 tbsp. butter
- 2 tsps. cocoa powder

Directions

1. Pour the water into the instant pot and place the steam rack.
2. Mix the remaining ingredients and mix in a mug. Cover with foil.
3. Place the mug onto the steam rack and close the lid.
4. Press the MANUAL and cook for 20 minutes.
5. Do a natural release.
6. Serve.

Nutrition Calories: 384 Fat: 28.5 g.Carb: 7.4 Protein: 9.1 g.

479. Mini Bread Puddings

Preparation time: 5 minutes
Cooking time: 35 minutes
Servings: 12
Ingredients

- 6 slices cinnamon bread, cut into cubes
- 1 1/4 cup skim milk
- 1/2 cup egg substitute
- 1 tbsp. margarine, melted
- 1/3 cup Splenda®
- 1 tsp. vanilla
- 1/8 tsp. salt
- 1/8 tsp. nutmeg

Directions

1. Heat the oven to 350°F (180°C). Line 12 medium-size muffin cups with paper baking cups.
2. In a large bowl, stir together the milk, egg substitute, Splenda®, vanilla, salt and nutmeg until combined. Add the bread cubes and stir until moistened. Let rest for 15 minutes.
3. Spoon evenly into prepared baking cups. Drizzle margarine evenly over the tops; bake for 30–35 minutes or until puffed and golden brown. Remove from oven and let cool completely.

Nutrition Calories: 106 Fat: 2.0 g.Protein: 4.0 g. Carbs: 16.1 g.Fiber: 1.0 g.Sugar: 9.1 g.Sodium: 118 mg.

480. Raspberry Peach Cobbler

Preparation time: 15 minutes
Cooking time: 40 minutes
Servings: 8
Ingredients

- 1 1/4 lbs. (567 g.) peaches, peeled and sliced
- 2 cups fresh raspberries
- 1/2 cup low-fat buttermilk
- 2 tbsp. cold margarine, cut into pieces
- 1 tsp. lemon zest
- 3/4 cup plus 2 tbsp. flour, divided
- 4 tbsp. plus 2 tsp. Splenda®, divided
- 1/2 tsp. baking powder
- 1/2 tsp. baking soda
- 1/8 tsp. salt
- Non-stick cooking spray

Directions

1. Heat oven to 425°F (220°C). Spray a baking dish with cooking spray.
2. In a large bowl, stir together 2 tbsp. Splenda® and 2 tbsp. flour. Add the fruit and lemon zest and toss to coat. Pour into prepared baking dish. Bake 15 minutes, or until fruit is bubbling around the edges.
3. In a medium bowl, combine remaining flour, 2 tbsp. Splenda®, baking powder, baking soda, and salt. Cut in margarine with a pastry cutter until it resembles coarse crumbs. Stir in the buttermilk just until moistened.
4. Remove the fruit from the oven and top with dollops of the buttermilk mixture. Sprinkle the remaining 2 tsp. of Splenda® over the top and bake for 18–20 minutes or top is lightly browned. Serve warm.

Nutrition Calories: 131 Fat: 3.0 g.Protein: 2.0 g.Carbs: 22.1 g.Fiber: 3.0 g.Sugar: 10.1 g.Sodium: 135 mg.

21 Day Balanced Plan

DAY	BREAKFAST	LUNCH	SNACKS	DINNER
1	Zucchini noodles with creamy avocado pesto	Almond-crusted salmon	Spicy sweet potatoes	Asparagus frittata
2	Avocado chicken salad	Chicken & veggie bowl with brown rice	Crestless berry cheesecake	Avocados stuffed with salmon
3	Pancakes with berries	Beef fajitas	Almond butter fat bomb	Bacon and brussels sprout breakfast
4	Omelette à la margherita	Italian pork chops	Chocolate chip fat bomb	Onion and zucchini platter
5	Omelet with tomatoes and spring onions	Chicken mushroom stroganoff	Chocolate mousse	Lemon flavored sprouts
6	Coconut chia pudding with berries	Cheesy mushroom and pesto flatbreads	Blackberry crunch	Avocado and caprese salad
7	Eel on scrambled eggs and bread	Roasted brussels sprouts with wild rice bowl	Peanut butter cheesecake bites	Cilantro and kidney beans
8	Chia seed gel with pomegranate and nuts	Sautéed zucchini and tomatoes	Pecan clusters	Ginger soup
9	Lavender blueberry chia seed pudding	Butternut noodles with mushroom sauce	Classic fudge	Buttery garlic shrimp
10	Yogurt with granola and persimmon	Homemade vegetable chili	Lemon poppy seed cake	Bacon and lemon spiced muffins
11	Smoothie bowl with spinach, mango, and muesli	Wilted dandelion greens with sweet onion	Brownies	Salmon stew
12	Fried egg with bacon	Collard greens with tomato	Peanut butter fudge	Asparagus salmon fillets

13	Smoothie bowl with berries, poppy seeds, nuts, and seeds	Cheesy summer squash and quinoa casserole	Chocolate pudding	Crispy baked chicken
14	Porridge with walnuts	Creamy macaroni and cheese	Chocolate cheesecake	Creamy chicken
15	Alkaline blueberry spelt pancakes	Roasted tomato and bell pepper soup	Chocolate mug cake	Paprika butter shrimp
16	Alkaline blueberry muffins	Spaghetti puttanesca	Vanilla tea cake	Almond flour burger with goat cheese
17	Coconut pancakes	Black bean and tomato soup with lime yogurt	Gingerbread soufflés	Stuffed bell peppers with quinoa
18	Quinoa porridge	Grilled tuna kebabs	Mini bread puddings	Mediterranean burrito
19	Amaranth porridge	Strawberry-arugula salad	Mini key lime tarts	Prosciutto wrapped mozzarella balls
20	Banana barley porridge	Blackened spatchcock with lime aioli	Moist butter cake	Garlic chicken balls
21	Apple cheddar muffins	Citrus chicken thighs	Peach custard tart	One-pot roast chicken dinner

Conclusion

We hope you enjoyed this book about diabetic cooking recipes that will benefit diabetics, but remember that our ultimate objective is to help you learn how to cook healthier for yourself. We are glad to have helped you on your way and hope you've found this book beneficial. Thank you for reading!

Over time, diabetes remains an issue in more and more people, this is because the so-called "diabetic diet" changes depending on what foods are healthy, which parties are expressed or digested, etc. If this becomes a problem, you can try some good diabetic recipes for good results.

But the best way to know that you are on the correct diet if you have diabetes is to check with your doctor or a certified diabetic educator.

Important Issues to Deal With Diabetes

- Trying and achieving the best blood-sugar control and maintaining it, especially when maintaining an overnight blood sugar level within normal limits, this will help lower blood sugar levels and help avoid risks associated with high blood sugar.

- For people with diabetes, it is essential to make sure the diabetic diet has enough carbohydrates and protein, this will help manage your body's nutrition better.

- Do not forget that it is essential to have a well-balanced diet since you have diabetes, but remember that you don't know everything about it if you try to limit your carbohydrate intake. You should talk with a qualified or licensed dietician to learn more about the diabetes diet. But also remember to read labels and check food labels, so you know what's in the food you eat. Also, you should make sure to read the information on the products you use for your diabetes medicine.

- It is critical for people with diabetes to engage in an exercise regimen that includes both aerobic and strength training. Remember that when you are exercising with diabetes, it is better to do it with a friend or family member to help keep an eye on what you are doing. Workouts for diabetics should also be limited because they will increase blood sugar levels, which if not controlled would be dangerous, especially in younger people who have not yet developed diabetes.

- You must have a proper way of educating yourself on diabetes. Reading books and other online resources is excellent to help people learn how to manage diabetes. Also, before beginning any type of diabetic therapy, you should always see your doctor. If the issue is due to something other than diabetes or any complications involved, it would be necessary to consult a physician about this.

- Diabetics who are using insulin injections need to regularly check their blood sugar levels to keep track of how well they are controlling their condition. They should also make sure they are well educated about how to check their glucose levels.

- Remember that it is essential for people with diabetes to check their blood sugar levels regularly. You can read about diabetes and diabetes detectors on the Internet, this will help you learn how to manage your condition, especially if you are not yet diagnosed with diabetes. Also, you may want to talk with your doctor before taking any medications because some medicines may affect blood sugar levels.

- Diabetics who have any surgery should always speak with their doctor beforehand to know what they can expect from the surgery and whether they have special needs associated with diabetes. If you have sickle cell disease, you should know how it may affect your condition and what may happen if you need to take insulin while having the surgery. Also, suppose you are allergic to any anesthesia medicine. You should seek medical guidance in this instance since the anesthetic may influence blood sugar levels after it has been delivered.

- Diabetics who have diabetes should know that they need to realize that medications may affect blood sugar levels when it comes to medicine. They need to know what effect the medication will have on their diabetes and monitor their blood sugar levels.
- One should be sure to eat foods that are rich in fiber. People with diabetes should also be sure to have a well-balanced diet every day.

This Diabetic cookbook for beginners will boost your knowledge of what foods are good for people with diabetes, bad, and in between or gray areas. You'll also get access to a handy food list that breaks down carbs versus protein versus fat for every single food in the grocery store.

Manufactured by Amazon.ca
Bolton, ON

24597817R00103